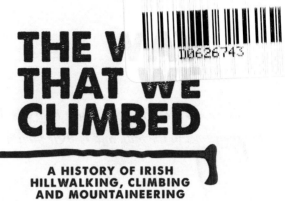

THE WAY THAT WE CLIMBED

A HISTORY OF IRISH HILLWALKING, CLIMBING AND MOUNTAINEERING

This book is dedicated to all those Irish who have lost their lives in the hills, and to their families.

THE WAY THAT WE CLIMBED

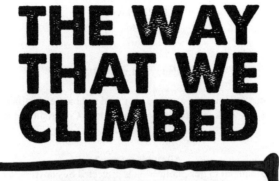

A HISTORY OF IRISH HILLWALKING, CLIMBING AND MOUNTAINEERING

PADDY O'LEARY

The Collins Press

FIRST PUBLISHED IN 2015 BY
The Collins Press
West Link Park
Doughcloyne
Wilton
Cork

© Paddy O'Leary 2015

A CIP record for this book is available from the British Library.

Paperback ISBN: 978-1-84889-242-2
PDF eBook ISBN: 978-1-84889-883-7
EPUB eBook ISBN: 978-1-84889-884-4
Kindle ISBN: 978-1-84889-885-1

Typesetting by Patricia Hope, Dublin
Typeset in Garamond

Printed in Malta by Gutenberg Press Limited

Contents

Acknowledgements

I must express my thanks, and apportion some blame, to two of my friends, Sé O Hanlon and Gerry Galligan, who challenged me to research and write this history. I imagine that they were tired of listening to my complaints about the lack of a comprehensive history.

Sé gave invaluable advice and support throughout the research and writing process. The list of other people who so generously gave of their time to assist me is so long that it is simply not feasible to single out the specific contribution of any individual listed below. I was kindly allowed to interview some people; others wrote, emailed, phoned, advised me, proof-read chapters, lent me photographs or allowed me to quote from something they had written. Still others did a combination of some or all of those things and even did some research on my behalf. To all I am extremely grateful. I list them without distinction. If I have forgotten anyone I apologise and trust that their names appear in the text or can be seen in the reference notes. None of them is responsible for what I did with the material they gave me, or for my errors: Mike Barry, Jack Bergin, Bernagh Brims, Noel Brown, Gerry Cairns, Con Collins, Dave Coulter, Ricky Cowan, Aleck Crichton, Willie Cunningham, Pat Falvey, Robbie Fenlon, Trevor Fisher, John Forsythe, Bill Gregor, Noel and Nora Hall, Paul Harrington, Sam and Olive Hawkins, Elizabeth Healy, Howard Hebblethwaite, Kevin Higgins, Ken Higgs, Pat Holland, Emmett Goulding, Phil Gribbon, Lindsay Griffin,

Tony Ingram, Tommy Irving, Matthew Jebb, Gareth Jones, Brian Kennedy, Anthony Latham, Jim Leonard, Sean Maguire, Pat McMahon, Ingrid Masterson, Con Moriarty, Norah and Brian Moorhead, Gerry Moss, Humphrey Murphy, Shay Nolan, Frank Nugent, Harry O'Brien, Conor O'Connor, Dónal Ó Murchú, Peter Owens, Orla Prendergast, Ken Price, Vera Quinlan, Bénédicte Reau, Christy Rice, Niall Rice, Brian Rothery, Sean Rothery, Kevin Shelley, Clare Sheridan, Shay Sheridan, Peter Shortt, Bert Slader, Dermot Somers, Dawson Stelfox, Alan Tees, Calvin Torrans, Brendan Walsh, David Walsh, Sheila Willis, Sean Windrim and Steve Young.

Glossary of Mountaineering Terms

Many mountaineering terms have entered the public vocabulary so this list is confined to more arcane terminology.

Aid climbing	Making progress by exerting one's weight on devices such as pitons, metal wedges or bolts (see below) fixed to rock.
Bergschrund	A crevasse at the junction of a glacier or snowfield with a steep upper slope.
Bivouac (bivvy)	Sleeping in the open beneath or on a climb, sometimes under cover of a flimsy, tent-like structure without poles.
Bolt	Metal bolt usually left permanently in drilled hole in rock face and to which rope can be attached or run through.
Bouldering	Climbing unroped on boulder or at low height on rock face or indoor wall.
Dry tooling	Using ice axe and crampons to make progress on rock, usually on mixed climb (see below).
Etrier	A stirrup or short set of rope steps used for aid climbing.

Fall factor As applied to climbing ropes, Ff is a measurement used to evaluate the shock load generated on a climber, his belayer and their associated equipment in the event of a fall. Ff = length of fall divided by length of paid-out rope.

Free ascent A climb completed without the use of aid.

Friend A spring-loaded camming device used in cracks as protection (see below).

Front pointing Climbing on ice using the forward-pointing spikes of crampons.

Mixed climbing Climbing which entails dealing with a mixture of ice, snow and rock.

Pitch Portion of climb between two fixed belay points.

Protection Equipment or anchors, usually a running belay (see below), used to arrest falls.

Red-point To free climb a route having already ascended either on a top rope or by frequently resting on the rope. Generally not applicable to long climbs.

Rimaye (or Randkluft) Similar to a bergschrund but with rock on one side of the cleft.

Running belay (or runner) A device anchored to rock or ice through which rope runs in such a way that a falling lead climber is held as on a pulley.

Serac A block or tower of ice, usually unstable, formed by intersecting crevasses or at the end of a hanging glacier. An icefall can consist largely of seracs.

Sports climbing   Rock climbing which depends for protection on anchors, usually bolts, fixed permanently, often at frequent intervals. Safer than traditional climbing.

Top-roping   Climbing that has the rope preset at the top of the climb. This results in much shorter falls than when a climber leads with rope trailing behind.

Traditional route   Rock climb on which a climber places protection as he progresses and which is retrieved by the second climber. Method in general use in Ireland and UK.

Tricounis   Before the introduction of moulded rubber soles during the 1950s, the soles of climbing boots were fitted with suitably designed nails. Tricounis were a particular type of such nails.

Yo-yo   To climb by repeatedly falling on protection and returning to the ground for a rest before making next attempt. Generally not applicable to long climbs.

Climb Gradings

It is not necessary that the general reader should be aware of all the fairly complicated grading systems as applied to rock climbing, ice climbing and alpinism. Those listed are those of relevance to this book.

Rock Climbing (traditional Irish and British)

Diff   Difficult. Actually quite easy.

Very Diff   Harder than Diff. but still fairly easy.

Severe   More demanding than above. Can be subdivided into Mild and Hard Severe.

VS   Very Severe. Historically, was the domain of only the best climbers. Still requires skill and some strength.

HVS   Hard Very Severe. This is the entry grade to higher-grade climbing.

XS   Historically the highest grade, mastered by few.

E grades   These are the grades to which the modern climber aspires. E1 would roughly equate to an easier XS. This is followed by E2, E3 and so on in an open-ended system.

In addition to these overall grades which take into account the general seriousness of a climb, individual sections have numerical technical grades which reflect the physical or technical difficulty without reference to height or danger. These begin with 3a, 3b, 3c and continue through 4a, b, c, and so on. A climb can thus be graded HVS, 5a.

Alpine Rock

Graded using Roman numerals. Grade III/IV is roughly equivalent to Severe. Grade V is about the same as VS/HVS; VI is conventionally the hardest grade. There is also a grading applied to aid routes or pitches: A1, A2, etc.

Ice (Scottish grading used by British and Irish climbers)

Graded I to VI beginning with straightforward but steep snow, going on to vertical or overhanging ice and rock, probably with some dry-tooling involved. Climbs vary in severity according to weather and ice conditions.

Alpine (and great ranges)

Alpine routes, which may be of rock, snow, ice or a combination of these, are graded descriptively in French. Grading takes into account rock and ice gradings along with overall seriousness. There are six grades; the ones relevant to this book begin with D (*Difficile*) and go through TD (*Très Difficile*) to the hardest ED (*Extrêmement Difficile*). This is not a precise grading when applied to some demanding routes which do not have ice or rock pitches of a high grade.

Introduction

How did Irish mountaineering arrive at the state in which it now finds itself? What factors, including socio-economic ones, affected the development of this somewhat esoteric activity? These are the kind of questions to be answered in any history. In mountaineering there is, in addition, a fascination with the ways in which climbers respond to challenging situations. In this history, that interest is only partly focused on the talented, single-minded individuals who push at the extremes of physical and imaginative capacity. It also extends to the doings of 'the ordinary man'. Too often, histories have to do with the elite or the famous to the detriment of an understanding of the experience of the majority. An interest in what have come to be called 'subaltern' themes, those dealing with the common lot, has been growing in conventional histories; why not in mountaineering?

During research I became aware that a really comprehensive mountaineering history is not possible. Given the nature of mountaineering, much of what is done is not recorded or widely known. So my hope is that research will continue and that those with stories to tell will put them in writing.

No attempt is made to define the term 'mountaineering'. Anything that happens indoors cannot be so described, even though the modern mountaineer spends a great deal of time on indoor climbing walls. Not all activities which take place mountains are included; hillwalking is, but not hill running or mountain biking. Traversing of waymarked trails, even through the hills, is not considered to be mountaineering but, contrarily perhaps, the scaling of sea cliffs and quarry faces far from the hills is generally regarded as being an integral part of the sport. The application, unroped, of advanced climbing techniques to near-impossible problems on boulders in or outside of mountainous regions – a practice of long standing – is a grey area which is outside the scope of this book.

It may be disconcerting for some who are still with us, and in some cases quite active, to find themselves referred to in the past tense, but that's history. The stories of most early Victorian Irish alpinists are not included, partly because they have been dealt with comprehensively by Frank Nugent in his *In Search of Peaks, Passes and Glaciers* (2013), but also because their considerable achievements added little to the development of Irish mountaineering. For that latter reason I have omitted, with some regret, the doings of some fine British-based Irish mountaineers such as Paul Nunn, Brendan Murphy and John Barry.

Standards improve from decade to decade, so references to climbs being hard, of medium difficulty or easy, must be read in the context of the time. A hard climb in the 1960s may become one of middle grade in the 1970s and 1980s.

Throughout the book reference to first ascents or fastest times can be assumed to mean the first such achievement on record. The recording of Irish firsts on previously climbed routes is not merely an exercise in chauvinism. There is the mountaineer's knowledge, rather than the historian's, that such information enhances the experience of those climbing compatriots who follow. Where climbing routes, first ascensionists and gradings are referred to without a source being mentioned, it may be assumed, unless otherwise stated, that such details can be found in the relevant guidebooks or climbing websites. Page numbers of club journals, magazines and guidebooks are not routinely referenced. Whenever possible, oral accounts are complemented by contemporary written sources. Guidebooks usually use initials instead of first names, authors of climbing journal and magazine articles frequently refer to their companions by their first names only so it is sometimes not possible because of distance in time or location to give full names. I apologise to any of those mentioned in the book whose full names do not appear.

A particular problem arises when dealing with one's own doings. It is hoped that the reader will forgive the rather stilted use of 'the author' or of my surname, but such use is infinitely preferable to the repeated use of 'I'. An effort is made to present these doings as if they were those of any other climber but occasionally a personal insight is thought to be useful.

The first chapter deals with the period from the 1870s to the late 1940s. Thereafter the narrative is fitted roughly into separate decades. As the numbers participating increase decade by decade, doings at home are separated from those in the Alps and further afield so that three separate chapters are required for the 1990s. Chapter 11, which is squeezed in non-chronologically, comprises of short and by no means comprehensive pieces dealing with topics that are closely although not integrally connected to modern-day mountaineering – topics such as mountain rescue, training and the national governing body. A glossary and a section on climbing grades are included (pp. viii – xii) for the non-specialist.

Prologue

Dublin was a smaller town in the 1950s so the group walking from Dublin Castle were soon clear of the suburbs and on to the 4-mile-long rise to the Featherbed Pass over the Dublin Hills. There was no traffic on the rural road at this late hour. At the bitterly cold summit, as they crossed the county boundary into Wicklow, the walkers were aware that down there in the darkness on the right was Glenasmole, a still-secluded valley less than 10 miles from the city centre, a valley which had been a legendary hunting ground of Fionn Mac Cumhaill and his warriors. On the left lay the monument that recalled the dumping here of the ravaged body of Noel Lemass in 1923, several months after the ending of the Civil War in which he had served as a captain on the republican side. They could not know it then but that murder was an ugly precedent for the gruesome killings and body disposals for which this lonely place would be used by the Dublin criminal underworld.

As they descended into Glencree, the hard-frozen road ringing under their metal boot heels, one of the party dropped out due to the fast pace, and at a fork in the road made his way down to the youth hostel that stood opposite the old reformatory which had been built as one of a chain of barracks along the Military Road. This road, the very one on which the group were now walking, had been built in the years following the 1798 Rebellion in order to deprive insurgents of the hitherto almost unassailable refuge of the wild uplands. There was ice on the steep pull up to the high, uninhabited and windswept ground of the Liffey Head bog so they walked on the crunching gravel at the road's edge as they passed peat cuttings where a wartime generation of Dubliners had harvested their fuel. To the right across the bog and up in the darkness were the mouldering megalithic tombs on the summits of Seefin and Seefingan. As they approached the Sally Gap where the road onwards deteriorated to little more than a grassy track they walked on crisp snow. Two more of the party returned to Glencree. The rest of the group, now numbering about five, turned left towards Luggala and after a hurried meal in a windowless old stone shack with a disintegrating rusty roof they left the road and dropped down through pathless woods to the shelter of the deep Cloghoge River valley. They maintained silence as they passed near the lodge owned by the Guinness family. Having skirted Lough Tay, on the other side of which rose the looming bulk of the crag which will feature prominently later in this history, they followed a grassy cart track that ran along the floor of the virtually unpopulated glen which in the nineteenth century had housed so many Scots settlers that a Royal Irish Constabulary barracks had been built there.[1] Before that, the glen had been a gathering place for rebels in 1798.[2] Only a short distance away some of those involved in the IRA campaign of 1956–62 were surreptitiously training occasionally at the remote shooting lodge which then existed in an isolated copse under the cliffs of Carraig Seabhach.[3]

A few hundred metres before the track reached Lough Dan they crossed the Cloghoge River on stepping stones. One of the party missed his footing at the far bank and wet his trousers to mid-thigh level. Within seconds the fabric froze stiff and the noise of his clacking trouser-legs set off the barking of a dog as they tried to quietly circumvent the only inhabited house at this end of the valley. As they crossed the open hillside on the east side of Lough Dan – there was no state forest there then – the cold and lack of sleep sapped energy levels and it was a subdued group which huddled at Oldbridge to discuss the next stage. The journey had been inspired by research carried out by one of the party who had concluded that the route followed by the Donegal princes, Art

O'Neill and Hugh O'Donnell, as they escaped from Dublin Castle in early January 1592 was more likely to lie along the approximate line this group was following than the more usual itinerary followed by walkers far on the west side of the hills.[4] His theory was discussed as the party skirted around the Barton estate where government forces during the Civil War had conducted the raid that led to the capture and execution of Erskine Childers. Somewhere there, in 1591, in what was then deep forest, the northern princes had sheltered during their first unsuccessful escape attempt. This part of the modern journey was on byroads through upland farms as they approached monastic Glendalough in its deep valley, situated there in keeping with the old Irish practice of locating sacred sites in secluded places.

They passed through the then tiny hamlet of Laragh with its collapsing thatched roofs and small shop-cum-pub. Back now on the Military Road, they followed it to a spot called the Clowran on the pass between Kirikee and Cullentragh mountains. On one side of the road lay the twelve graves of local people killed by a Cromwellian patrol whilst clandestinely attending Mass on the hillside. On the eastern side, at the edge of the old road to Kirikee which was still visible then, a cairn marked the spot where local lore had it that a prince was buried.[5] Here also was obtained the first glimpse, in the early morning light, of their destination: the site of Hugh O'Byrne's stronghold at Ballinacor. This was the safe haven towards which the Donegal princes had striven and which the unfortunate O'Neill would not reach. Perhaps it was he who lay beneath the cairn.

Glenmalure, scene of battle and rebels' lair, stretched north-westward below them. Down there was the hotel at Drumgoff at which the noted Victorian alpinist H. C. Hart had rested and eaten during his marathon walk from Dublin to Lugnaquilla and back.

I was one of that 1950s group, on one of the coldest nights I have experienced. I can't remember everyone in the group but do recall Tom Quinn and Eddie Ferran. It was Tom who proposed taking this eastern route. Even then I had begun to realise that the Wicklow hills – and other ranges as we shall see – did not merely feature in many aspects of Irish life and history but were knitted closely into the causes and effects of that history, and of societal trends, in ways more intimate and unexpected than normally applies between man and the upland landscape in our neighbouring island and even, perhaps, than in many other countries. What I did not then grasp was that this connectedness of the uplands with politics and a changing society had affected the development of Irish mountaineering and would do so up to recent times.

It was not until a small group dominated by Hart came along that this interaction between hill and history extended also to the doings of mountaineers, so this history will begin with that remarkable man.

1

A Break in a Day's Walk

Henry Chichester Hart (1847–1908) was of the landed gentry and one of the Irish alpinists of Victorian times. A member of London's Alpine Club, he spent several seasons in the Alps, during one of which, in 1889, he climbed, with guides, the Weisshorn and Dent Blanche, introducing a competitive element by giving other parties an hour's start and arriving at the summits of both peaks well ahead of them.[1] Handsome and of magnificent physique, he had served as a naturalist on a polar expedition in 1875 and eight years later was on a scientific expedition to Palestine. Unlike almost all of his fellow Irish alpinists, some of them quite famous such as John Tyndall, John Ball, Anthony Adams-Reilly and that excellent rock-climber V. J. E. Ryan, most of Hart's endeavours focused on Irish hills. The doings of these other worthies properly belong to the history of British alpine mountaineering and are treated as such in British accounts, although Frank Nugent's recent book stresses their Irishness.[2] Most of them had little contact with Ireland as they forged careers in London and they certainly displayed little enthusiasm for the Irish hills beyond a brief passing interest in Kerry hills on the part of

Tyndall.[3] They had no impact on the development of mountaineering in Ireland. Hart's legacy, and that of his friends, the Barringtons, lies in their exploration of the Irish hills and in the various long hill walks which they pioneered and which are emulated to the present day. Although not a professional academic, Hart's botanical expertise, his scrambling skills and daring, his leisure time as a landowner and, above all, his remarkable powers of endurance were invaluable to a national botanical survey directed from the Natural History Museum in Dublin. Somewhat arrogant and aware of his social position, Hart usually worked alone as he strode over Irish hills at speeds which others could not match, climbing down cliffs such as those on Slieve League in his native Donegal, to stuff specimens in his pockets.[4]

Hart's notable walk from Dublin to Lugnaquilla and back, a distance of about 75 miles (120km), arose out of a wager with fellow mountaineer and botanist Richard Barrington, who had been with him in the Alps, that he could not complete the walk in less than twenty-four hours. Together with Sir Frederick Cullinan, Hart left Terenure on the evening of 20 June 1886 and walked along the Military Road to Glenmalure, from which they ascended Lugnaquilla and then made their way back over the hills to Mullaghcleevaun. Cullinane was a member of the Alpine Club, an early ascensionist of the Matterhorn in 1877 and a first ascensionist of the Aiguille de Taléfre, both guided as was normal in those days. From Mullaghcleevaun they went through Ballinascorney Gap, arriving at Terenure 23 hours 50 minutes after setting out. This feat was not equalled until 1917, and subsequently until the 1950s, since when it has become a relatively frequent test piece for mountaineers and athletes.[5]

Hart's competitiveness and hardiness were well illustrated during a botanical outing to the area of Powerscourt waterfall undertaken with Barrington, whom he regarded as his social and climbing peer. In heavy rain, Hart walked through thick, sodden vegetation along the riverbank in an attempt to deter his companion who, in response and with an air of nonchalance, waded into midstream where he sat on a submerged rock to eat his lunch. Hart silently joined him. Barrington, whose older half-brother Charles had made the first ascent of the Eiger, wrote: 'All rivalry ceased and friendship prevailed during the remainder of the day.'[6]

Barrington, besides being a keen walker of the Irish hills, also made a difficult crossing of the Canadian Rockies as well as repeating his brother's Eiger ascent. He made several outings to Killarney where he ascended Corrán Tuathail (Carrauntoohil) twice and also climbed Purple Mountain and Mangerton. With a member of the Shackleton family he turned back in mist just short of the summit of Mount Brandon.[7] Socially, he was very different from Hart, being, according to Lloyd Praeger, 'full of enterprise, originality, humour and a never failing friendliness'.[8] His brother Charles organised what was probably the first mountain race in Ireland (if one discounts myths associated with Slievenamon), when, in 1870, he donated a watch as a prize for the fastest time for an ascent and descent of Sugar Loaf Mountain.

Hart was asked by W. P. Haskett-Smith, one of England's earliest rock climbers, to contribute the Ireland section of his *Climbing in the British Isles* published in 1895. In his wide-ranging but cursory survey of the possibilities in various hill areas and on coastal cliffs, Hart confessed to having no experience of roped climbing outside of the Alps – although he had made the third ascent of the Inaccessible Pinnacle in Skye which probably called for the use of a rope – but it is obvious from his descriptions that he engaged in fairly risky scrambles. He seems to have climbed the Inner Stack on Ireland's Eye probably by the North Chimney.[9] Like others who came after him he was dismissive of Ireland's potential for rock climbing. It is clear from his comments on such places as Fair Head, the Poisoned Glen and the Twelve Bens that at this time, when rock climbing on open faces was a very new activity, he simply did not have the eye or the experience for this task.[10]

It is difficult to ascertain if there was much interest at this time in the Irish hills apart from that of naturalists and other scientists. However, one can surmise, because of the scope and difficult of Hart and Barrington's wanderings in places such as the MacGillycuddy's Reeks and Mweelrea as well as the elder Barrington's sponsoring of

Henry Chichester Hart. *(The Irish Naturalist, vol. xviii, 1908).*

Painting of Robert Lloyd Praeger by Anna O'Leary (2000). (COURTESY OF THE NATIONAL BOTANIC GARDENS, GLASNEVIN).

Richard Manliffe Barrington. *(Journal of Botany, 1915).*

the Sugar Loaf race, that there was some inclination to see the hills as places of recreation. Shepherds would be familiar with their local hills. Many hilltops, even the highest, were well trodden as pilgrimages to such sacred summits as Croagh Patrick and Mount Brandon, and attracted large crowds. Field clubs in Dublin, Cork, Limerick and, in particular, Belfast, brought members into adjacent hill areas where walks of considerable length were not unusual. Lloyd Praeger, as a member of some of these clubs, and later in a more formal academic way, ranged the hills of Down, Wicklow, Kerry, Mayo and Donegal in the manner of Hart and at a time which overlapped that of his energetic predecessor. He continued in that fashion well into the twentieth century and his book, *The Way That I Went*, with its descriptions of mountain wandering mixed with natural history, archaeology and geology would later inspire many to follow his rambles.[11] However, in a situation reminiscent of that which pertained in the early years of alpinism, hillwalking as a recreational activity separate from displays of athletic prowess or as an incidental necessity in the course of scientific research does not seem to have been widely practised.

Nevertheless, some knowledge of this somewhat esoteric activity must have been gained at a slightly later stage from the likes of that great alpinist and mountaineering author Geoffrey Winthrop Young (1876–1958) who had strong Irish connections. As a child he often stayed with his cousins at Belgard near Tallaght and had walked in the Dublin Hills. Sometime in his teens – it is not quite clear just when but it must have in the early 1890s – he left the railway station in Killarney, walked round Lough Leane and up the Hag's Glen. He traversed Corrán Tuathail (he wrote it as Carran Thuoile), and descended, it would seem, to Glencar. He continued walking to either Kenmare or Cahirciveen if one is to judge from his claim to have completed a total of 60 miles ending at a railway station by the sea with most of the journey being over open bog.[12] Around this time, according to Con Moriarty, the well-known Kerry mountaineer, a few Englishmen had begun what was to become a fairly frequent practice of coming to Con's home hills to include Corrán Tuathail in their endeavours to ascend the

Con Moriarty, 1885–1940.
Corrán Tuathail guide. c. 1940.
MUIRCHEARTAIGH COLLECTION

four highest 'home peaks' (Ben Nevis, Scafell and Snowdonia being the others) in the then United Kingdom. It was even possible for Con's grandfather, also Con Moriarty, to supplement his part-time jarvey and hill farmer's income by guiding some of these and other tourists up Ireland's highest peak. Con's usual practice was to start from Kate Kearney's Cottage before midnight in order to reach the summit at dawn.[13]

Young was to return to Ireland on several occasions. In 1903 when weather precluded an Alpine visit he went to Donegal to hill walk and cycle,[14] and at some time he also visited Connemara and other ranges in the west.[15] Later, in 1913, along with Mallory of Everest fame, he would climb Mount Brandon using Conor O'Brien's yacht as a mobile base.[16] Perhaps it was on one of the earlier visits, which usually included a stay with his cousins, that he persuaded or inspired his first cousin, Page Dickinson, to take up climbing (see below).

The first example of mountaineering skills being deliberately applied for sport in Ireland seems to have been on a climb on the steep slope beside the frozen Powerscourt Waterfall (121m) in Wicklow in February 1895. *The Irish Times* reported that 'a member of the Alpine Club and two experienced mountaineers', using ice axes and other mountaineering equipment climbed up the steep left-hand side, which was covered in deep snow and ice. They avoided the cornice on top and continued in nasty conditions to the summit of Djouce.[17] Nugent thinks that it was likely that the Alpine Club member was Richard Barrington.[18] Just a few days afterwards, on 28 February, the same paper gave details of a fatal accident on the same slopes when a young medical student, Louis Pomeroy, fell to his death. Perhaps he was trying to emulate the doings of the climbers a short time before.[19]

Early Twentieth Century

The early years of the twentieth century saw a rapid growth in interest in hillwalking and the first tentative ventures on to Irish crags. Ascents of Mangerton and Corrán Tuathail were common, according to *The Irish Times*.[20] 'Great mountain and open-air tramps' were said to be a feature of Dublin life, with civil servants and others spending time on the hills during the century's first decade.[21] In 1902 'a small band of mountain lovers' formed a club grandiosely called 'the Most Illustrious Brotherhood of Lug' which some years later would be described as the 'only mountaineering club in Dublin, perhaps in Ireland' by J. W. Redmond of Sandycove, a stock exchange clerk and the club's then 'grandmaster'.[22] However tongue-in-cheek their title, however open to interpretation was its description as a mountaineering club, and however confined the club's official activities were to annual ascents of Lugnaquilla, the club's members were serious hillwalkers judging from Mr Redmond's descriptions of various ascents in severe wintry conditions. The club is still alive as this is written and, if its claim to be a mountaineering club is taken to be valid, it is by far the oldest mountaineering club in Ireland.

There were several notable Irish members of the Alpine Club at about this time including a former president of that club, Belfast-born James Bryce, who, as Lord Bryce, served as Chief Secretary for Ireland for a brief period in 1905–06. He had, at the age of eleven, been brought up Trostan hill in County Antrim, an experience which aroused his passion for high places,[23] and he subsequently made ascents in many parts of the world.[24] He led some of his officials up Croagh Patrick in County Mayo and Croaghan, County Antrim, in 1906.[25] There is no record of what they felt about being dragooned – well, perhaps they were simply persuaded – to the summits, but, weather permitting, the vistas from these

A page from the log of The Most Illustrious Brotherhood of Lug depicting their first official outing to Lugnaquilla in 1902 *(left)* and members of the Brotherhood of Lug on their first outing *(below)*.
COURTESY DERMOT QUINN, BROTHERHOOD GRANDMASTER

peaks should have moved even the most soulless of Dublin Castle bureaucrats.

W. T. Kirkpatrick from Celbridge in County Kildare and his Scots friend R. P. Hope were among the pioneers of guideless alpine climbing and led the way in saving weight 'with silk shirts and shorts, a 6-ounce sweater, 11-ounce crampons and an aluminium shirt-stud!'[26] They carried an aluminium stove, and descriptions of their many climbs – some of which were first ascents – frequently included details of prolonged halts for cooked meals. Not surprisingly, during their many productive seasons in the Alps they were often forced into impromptu bivouacs. The pair had an alpine career extending over thirty years and through their guideless experiences acquired attitudes towards mountaineering that were well in advance of their time. A flavour of a rather different spirit of that time can be gleaned from Kirk-patrick's remark, 'the first English traverse of the Meije without guides – done by a Scotsman and an Irishman'.[27] According to *The Irish Times*, Kirkpatrick would have been a member of the first expedition to Mount Everest were it not for an age restriction (presumably he was considered too old).[28] He took part in the first climb on the Baravore crag (see page 20).

William T. Kirkpatrick of Celbridge, County Kildare, on the East Arête of the Weisshorn c. 1900. *(Alpine Journal XXII).*

In 1908, Page Dickinson (G. W. Young's cousin), wrote:

During the last three or four summers, a small group of us living in Dublin have, inspired by Easter and Xmas spent in Wales and Cumberland, been exploring the Wicklow mountains, with a view to ascertaining what could be found in the way of rock climbing. The result has been on the whole disappointing, as although numerous crags occur, notably at Lough Bray, Upper Valley Glendalough, the Scalp, the Rocky Valley and at Lough Dan, hardly anything has been met with what one can dignify with the name of a climb, and what does occur may be only regarded as a break in a day's walk.[29]

He then goes on to describe finding the crag at Luggala (which he mistakenly says rises above Lough Dan rather than Lough Tay) and a return a week later to do the first few pitches of what is usually regarded as the first roped rock climb in Ireland. The climbers were Dickinson, Frank Sparrow and Edward Evans, accompanied by a well known English motor-sport enthusiast called Earp. (Contrary to some accounts G. W. Young was not there and there is no evidence that he ever climbed at Luggala.) At the first attempt, using a 60-foot (18m) rope they got about 50m high on what is now surmised to be Intermediate Gully route. Without Earp, they returned a month later, and, with Evans doing most of the leading, they continued to the great terrace which runs across the face at mid-height (Conifer Terrace) and from there to the top, probably via the line of Sweet Erica.[30]

This little group, along with Conor O'Brien a little later, were associated with the newly formed United Arts Club, 'a high-spirited, non-sectarian, non-political social club' in Dublin.[31] Dickinson, Sparrow and O'Brien were architects, while Evans was a recluse and religious eccentric known as the Bishop who later became a lay brother in an Anglican Franciscan order.[32] In 1907 Dickinson and probably Sparrow attended one of the first of G. W. Young's famous gatherings at Pen-y-Pass in Snowdonia. Over the next thirty years, these assemblages included many of Britain's outstanding climbers, especially those in the newly formed Climbers' Club, along with selected artists and intellectuals, who came together for climbing and fun whetted by intellectual jousting. The four Irishmen used to sail across to Wales in O'Brien's boat *Kelpie* – he went on to become a noted round-the-world sailor – and feature prominently in accounts of Pen-y-Pass gatherings by Young and his wife. The couple believed that the Irish added much in gaiety and good conversation as well as a certain eccentricity when O'Brien climbed, as was his wont, in bare feet.[33] Young wrote drily about discouraging W. B. Yeats, one of the several literary giants of the Arts Club, who wanted to sail with O'Brien to one of the Pen-y-Pass parties, presumably because of the likelihood of meeting some of the Bloomsbury set or one of the Huxleys. Young seems to have feared that Yeats, if he climbed: would in mid-pitch lose concentration in some poetic or metaphysical reverie.[34]

Members of the United Arts Club, including climbers: Dickinson on left, climbing wall; Sparrow standing with banjo; Conor O'Brien in centre sitting in miniature yacht. Non-climbers easily identifiable include W. B. Yeats, William Orpen and a pipe-smoking Count Markievicz. *(A cartoon by Beatrice Elvery.)* COURTESY OF THE UNITED ARTS CLUB

E. L. Julian. *(Henry Hanna, The Pals at Suvla Bay, 1917.)*

Young later included E. L. Julian, a young Reid Professor of penal legislation at Trinity College Dublin (TCD) and also a member of the Arts Club, in his list of Irish climbers of that era. Julian, in common with Sparrow and others, was also a member of the Climbers' Club.[35] Dickinson tells of a harrowing experience when Julian and a young friend became lost during a winter ascent of Parson's Nose on Snowdon and were forced to spend the night in the open high up (possibly on Crib Goch).[36] In 1915, Julian was involved with several others, including Robert Booth, Norman Chance and the experienced alpinist W. T. Kirkpatrick, in the ascent of a gully on the cliff of Ben Leagh now known as Baravore crag. Julian was stuck near the top, not wishing to use the only available foothold because it held the nest of a peregrine falcon, so, after a long delay, some of the others climbed up the side of the gully to a point above Julian from which they threw him a rope.[37] The young professor was probably on leave from his wartime regiment, the Dublin Fusiliers.[38]

A spate of letters to *The Irish Times* in October 1911 made it clear that hillwalking had become widely practised among the city's middle classes. Willie Redmond MP described a route up Lugnaquilla from his shooting lodge in Aughavannagh. An aptly named George Hill wrote of 'a new route, and, as we know, a terribly trying one' from Glendalough to Lugnaquilla. Standish O'Grady, the unconventional writer associated with the Celtic Revival, suggested the founding of a County Wicklow Mountaineering Club with its headquarters in Glenasmole.[39]

The United Arts group, particularly Dickinson and O'Brien, explored widely in Ireland looking for likely looking crags. They noted from a distance some possibilities in the Burren and on

Slieve Anieran. On Ireland's Eye they climbed 'the smaller pinnacle
. . . from the seaside'. But, as they wrote in an article in the
Climbers' Club Journal in 1912, 'rock suitable for serious climbing
is almost entirely lacking' and there was 'nothing to repay a definite
climbing visit'.[40] O'Brien, although of an Ascendancy landowning
family, was a fervent nationalist who became a member of the Irish
Volunteers and used *Kelpie* to help run German guns into Kilcoole,
County Wicklow, in 1914. Dickinson, who professed to believe
that the more refined forms of culture in Ireland were entirely those
of the Anglo-Irish,[41] was a unionist who would leave Ireland during
the War of Independence, as did V. J. Ryan.[42]

Climbing, a love of the arts and membership of the United Arts
Club helped this group, of diverse political views, to maintain a
friendship. Poignantly, despite O'Brien's return to Young's gatherings
after the war, the influence of the little group on Irish climbing ceased
as Sparrow and Julian were killed during the First World War while
Dickinson suffered from shell shock. O'Brien served in the Royal
Naval Reserve during that war and in 1922 embarked on a round-
the-world cruise on his new yacht *Saoirse*. He does not seem to
have climbed again except for an ascent of Table Mountain with
Cape Town climbers.[43]

Mountaineering was inevitably curtailed due to the outbreak of
war and the effects it had on the small group of rock climbers.
Moreover, the combined effects of political and labour unrest from
1913 onwards, the tensions associated with the signing of the
Ulster Covenant, the 1916 Rising, the War of Independence
followed by the Civil War, along with sectarian violence in what
had become Northern Ireland, engaged the energies of many of
the kind of vigorous people who then took part in one or other
forms of mountaineering. Some of those associated with the
United Arts Club were involved in the Rising and its aftermath.
Several – MacBride, Plunkett, Markievicz – were executed or
imprisoned. Erskine Childers would, shamefully, be shot during the
Civil War. It is not surprising that there was also opposition in the
club to what was done in Ireland's name during Easter Week.[44]
Yeats, of course, was highly exercised but ambivalent. That some

mountain activity continued during the world war, in Wicklow at any rate, is shown by the spirited performance of J. J. Cronin, a Corkman living in Dublin who, in 1917, beat Hart's time for the walk from Terenure to Lugnaquilla and back by 3 hours 32 minutes. His time was 20 hours 18 minutes, a remarkable feat. It was his third attempt that year, on the previous two of which he was accompanied by the equally capable Sam Cunningham from Sandymount. They had been thwarted by bad weather, going astray on one occasion in rough weather on Lug's summit.[45]

Whatever hope may have existed that mountaineering in the general sense, or even hillwalking, could again be taken up after the war quickly vanished as almost all the hill areas became guerrilla refuges during the conflicts which raged from 1919 into 1923. Fighting or unrest broke out in the Galtees, Knockmealdowns, all the Connemara ranges, the hills of west Cork, Sligo, Mayo, Donegal, as well as in the Sperrins, Kerry and the Dublin/Wicklow hills.[46] It would have been a foolhardy soul who ventured into any of these places, particularly in poorer areas like Connemara, for some time afterwards, when bitterness and suspicion were heightened beyond the habitual distrust displayed towards outsiders by poteen makers and those hugging residual resentment from the land wars of the late nineteenth century.[47] Accounts of various activities, military or nefarious, in places very familiar to today's mountaineers offer fascinating if sad reading.

Perhaps hillwalking gradually recovered some of its popularity in safer places close to cities, as happened in the case of Claude Wall and his friends who in the latter part of 1923 ventured into the nearer Dublin and Wicklow hills.[48] But Dublin's exceptional geographic position, and Belfast's to a lesser extent, allowed such walks to begin and end in the city environs. No rock climbing seems to have been practised throughout this time.

The first revival of interest in rock climbing occurred in 1925 when an enterprising fourteen-year-old boy began climbing in the Scalp about 11 miles (17km) from Dublin. Harold Johnson, a native of Dublin, was at the time at school in Kendal in the English Lake District. In the following year he helped in the development of Buckbarrow Crag with the almost equally young Maurice Linnell, a local lad who would become a leading English rock climber.[49] Harold wrote about how lonely it was to have in those days in Ireland 'no one to climb with and even no one even to talk about mountains'.[50] If only he had known, he might have contacted people like Dr Healy who hillwalked in Ireland in the 1920s and climbed in the Alps, usually with guides, throughout the 1930s. Healy would later join the Irish Mountaineering Club. Johnson would induce unsuspecting friends or relatives to come to the Scalp or the Rocky Valley and then produce a rope and a spare pair of nailed boots for his reluctant second. He put up at least four climbs at the Scalp in 1925, mostly of about 12m, but one, Steep Slab, was 38m in length. All were graded V. Diff. because, according to Joss Lynam, Harold underestimated his own abilities.[51] Harold, as one expects of pioneers, was a youngster with special qualities. These became more obvious as he matured and we will meet him again as an adult.

Harold Johnson, on left with rope, on an Alpine glacier in 1957. COURTESY OF PETER JOHNSON

Almost all the climbers and walkers mentioned so far were middle class – academics, professional people and civil servants, with a few landed gentry. The likelihood of working-class people, especially the unskilled poor, being involved in these activities was remote indeed. In 1911, when there was plenty of evidence of middle-class engagement in the hills, the living conditions for others in Dublin were horrific even by the standards of the time, with tens of thousands of inner-city dwellers living in teeming tenements. Who in Strumpet City could afford a rope, boots or tram fare to the suburbs? Many were unemployed or reliant on occasional day-labouring jobs. The standard and poorly paid working week was sixty hours.[52] Belfast was a wealthier city enjoying an industrial boom but it had its share of unskilled poor with women and children employed in unhealthy and dangerous mills.[53] There was industrial unrest in the city during the century's first decade, while some would have religious scruples about enjoying useless and frivolous pursuits on their one day off a week.[54] However, Belfast artisans who, according to D. A. Webb, were 'dogged and determined self educationists', were active in the already-mentioned field club outings.[55]

Even when the two parts into which Ireland was newly divided gradually settled into a shared mediocrity, or, more accurately, into separate mediocrities, the plight of the less well-off did not appreciably change, nor did the likelihood of their participating in an activity which required both a means of transport and some expenditure.[56] Early in the 1930s this began to change as what *The Irish Times* called the 'cult of hiking' grew increasingly popular,[57] and youth hostelling organisations were founded in Belfast (YHANI) and Dublin (An Óige), while early signs of an interest in rock climbing became apparent, especially in Northern Ireland. Although there were some odd manifestations of the new tendency, such as the Army Comrades Association Hiking Club in their blue shirts and black berets, and a Cumann na nGaedheal South City Hiking Club,[58] both hostelling associations quickly fulfilled their founders' non-sectarian and non-political objective by enabling young people to get into the countryside through providing cheap, simple accommodation. Although the founders of the associations north and south of the border were middle class, the countryside and hostelling 'increasingly attracted apprentices and other industrial workers as well as the white-collar workers with which it had largely started'.[59] However, living conditions, North and South, were still dreadful due to the Great Depression of the early 1930s, the economic war with Britain brought about by de Valera's withholding of land annuities, and Northern Ireland's position as the most disadvantaged region in the United Kingdom with high unemployment and atrocious housing aggravated by sectarian strife.[60] It is probable therefore that working-class participation in countryside recreation was confined to the artisan classes and their white-collar counterparts. Throughout the 1930s Dublin newspapers carried photographs of groups of young people venturing into the Wicklow Hills, while other cities such as Waterford and Cork started their own groups within An Óige.[61] Claude Wall and his friends had graduated from longer excursions into Wicklow, where they cycled to the jumping-off point of their walks or used the Blessington Steam Tram and the railway network. They were now tackling ambitious outings throughout the country, ascending peaks such as Slieve Donard, Ben Bulben and Corrán Tuathail.[62]

There was a walking club in Clonmel, County Tipperary, whose tweed-clad members used to walk to the Nire valley,[63] although it is not recorded that they ventured higher. There were similar groups in other towns such as Omagh, County Tyrone.[64] There were four hiking clubs in University College Dublin (UCD) in the early 1930s,[65] but it is not clear how many of these gown-or-town groups extended their activities to the hills. Inevitably, with increased

Claude Wall. IMC ARCHIVE

participation in the 1930s, came greater risk. Fatal accidents to hillwalking English tourists were recorded on several occasions.[66]

It is not to be supposed that during this time the old Anglo-centric, or, let us say, the better-off middle-class interest in the Alps ceased altogether. Some Alpine Club members were Irish residents, such as Col. O'Brien of Dalkey who had a number of guided alpine seasons. He does not seem to have been at all involved in climbing in Ireland although he later became an early member of the Irish Mountaineering Club.[67]

In 1933, Harold Johnson with David Weir and Cyril Hill, climbed Central Gully on the great cliff of Ben Leagh (Baravore Crag), in a hanging valley above Glenmalure. They thought that it was a first ascent but it later transpired that this was the gully climbed by Booth, Julian, Kirkpatrick and friends in 1915. An added confusion was Harold's later mistaken belief in 1952 that Central Gully and Great Gully on the same crag were one and the same.[68] Harold was different in a number of ways from the kind of people who had rock climbed in Ireland earlier in the century. He was a successful businessman from a well-to-do family. A convert to the Society of Friends (the Quakers) he exemplified the modesty and strong social conscience associated with that community, attributes which would later be of much service to Irish mountaineering when the activity became more popular. In that same year of 1933 two members of the Cambridge University Mountaineering Club climbed a spur on the left edge of the huge cliff in Glen Inagh in the Twelve Bens. This was to become Carrot Ridge (286m), one of the country's easy classics.[69] They also put up 'four climbs of moderate difficulty . . . on a spur of Lugnaquilla called Percy's Table'. (This was on the scrappy rock on the South Prison). They climbed two 'rather hold-less slabs' at the Scalp.[70] Interest in the hills was not confined to people from the two major cities, judging from a *Cork Examiner* report in 1935 of an ascent of Corrán Tuathail, 'by a new route by way of the cliff rising from the Hag's Glen direct to the summit'. This scramble up the north face was done by J. Kerrigan of University College Cork (UCC) and G. S. Adair of King's College Cambridge.[71] Kerrigan, known as Joey, would become noted in the next few decades for various stunts on Corrán Tuathail including bringing a motorbike to the top and later, in 1977 when he was in his sixties, hang-gliding from the summit. In a published interview with Con Moriarty, which has photographs of both these escapades, Joey made it clear that the ascent of his indefinite line on the face was a roped one. Kerrigan, having cycled to the Alps, also did solo ascents of the Matterhorn and Mont Blanc.[72] (Those last feats, if Con properly understood Kerrigan, seem unlikely in the 1930s but in view of his other proven achievements his claim cannot be perfunctorily dismissed.) Around this time also, the walking possibilities of Cork and Kerry hills were being explored by J. C. Coleman who was to become a noted speleologist and an early president of the Irish Mountaineering Club. He and his friends based in Cork were very active, giving rise to his books, *The Mountains of Killarney* and *Journeys into Muskerry*.[73]

In 1935, some of the founders of YHANI, in particular Wilfred Capper and Fred Martin, founded a rock-climbing group which was not directly connected with that organisation. As it quickly became apparent, the little middle-class group (there were nine people at its inaugural meeting) was a club in all but name and was the first group to systematically seek out and climb or scramble routes in the Mournes, other parts of Northern Ireland and Donegal. Joss Lynam felt that the group should be regarded as the first Irish climbing club.[74] Its members ascended gullies on Slieve Commedagh and Eagle Mountain in the Mournes and, within six months of the establishment of their little group, had ventured abroad to the Lake District, Snowdonia, Skye, the Bernese Oberland and Austria. At home they tended to use a top rope when trying various routes such as York Street on Slieve Binnian and the first routes attempted on Eagle Rocks on a shoulder of Slieve Donard. They explored various gullies in Donegal's Poisoned Glen. They visited Idwal in north Wales at Easter in 1936 where they climbed on the Idwal Slabs and Tryfan as well as on Milestone Buttress. Their best performer was Charlie Brims who, without a top rope, led a number of climbs, including two on Bernagh Slabs, and he soloed Shark's Nose (45m, Diff.) on Upper Cove besides doing the first recorded circuit of the 35km-long Belfast Water Commissioners Wall (The Mourne Wall) in May 1935. The latter round, which includes 3,048m of ascent, was done in 13 hours 50 minutes. In July of that year, Norman Capper, Fred Martin and Barbara Catford also completed the circuit, the first two in 10 hours 59 minutes with Ms Catford coming in 40 minutes later.[75] In 1936 Brims, Norman Capper and Martin climbed Belly Roll on the Summit Tor of Bernagh, the line of which has since misleadingly become entangled with the lines of Wounded Knee and Chinook. This energetic and enterprising group explored climbing possibilities on the north Antrim coast at Carrick-a-Rede, Runkerry, Doon and the Giant's Causeway, and elsewhere at Ballygally, Port Muck, Ballintoy and Whitepark. In Donegal they noted possibilities at Malin Head and Dunaff but dismissed Malinbeg.[76] In summer 1935, members were in the Bernese Oberland, as well as the Stubai and Oetzthaler Alps. Norman Capper, Martin and Catford were particularly active in these last-named Austrian areas. Capper and Catford were in the Oberland in the 1936 where their peak list included the Jungfrau and Finsteraarhorn. Martin and Brims climbed above Arolla in 1937 while Haddon Common reached nine summits in the Oberland including three 4,000m tops. At home Brims and Martin were on the Reeks, Brandon and Twelve Bens in 1938, Common was in Skye, Glencoe and in the Oberland. In 1939 Martin and Brims were at Saas-Fee in Switzerland

Charlie Brims.
COURTESY BERNAGH BRIMS

but had to be satisfied with a number of lower peaks because of bad weather. At home R. Ibison made his mark and G. J. Bryan made the first ascent, solo, of Spellack Chimney in the Mournes in April 1938,[77] a good effort for its time which is unintentionally tarnished by later Mourne guidebooks which give 1963 as the date of ascent. The group continued climbing into 1939 and 1940 but, as Phil Gribbon says, by then their era had passed, never to return.[78]

By the end of the 1930s, walking in the hills had become so popular that a readership had developed for the writings of people such as J. B. Malone, Claude Wall and Coleman who produced guidebooks or wrote for newspapers.

It would seem inevitable that a slowing of pace would occur during the Second World War despite the southern state's neutrality. Petrol and clothes rationing on both sides of the border militated against easy access to the hills and to equipment. But there was a very significant development, one instigated by a small group of friends in their teens and early twenties, most of whom were aged between sixteen and eighteen.[79] Bill Perrott, J. R. Greening and other members of this founding circle calling itself the Irish Mountaineering Club (IMC) began to climb in Dalkey Quarry, Bray Head and Ireland's Eye, all crags easily accessible from their homes in the Blackrock area of County Dublin. Within two years they claimed to have put up over 100 new routes.[80] Besides the discoveries of Bray Head and Dalkey Quarry these young men brought Irish rock climbing to a level far beyond that which had been reached hitherto. Their first guidebook to the quarry, handwritten in 1942, included thirteen climbs of which some, such as Fifth Avenue and especially Gwynne's Chimney, would still pose problems for aspiring rock-jocks in the twenty-first century.[81] Other routes were added but there is lingering doubt as expressed in a succession of guidebooks about the authenticity of claims in regard to the leading of a small number of these. Joss Lynam, a contemporary of Perrott, has written: 'Doubt has been cast on some of the ascents – Asterisk, Great Central.'[82] Perrott, whose contribution to Irish mountaineering has not received sufficient public recognition, had lived for

Bill Perrot, initiator and co-founder of the IMC at Ireland's Eye,
c. 1950. IMC ARCHIVE

some time in the Lake District where he learned to climb and
picked up some names of routes which he transferred, perhaps too
liberally, to new climbs in Dalkey. In Lynam's words 'he did not
claim to be a tiger . . . but the dream of the Irish Mountaineering
Club was his.'[83]

The Club went into abeyance from about the end of 1943 as its
members scattered and Perrott joined the British Army. He served in
India where he met Joss Lynam, a fellow engineer, and as the war
ended they climbed Kolahoi (5,425m) in Kashmir together. On that
trip Perrott inducted Lynam into the IMC as an honorary member,
even giving him a membership card. He told Lynam that the club

did not exist just then but he pledged that he would re-form it when he returned to Ireland.[84] They would pursue their common interest when Lynam came to TCD in 1948.

Lynam (James Perry O'Flaherty Lynam) was born and educated in London. His mother was from Galway as were his paternal grandparents who were both Irish-language enthusiasts. His father was superintendent of the map room at the British Museum.[85] In 1942, at age eighteen, Joss was sent by the army on an engineering officers' course at Manchester University and climbed with the college club in the Peak District and Wales. He was delighted when he was posted to India but found himself in the hill station of Mussoorie training recruits in, of all things, jungle warfare. Before being demobilised in 1947 he and Perrott joined an engineers' team to climb Kolahoi. This was Joss's first 'real' mountain and he afterwards recounted how he sneaked away from the rest of the team with a mountaineering book to learn how to cut steps.[86]

Another figure who had climbing experience was Aleck Crichton. Aleck was the scion of a landowning family in Sligo and grandson of the head of the Jameson whiskey firm, a firm he himself would one day run. He began climbing as a member of the Cambridge University Mountaineering Club during his sojourn at King's from 1936 to 1939 and was one of that slightly disreputable band who made illicit night-time ascents of various college buildings. He later liked to relate how he brought Eric Shipton up a chimney at the back of the Fitzwilliam Museum. He also attended one of the last of Geoffrey Winthrop Young's gatherings at Pen-y-Pass where the great man told him of his exploits on Brandon with Conor O'Brien.[87] Aleck was a tank commander with the Guards Armoured Division during the war, arriving in France shortly after D-Day. He was wounded and ended the war as acting Lieutenant-Colonel with the substantive rank of Major.[88] With that background it might be expected that Crichton would turn to England or to the Alps for most of his climbing, ignoring the Irish hills as so many of his status had done, but, in fact, he was to make a considerable contribution to Irish climbing. In July 1947 he made what was probably the first post-war ascent of a rock climb in Ireland when he and his brother-in-law slipped around the shoulder of Bencorrbeg in Connemara's Twelve Bens from where they had been fishing on Lough Inagh and completed the second ascent of Carrot Ridge. (Aleck's father was a game-shooting and fishing enthusiast so rods had to be brought to avoid disapproval.[89]) Crichton can thus be seen as a noteworthy link between the earlier mountaineers of the leisured classes and the modern Irish rock climber.

With Johnson, Perrott, Lynam and Crichton having acquired the necessary experience and skill, with Wall and others having built up a wide knowledge of Irish hills, and with Perrott anxious to fulfil his pledge to Lynam when the latter came to do engineering at TCD, the time had come to revive the Irish Mountaineering Club. Bill and Joss placed an advertisement in *The Irish Times* and in December 1948 the IMC was reborn at a public meeting of over sixty people in a Dublin hotel. The club

First IMC meet atop Sugar Loaf, 28 November 1948. Front row sitting *(l–r)*: Bill Carroll, Bill Perrott; Back row, far right: Claude Wall. In front of Wall, in shorts and glasses, is Frank Winder. Joss Lynam with glasses at centre of the group. IMC ARCHIVE

was formed with fifty members and soon acquired Lloyd Praeger as its first president.[90] From the beginning it was open to all those interested in the hills regardless of gender (most unusual in climbing clubs in those days). Within a very short time new climbs were being put up on various crags, a new rock-climbing guide to Dalkey was produced in the first year and Lynam led the club's first organised outing to the Alps eight months after the club's foundation.[91] At the club's meet on Sugar Loaf just a few days following the inaugural meeting, a photo was taken of a group, some of whom were incongruously dressed. Perrott, Lynam and Wall were there and also, sitting high up near the back, a slight, bespectacled figure with a high forehead.[92] This was Frank Winder.

2

Comrade Lysenko and The Affables

To the south-west of Ireland's highest peaks in the MacGillycuddy's Reeks, there is a secluded, tangled country of deep-cut cooms and corrie lakes with evocative, albeit anglicised, names such as Coomcallee, Iskanamacteery, Lough Nambrackdarrig. One of the most impressive places is Coomanassig which, in 1946, was the sombre amphitheatre in which Frank Winder almost lost his life. Looming over Eagles Lough, the larger and lower of two lakes in the coom, there is a long cliff broken by vegetated ledges. The crag increases in height to about 300m at its southern end where it is cleft by a deep, damp gully that promised botanical riches to eighteen-year-old Winder who was spending his summer searching for a particular rare fern and other specimens.

Frank scrambled up the gully to reach a promising habitat. He fell, losing his sandals in the process, and tumbled about 20m to a ledge where he lay semi-conscious for some time before staggering, bleeding and barefoot, back to his tent where he remained recuperating for several days.[1] He resolved not to repeat such vertical explorations, given that he lacked climbing techniques and had no like-minded companions. Those two deficiencies were remedied two years later with the founding of the IMC.

Winder's exceptional talents, along with a certain eccentricity and individuality in other facets of his life, were evident for some time before he took up rock climbing and were to be displayed throughout his life: in student politics; as a successful scientist and academic; as an advocate of social, political and environmental causes, as well as being an exceptional performer and pioneer on steep rock. That early trip to Kerry had come about because his promise as an amateur naturalist had been recognised by Arthur Stelfox of the Natural History Museum who, by happy coincidence, was to become grandfather of another influential Irish mountaineer. That recognition resulted in Frank being sent by a colleague of Stelfox's on an entomological outing to mountains near Killarney where he discovered a dragonfly previously unknown in Ireland and, following that, to his botanical wanderings in the wild country of south Kerry.[2] The young naturalist sometimes wandered naked in the little-frequented hills during that fine summer.[3] When he joined the IMC at its foundation, he quickly became an outstanding rock climber, but not the only one.

Within a very short time following the IMC's formation the standard of climbing reached a remarkably high level. Of the fifty or so people who joined the club at or shortly after its inaugural meeting,[4] only five had experience of roped climbing.[5] Yet, within months, newcomers Winder and Fred Maguire had put up routes of considerable technical difficulty such as Bracket Wall and Central Rib in Dalkey, and Winder had found Hobnail Buttress at Glendalough where he climbed a route in nailed boots. A few more experienced members of the club had rediscovered the great crag in the Guinness estate at Luggala on which Dickinson had climbed forty years previously, and were taking part in exploits which would become the stuff of oft-told sagas. Joss Lynam led Pine Tree Buttress, of middling difficulty, in 1949, tackling the crux pitch while belayed to the pick of a slater's hammer jammed into vegetation by Pat Crean who was simultaneously leading his own climb, Crean's Crawl. Having overcome the crux, Joss suffered a lengthy fall on the final pitch, recovered, and finished to the eponymous lone pine on the grassy esplanade, Conifer Terrace, which runs across the face at mid-height. On that same day, Welshman Bryan Hilton-Jones fell while attempting the last part of the final pitch of another new climb, Crevasse Route, even though he had already overcome the crux. He then top-roped the final section.[6] Hilton-Jones, yet another ex-British army officer, a former commando and stalwart of the Climbers' Club, had a remarkable wartime record while in charge of the cloak-and-dagger X-troop of German-speaking Jews.[7] He was one of the five IMC members who had previous experience of roped climbing, but his stay in Ireland with ICI, the British chemical company, was curtailed when he was transferred back to the UK. On this day he was probably lucky that the rough hemp ropes in use at the time were too short to allow long run-outs. Aleck Crichton, his belayer, has described how Hilton-Jones turned around just before he fell, announced with his back to the crag that he was about to fall and then came down taking short running steps like a goat, finishing with a jump on to a grass ledge. There is the impression of pioneers pushing a little harder perhaps than was warranted by the poor equipment available at the time, but also of excitement at making new routes on this complex and beautifully situated crag.

Winder has written ruefully about the shortage of transport at that time, when trips such as those to Luggala, distant from the nearest road and bus route, were usually available only to those lucky enough to be taken by car owners such as Perrott.[8] Even the crags at Glendalough were difficult to access, bearing in mind the infrequent and inconveniently timed bus service and the long distance from the terminus. For a while, then, most of the early pioneering was confined to Dalkey Quarry as a group of exceptional ability formed around Winder and Maguire.

In the early 1950s, Peter Kenny, André Kopczynski, John Morrison, Sean Rothery, all in their early twenties, all students or recent graduates in the sciences or architecture, were an unusually talented bunch. With virtually no contact with climbers from

Britain or elsewhere, these young men put up a series of routes which retain their reputation and fine qualities into the twenty-first century. Indeed, forty years later, Winder's Bracket Wall was upgraded as were two fine routes, Helios and Hyperion, first led by Kenny in 1951 on the clean, steep granite of a section of Dalkey called White Wall. In that same year Maguire plotted a devious but elegant route through the overhangs on the highest face in the quarry to create Central Buttress, a route of considerable quality. The route was at the top of the middle grades for some time, so its complexity and airy situations were enjoyed by climbers who were not quite of the highest standard, but the breaking sometime in the 1970s of a vital hold at the start of the second pitch brought the climb into the top grades. By 1951 there were new routes also on Bray Head and Ireland's Eye.

Over the next few years Dalkey continued to act as a forcing ground for Irish climbers, particularly those based in Dublin, providing opportunities to develop skills on crags which could easily be visited in the evenings and which were of a sufficiently modest height to allow time to work on tricky moves. In 1952, Kopczynski and Ruth Ohrtmann put up In Absentia (they were absent from college lectures),[9] on White Wall between Helios and Hyperion. It was the hardest and probably the finest route in the quarry at that time and remains as a test piece. Kopczynski, a physicist, was a Polish war veteran and Ohrtmann, also a daring lead climber, was German: a roped partnership which, so soon after the war, might have seemed odd in another setting. At that time most climbers were happy to limit themselves to routes in the middle grades or lower. With little or no facility for running belays a leader's fall usually resulted in injury or worse. The second man on the rope was often belayed very close to crux moves. In the following year, Paul Hill led a bold route on the right edge of the slab in the West Valley which contained several routes named after their reputed first ascensionist, Winder, (although it is probable that Winder's Crack was first climbed by Harold Johnson).

Irish mountaineering would have developed in a very different way, and certainly not so rapidly, had it not been for this small, gifted group. Ireland at the time could not be thought of as adventurous. More than one commentator has remarked on the enervating effects of what came close to economic despair,[10] and of the essentially conservative nature of Irish society which had little inclination to frivolous endeavours such as mountaineering.[11] Some of the club's hillwalkers had a somewhat decorous approach, as witnessed by their dress on the first hillwalking meet atop Sugar Loaf, and by one individual who was known to carry his sandwiches in a briefcase. But Sean Rothery has stated that the top climbers of the time thought of themselves as daringly unconventional,[12] bohemian perhaps. Their climbing gear, consisting of wartime surplus clothing, deteriorated with hard use to ill-fitting tatters. Then, and for more than a decade afterwards as Korean War surplus became available, the unspoken belief (or youthful affectation?) was that the grottiness of one's britches was directly related to one's climbing ability. Their nonconformity may have been a little callow but the initiative of these pioneers, their shrugging-off of societal norms, required spirit in an Ireland pervaded by a narrow religiosity and lack of enterprise.[13] However, this display of spirit does not entirely account for their extraordinary abilities and their dominance over others attracted to climbing at that time.

Winder – slight, scholarly, keen – had, in 1950, joined a small team at TCD engaged in research which led to a breakthrough in the chemotherapeutic control of the then common scourge of tuberculosis. He went on to academic eminence and a professorship. He could not by any means be described as muscular even though some of his routes, at that time and later, were steep and strenuous; compared to most climbers his legs were matchstick thin. No doubt his weight/strength ratio was good and he later suggested that he climbed from stance to stance in bursts of nervous energy,[14] which may be why he also said that he never really enjoyed the Alps, where long stints of speed and steadiness are required.[15] Elizabeth Healy, a long-time climbing partner of his describes how, in the hills:

He revealed the significance of the apparently insignificant – a slight change of colour in a brackish pool, a little movement in the grass. He knew the name and habits of every shy leaflet and rare blossom, and every small creature that rustled in the heather. Even climbing up some wet and vegetated gully, he would be heard to exclaim with the delight of discovery – 'Ah, Adelanthus lindenbergianus' or some such. Or, instead, the voice might float down from above, declaiming, as the rope ascended slowly – interrupted by many grunts – 'the unpurged images of day recede' or other Yeatsian stanza . . . I can see him towards the close of an Annual Dinner . . . quartering the dance floor on roller skates, intoning 'Because we love bare hills and stunted trees' . . . not to an audience, just to himself.[16]

Oddly, his writing on mountaineering was matter-of-fact and reflected neither his passion for the activity nor his poetic sensibility.

Kenny was taller, robust, ebullient, and given to wild bursts of enthusiasm which tended to sweep others along. He had what he considered a purist's approach to climbing, disdaining top-rope inspections and being abstemious in his use of protection.[17] He even voiced objection to the use of running belays which were placed above head height and was prepared, probably more than any other climber of that era, to face long, unprotected run-outs.[18] He climbed gracefully, methodically, seemed always to be in control. He was given to

Frank Winder. IMC ARCHIVE

Peter Kenny. KENNY, IMCI 1958–59

enthusing loudly, almost fiercely and in an asthmatic rasp, on the quality of the climb or the performance of his partner. In the pub his humour was boisterous as he sang, to the tune of Handel's *Water Music*, his own satirical composition, 'Comrade Lysenko', about a notorious Soviet 'geneticist' of the Stalinist era (this despite Kenny's early Marxist leanings).[19] His drinking sometimes got out of hand, as it did with many young climbers, and he was not above the harbouring of grudges. He was withering in his contempt for what he called 'the nylon and hand-bag brigade', a small section of female IMC members who so typically represented the contemporary prim nature of middle-class Irish society. (However, the only written record to be found of such pietism is of a male club member writing in shocked tones to the club committee about men and women sharing tents,[20] a prudishness directed against climbers to be echoed later, again by men rather than women, in a submission to the so-called Morals Committee set up in An Óige.) Kenny related better than most of his peers to the working-class climbers whom he encouraged to take up climbing, and he was highly regarded by them. He was a physicist, born in Penang and brought up in Dalkey and, like Winder, would become a very successful researcher. As Professor of Radiology at the University of Miami he was to build a world reputation for pioneering a fresh approach to nuclear magnetic resonance imaging. His work with radiation may have led to his early death, aged sixty-one, in 1989.[21]

By 1950, the pleasant south-facing Twin Buttress on the Camaderry crag at Glendalough, and the adjacent more complicated

Upper Cliffs, had gone through their first stage of development as Kenny and Winder, having cycled from Dublin, did the first ascents of Quartz Gully and Cúchulainn Groove on the same weekend. Quartz Gully maintains its reputation as a classic Hard Severe with 'a character-challenging crux' despite the plenitude of running belays afforded by modern gear.[22] The ascent of streaming wet Cúchulainn Groove, actually a corner crack, was protected by precariously inserted pitons and at least one belay point consisted of a thumb-knot jammed into a crack. The climb was begun in nailed boots, with a single snap-link shared by the two climbers, and higher up entailed a precarious change into rubber-soled shoes at a small stance, one shoe being later shucked off while standing on a 'wrinkle'.[23] Irish climbers were unused to crack climbing so the route acquired a considerable reputation, being over-graded for some time.

Following this initial burst of high-grade activity at Glendalough things quietened down there for the next two years as Winder emigrated temporarily, as did Kenny to Scotland where he formed a bond with fellow iconoclasts in the Creagh Dubh, a mainly working-class group who mocked the prevailing hierarchy and were in the vanguard of Scottish rock and ice climbing.[24] Lynam began a longer absence in England and India. But things had been happening elsewhere: in the Mournes, Connemara and Kerry. The first tentative steps had been taken in Donegal, while in the Alps lessons were being learned.

An Easter meet to Connemara in 1950 led to return visits in 1951 which resulted in some easy climbs and scrambles near Doo Lough and in the Maumtrasna, and to the notable first ascent by Kenny, Kopczynski and Morrison of Seventh Heaven in Glen Inagh, a serious if not very technical route of about 330m on compact quartzite with small sloping holds and sparse protection on its thirteen pitches. Kenny, who recommended Tricouni nailed boots for the climb, thought it 'undoubtedly the best climb in Ireland to date'[25] and it has occasionally surprised strong parties. Winder and Hill were lucky to survive when a vegetated ledge high up on the route collapsed, leaving them hanging from a line casually looped over a small rock knob.[26] Some years later Vivian

Stevenson recalled 'the terror of poorly protected moves' when he completed Seventh Heaven in a thunderstorm in 1959 with Zeke Deacon, one of Britain's top climbers of that era.[27] Camping in bad weather in Connemara was a common abiding memory and Elizabeth Healy later recalled, 'the great days of Peter Kenny, the wild days of poteen, filthy, wet drunken poteen weekends'.[28] In 1951, Lynam and Rothery separately had put up some routes in the Gap of Dunloe in Kerry. Their easy routes seem to have been somewhere on the high cliffs on the west side of the gap overlooking the Black Stream bridge. In the following summer a pair of English climbers put up routes in that area and in Coomreagh in the nearby Black Valley.[29]

Northern Ireland

Before the formation of the IMC, student teachers and graduates from Stranmillis College in Belfast had revived interest in mountaineering in a province recovering from war. Maurice McMurray, Roy Johnston and Brian 'Gaspe' Gibson raised the standards and intensity of rock climbing activity beyond pre-war levels, climbing mainly on Eagle Rocks because of that crag's accessibility from Newcastle for bus- or train-reliant students. They slept under overhanging boulders or in the ill-designed US army bivouac tents which featured so much in tales of discomfort in the Irish outdoors of that time.[30] Further from the usual bus routes, and as early as 1947, Johnston led a hard climb for its time, Niche Route, on one of the several tors which project stegosaurus-like from the long crest of Slieve Binnian. In 1949, he led a party up the long but easy classic slab-route called FM on Slieve Lamagan, the name of which is explained by the last two lines of a doggerel:

> They started quite merry they thought it fine spree
> But before the day was over they were murmuring F. . .
> Me.[31]

Later, in 1954, Phil Gribbon, with his customary quirky humour, named an adjacent route Cherchez-La.

McMurray and Gibson must also be credited with a notable exploration of rock-climbing possibilities in Donegal when they ascended a gully at the head of the Poisoned Glen in 1950. The gully, which came to be called Green Grass Gully, is, strictly speaking, a scramble rather than a rock climb but was typical of early tentative approaches to big and unknown crags when the architecture and possibilities are being sorted out.

The founding of Queen's University Belfast Mountaineering Club (QUBMC) in 1950 had an important impact as it resulted in increased participation, as can be seen from the new names which appear in the various Mourne climbing guides. Among these were Phil Gribbon, Doug Sloan and the wonderfully named Ken W. W. Double who was one of several British ex-servicemen. More attention was given than hitherto to the recording of new climbs.[32] Gribbon, the acknowledged leading light of that time, suggests that there was now a new impetus to northern climbing even if this did not extend to pushing standards as high as those pertaining in the south. There is scarcely an account of this time which does not vainly attempt to explain this difference in standards but none focuses on the rather obvious reason that there was sufficient satisfaction to be had from exploring the numerous Mourne crags. This contrasted with Wicklow's two widely separated main cliffs, and allowed for routes of good quality and at a more reasonable grade than was possible in Wicklow where there was a paucity of climbs of any character which were below the middle grades. As Gribbon says:

In the beginning there was a wealth of untapped mountainy things to do and anyone in an idle whim could pioneer a new route on a new crag. Those folk who began climbing in those golden days realised unconsciously that they must be experiencing something unique and historical in their lives.[33]

As with all such pathfinding, there is a sad realisation that such an experience is in the past and can never be repeated. Much of the geniality of the narrative of that time, perhaps true myth would be a better term, owes its existence to Gribbon's wry insights. Laconic in conversation, self-deprecatingly funny in print, his early writings and later memories describe a time of discovery, of warm and eccentric camaraderie much at odds with conventional views of a solemn, even dour northern society. Gribbon, yet another physicist, revelled with his friends in their mountains, in the freedom to wander through the rugged if compact Mourne, to select untouched crags and winkle out delectable routes. They camped, bivouacked, stayed in youth hostels or made use of a rented cottage high on the slopes of Slieve Binnian which they named the Bloat House after the Bloat, an evil concoction of rice, spam, onions and whatever was handy and could be lived off for an entire weekend, and even the following one if it survived the intervening days in the drawer to which leftovers had been consigned.[34]

The Bloat House under Little Binnian in the late 1950s. BRIAN KENNEDY

As in the Dublin IMC there were women members, two of whom, Hazel Fitzpatrick and Emily Innes, each led a first ascent on rock, and the latter was prominent on at least one Alpine trip. As they settled into jobs the male climbers acquired motorbikes, the cumbersome British machines of the time, and travelled to the Bloat House swathed in newspapers as insulation beneath their outer clothing and wearing papier-mâché helmets.

Above all, they had fun.

They too wore ex-War Department camouflaged anoraks or Navy blast-protective smocks. They nailed their own boots and used triple hawser-laid nylon ropes 30m in length, having given up on the rough, hawser-laid hemp ropes which had been used for some time by McMurray and also by the founder members of the IMC. Perhaps even more than their Dublin counterparts they revelled in torn and patched clothing – possibly a necessity given the rough nature of Mourne granite.[35] Gribbon, in particular, who might be described as a conservative eccentric with features fittingly craggy, clung on to gear well past its sell-by date even into the 1990s. He is famously reputed to have surprised a Canadian lady as he descended from a climb in Ontario with one trouser leg missing from the knee down. On being asked if he had lost it on the climb, the future lecturer in physics at St Andrews loftily replied, 'No, in the war'.[36] Brian Rothery, Sean's brother, related how, on a roadside crag in upper New York state, Canada-based Gribbon instigated a near-riot when he shouted 'Go home, Yanks!' to gawking motorists lined up below.[37]

Many of the active climbers joined the Belfast Section of the IMC, which was formed with the active support of QUBMC members in March 1952. They began to think of themselves as the 'Affables', slightly rebellious, less mature than 'those others' who were keen on committees and other appurtenances of a club and whom they called 'Typicals', both terms conjured up by McMurray.[38] In line with their somewhat chimerical self-image, the 'Affables' continued the outwardly casual style already established but began to raise standards and look beyond the Mournes. A combined meet with their southern counterparts in Donegal very shortly after the formation of the new Section resulted in a joint Dublin/Belfast ascent of Jubilation on Castle Buttress in the Poisoned Glen in Donegal by Gribbon, Joe Madill, Sloan and Sean Rothery. Later in that year McMurray and Gibson continued their adventurous

pioneering by climbing Tuning
Fork Flake, the first route on one
of the fine crags at remote Lough
Belshade in the Bluestacks in
south Donegal.

Gribbon's unprotected and
delicate Nig Nog on Little
Binnian, a route which was then
in the upper grades, remains a
classic. It was top-roped prior to
first ascent. His ascents of
popular Third Corner on Lower
Cove and Asphyxiation on Pigeon
Rock were, surprisingly, the first
routes on these crags. But several
of the harder routes fell to
Dubliners with Kenny, Winder
and Sean Rothery all making
their mark. At a combined meet
in a campsite near Blue Lough
the northerners were appalled by
the Dubliners' use of belay pitons
and by their overt ambition. To
quote Gribbon again:

Tuning Fork Flake, Lough Belshade,
County Donegal, in 1958. Barry White
leading Phil Gribbon. GRIBBON COLLECTION

In the Mournes we didn't dash at it; if we could put up
one new route, and maybe repeat an earlier route, we were
satisfied. There was no rush, we had the scene to ourselves,
there was no competition from other climbers. We were
content with what we climbed within our limits and were
well aware that our standard fell well below that of our
fellow Dubliners [sic].[39]

Abroad

Both IMC sections inevitably progressed to Alpine climbs, the Belfast
group a little more slowly and tentatively and without losing their

anarchic approach. Joss Lynam led a meet to Arolla in Switzerland in 1949 which spilled over to the Mattertal where the Rimpfischorn and Zinal Rothorn were climbed.[40] In 1951 Frank Butler and Brendan Moss were sufficiently confident to forego another club meet at Arolla in favour of Austria,[41] which was to serve as an Alpine nursery for novice Irish alpinists for some years.

A problem faced by Irish climbers for quite some time, in the Alps as well as at home, was a difficulty in measuring their own abilities. The founders of the IMC had been schooled in British attitudes, techniques and climbing ethics, but they did not climb at a high standard and were not fully conversant with the rapid rise in standards taking place in the neighbouring island at this time. The more able climbers who were pushing up Irish standards were, perforce, rather tentative when it came to the Alps, not knowing if their doings at home would translate into success on the higher peaks. They were aware that British standards in the Alps had lagged behind those of their continental counterparts between the two world wars and for the latter part of the 1940s.[42] Where did this leave them?

By 1952, the confidence shown by Brendan Moss and Butler had spread and was matched by strengthened ambition. Some of the top climbers arrived in the Mont Blanc area intent on climbing on the Chamonix Aiguilles, a complex jumble of granite spires ranging from 3,000m to 3,600m in height. But they would not be the first newcomers with considerable rock-climbing ability to find that in this exciting stone jungle they would encounter unfamiliar dangers. In early August, while negotiating the Nantillons glacier on his way to do the Charmoz-Grépon traverse, Fred Maguire fell to his death in a crevasse,[43] the first Irish climbing fatality of the twentieth century in what would become a distressingly extended list. Kenny, Winder and Kopczynski in attempting the Chamonix Face of the Aiguille du Peigne wandered off route on what is an uncomplicated line and, although they reached the top, delay and poor route finding led to further adventures and confusion during a long-drawn out descent in darkness. Kenny's mettle showed through as he steadied the tired and dispirited party.[44]

(In early summer Maguire had fallen at Ireland's Eye. Club minutes of 12 June 1952 show that resultant rescue measures had cost the club £2 11s 0d. This was to be recovered from Maguire. Another meeting on 25 July 1952 recorded that as Maguire was dead his debt to the club was now cleared.[45])

Gribbon, innocently passing through France, was arrested and conscripted into the French Army, thus adding to his atypical repute. He had been born in France while his parents were on holiday so he was suspected of being a draft dodger. His arrest led to a minor international incident and his release after some months.[46] He had been with others of the Belfast Section making their Alpine debut in the Stubai. On their return they found that Joe Madill had met his death climbing in Glencoe. In the following few years the Belfast Section made trips again to Austria, to Val d'Isère and to Arolla but, while they were to have many adventures and their habitual relaxed fun, their ambitions and achievements lagged behind those of the Dubliners.[47]

The amount of club activity in the Alps in 1953 was remarkable even when compared with Alpine doings in later times. There were Irish climbers in the Mont Blanc massif, the Dauphiné, Arolla, Graians, Julian Alps and Austria.

The Chamonix Aiguilles were again tackled in 1953, this time with élan and improved competence, by Kenny, Winder, Rothery, Morrison and Hill. All but Hill attempted the north-west ridge of the Grands Charmoz, a route which had been climbed for the first time only three years before by two of France's foremost alpinists. The four-man Irish group teamed up with two Englishmen and, perhaps inevitably, the unwieldy party of six made such slow progress that dusk overtook them as they neared the crux pitch. They retreated until darkness forced a shivering, cold bivouac for which their poor equipment had left them unprepared.[48] One of the Englishmen, Harold Drasdo, who was to form a close bond with Ireland and its climbers, has recounted how Winder, unable to sleep having taken Benzedrine or some such amphetamine, stayed erect muttering Yeatsian verse for most of the night.[49] In various combinations, the group went on to complete the Aiguille de Roc, two routes on the

Requin, and the Ryan–Lochmatter Route on the Plan (the 1950 ascent of which by British climbers Bourdillon and Nicol was regarded as exceptional although Frank Smythe had climbed it in 1927).[50] Perhaps of equal importance in the acquisition of Alpine experience by Irish climbers in that same year was the success of a party with traditional mountaineering skills (Butler, Moss, McMahon and Masterson) who, following ascents of Les Bans, Les Écrins and Pic Coolidge in the Massif des Écrins in the Dauphiné Alps, moved to the Mont Blanc area where they traversed Dômes de Miage, the magnificent arête of Aiguille de Bionnassay, and Dôme du Goûter to Mont Blanc.[51] Given that the 'top men' were relying on their previous experience of rock climbing in concentrating on the magnificent granite of the Aiguilles, this showing on mixed snow, ice and rock routes by a competent party pointed the way to the many subsequent enterprising Irish parties whose rock-climbing skills were not of the highest order.

Tragedy again darkened the following year's alpine season when Kopzcynski fell to his death abseiling in the Peigne couloir. He had attached the abseil rope to just one of a number of lines attached to a much-used abseil point. The line, probably hemp, broke and he fell past Kenny who had to remain with him throughout the night as he died while the English pair accompanying them (one of whom was Drasdo again) had to wait for dawn on a lower ledge before

André Kopzcynski in Connemara in the early 1950s. IMC ARCHIVE

going for help.[52] Lessons were being painfully learned but they had done remarkably well bearing in mind that a number of the climbs they completed had been considered to be beyond the competence of British climbers (their only ready exemplars) until 1950.[53] Lynam and Gwynn Stephenson led an energetic trip to Zermatt this same year while Belfast climbers expanded their horizons on Grossglockner and other Austrian peaks.[54]

Wicklow

In 1953, Kenny and Winder, usually together and sometimes with others such as Rothery or Moss, laced Glendalough's Twin Buttress with bold routes like Prelude and Nightmare, Scimitar and Aisling Arête. If one stands close beneath the main face on Twin Buttress and looks upwards one cannot but be impressed by these pioneers who could imagine a way through the daunting bulges that guard the upper face. Admittedly, Nightmare was subjected to a top-rope inspection,[55] and Winder first top-roped the crux pitch of Scimitar,[56] but bearing in mind the lack of reliable protection and near-impossibility of a climbing retreat, theirs was a remarkable feat. And there was more to come.

In 1954, Kenny, Winder and Rothery firstly managed to find and climb the partially hidden and slightly overhanging Lethe, albeit with the aid of two pegs, and then moved on to what Lynam has called the 'apotheosis of Camaderry climbing',[57] the first ascent of Spillikin Ridge, a line which in its upper reaches follows a prow forming the right-hand edge of the main face.

There had been several previous attempts and some top-rope inspection before the climactic day, 13 June, when Peter Kenny led the crux pitch of this fine route. With Winder belaying from the top of the Spillikin, a 6m detached pinnacle, Kenny made a long stride from its tip to gain a shallow quartz crack which led to the first overhang where a piton placed on a previous attempt protected a tricky move. Kenny then moved up, eschewing the use of two further pitons previously placed by Winder, to make a long step into Scimitar Crack, which had proved too much for Winder in damper conditions, thus avoiding a second overhang. He climbed back out of Scimitar above this overhang to reach a small foothold on the edge of the arête which served as a very airy stance.

He brought up Winder while their waiting rope-companions Rothery and Hill dozed at the foot of the pinnacle. The use of combined tactics, even the use of Kenny's stubbly face as a hold and a wobbly move from atop his shoulders along with the use of a stirrup, all helped Winder to move up to where the angle and tension eased.[58] Those who have stood on one foot at this last stance will testify to the poor prospect of holding a fall when balanced so precariously – bearing in mind that there were no harnesses then in which to sit – but this method, *sans* stirrup, stayed in use on this pitch until ropes longer than 120 ft (36.5m) came to be used some time in the 1960s.

With this ascent of what the 1993 climbing guidebook called 'the most celebrated line in Wicklow'[59] a quite remarkable period of exploration and development came rather abruptly to an end. In the short space of six years a small group of climbers had produced some fine routes, and with Spillikin Ridge had achieved a level of rock-climbing difficulty (XS) which would have been regarded with considerable respect in international climbing circles only a few short years previously. Irish mountaineering, especially in Wicklow, should have been set for further development but, apart from a good season in Donegal in 1955, there followed an unfortunate hiatus. Spillikin would not have its second Irish ascent until 1959.

Little new of major significance was done in Wicklow in the following five years apart from Sean Rothery's addition of the crux pitch to the ethereal and felicitously named Spéirbhean, and his Facilis Descensus. The name of this latter climb came partly from Dante (to match nearby Inferno) and partly from Sean's potentially fatal flying descent from the top of the climb. He was stopped just short of the ground by his only running belay. In 1956, Kenny and Winder, climbing together for almost the last time, and accompanied by Rothery and Charlie McCormack, endeavoured – without lasting impact – to revive interest in Luggala by putting up Left Side Climb near Pine Tree Buttress.

Emigration and careers had their effects while, momentously and sadly, the prolific Kenny/Winder partnership broke up for reasons

Spillikin Ridge with semi-detached finger of Spillikin still intact. Note climber sitting on Nightmare Ledge at top of photo. PETER HEALY, IMCJ 1958–59

which need not be probed here other than to observe that an enduring antipathy was generated which lasted for over thirty years until a dying Kenny penned a letter of reconciliation.[60] In 1955, some working-class hillwalkers and middle-class mountaineers coalesced when a number of An Óige people were introduced to mainstream rock climbing and the IMC by Kenny and Sé Harmey. Following a weekend at the Glendalough crag when Kenny and Harmey brought thirteen of these tyros up some easy climbs, about six seriously took up the activity and began a gradual trend which led to the domination of Irish mountaineering by working-class climbers for nearly two decades but also to tensions which were to threaten the solidarity of the IMC, North and South.

3

Where Does the Fugitive Prince lie?

Hillwalking

The early fruitful period of rock climbing and alpinism had been matched by happenings in that more traditional, demanding, but less hazardous aspect of mountaineering fostered by Praeger, and by G. W. Young in his Irish outings. During the early and mid-1950s, many of what much later came to be called 'Challenge Walks' were completed for the first time and attained some measure of usage. There were in the IMC, North and South, members who had combined their rock climbing and trips to the Alps with hillwalking, a practice that would continue in Irish mountaineering for some decades. In Dublin, Pat McMahon and Ciaran Mac an Fhaile were each noted for their solo walks, often at night, and their predilection for bunking down in the rough.[1] Joey Glover, from 1955 onward, would embark on his stamina-demanding hill traverses in the north-west and west. Most of the hillwalking feats were completed by 'hard men' from outside the IMC who would not have thought of themselves as mountaineers in the commonly accepted sense: men, and some women, associated with An Óige or with Na Fánaithe, an Irish-speaking club which had a cottage near Valleymount in west Wicklow.

The Irish hills still offered opportunities for endeavours which were very much outside the ken of the average urban dweller. Even Wicklow, the mountainous county adjacent to Dublin, remained very rural, touching on the backward, in the early 1950s. Most of the mountain roads were unpaved, homes in the hills were still lit by oil lamps, there had been no new houses built in the Glenmalure and Aughavannagh areas since the nineteenth century. Turlough Hill power station and the television mast atop Kippure, both with their approach roads, did not yet exist and much of the forest, which would later cover large expanses of the hills, had yet to be planted. Most of the hilltops and ridges were pathless. Motor traffic was sparse and public transport infrequent. The more distant hills ranging down through counties touched by the Atlantic were little changed from the 1930s and were as remote and unfrequented as all but the most isolated parts of Scotland. The hills, then, were wild, free, challenging places 'robed in mystery',[2] to which the adventurous responded with imagination, vigour and readiness to tackle the unknown. An *Irish Mountaineering Club Journal* editorial said; 'Exploration remains the keynote of Irish mountaineering'.[3]

A practice grew among a few of the more enterprising of hitch-hiking to remote ranges, of 'shacking'– sleeping in farm outhouses, forestry huts, abandoned rail stations, upturned boats – completing an outing in the hills and making it back in time for work on Monday morning.[4] And these were times when most people worked for half a day on Saturday. In remote valleys, and even in Wicklow to an extent, one could count on a traditional welcome permitting the use of farm outhouses and which sometimes extended even to sharing meals and sleeping in the farmhouse or cottage.[5] It was an obvious outlet for adventurous but impecunious young working-class city dwellers. However, the movement was led initially by middle-class civil servants and a few professionals, mostly from rural backgrounds, who outdid some of Hart's feats and devised other long hill traverses and 'themed' walks which ever since have been the objects of emulation and competition. In 1950 Tom Quinn and John O'Keeffe, both civil servants, completed what became known as the 'Lug Walk', the 29-mile (46km) route from Ballinascorney Gap to Lugnaquilla, taking in all the intervening summits.[6] (Hart had reached Lugnaquilla mainly by road and had avoided many tops on the way back.) Including their subsequent descent to Aughavannagh the time taken was 16 hours.

In 26 May 1952, six members of Na Fánaithe repeated the escape route through west Wicklow which, supposedly, was followed by O'Neill and O'Donnell when they escaped from Dublin Castle in the winter of 1592. Because of some ambiguity associated with the location of Sliabh Rua which, according to the Annals of the Four Masters, was traversed by the young princes, this first repeat by Na Fánaithe differed in its first section from the route which subsequent parties followed. The starting party of nine joined the now commonly used route into the Wicklow Hills at Ballysmuttan and proceeded over Billy Byrne's Gap, through Glenbride and on to Glenreemore and finally Glenmalure. At Ballynulty, just before Byrne's Gap, they descended to attend Mass in Lackan. Three of the party dropped out here before the walk was resumed by ascending again to Ballynulty. There is no record of the time taken, which was obviously significantly lengthened by the diversion to Lackan.[7] Later that year Uinseann Mac Eoin, an architect, and Daithi Ó Scolaird, a civil servant who had been on the previous walk, decided with others to make the outing more in keeping with the original by starting at night from Dublin Castle in late December, a custom followed ever since, sometimes in extreme conditions which tax even hardened climbers. They took about 19 hours, having again diverted to attend Mass, this time in Valleymount. It seems they initiated the tradition of ending up at Ballinacor, the site of Fiach McHugh O'Byrne's stronghold, the final refuge of Hugh O'Donnell, the survivor of that terrible blizzard-beset escape.[8] Na Fánaithe again did the walk in January 1954, this time including the first woman, Nóra de Hal, to complete the walk.[9]

Earlier in 1952, in September, Mac Eoin and Ó Scolaird completed the traverse of the Maamturks in Connemara, in 7 hours 50 minutes.[10] This had already been done by Hart in about 14 hours,[11] and then by Praeger,[12] and was to become a popular outing and organised competition for many years. Mac Eoin had also paid his first visit to Scotland in April (with John O'Keeffe) where he ascended the first peaks of what would become – without his realising it then – the odyssey which eventually led, in 1987, to his being the first Irish-based person to complete all the Scottish Munros, (peaks over 3,000 ft).[13] (According to Alan Tees, his brother Jimmy Tees based in Inverness had previously completed the Munros.)

Most of these long walks, and this was the case for those who followed for some years later, were unsupported; the walkers carried food, a change of clothes, sometimes a stove and cooking pot, and whatever was necessary for self-sufficiency until infrequent public transport was boarded, perhaps as much as eight hours following walk's end. Boots were then of poor quality so that in cold or snowy conditions it was essential to keep moving and snack breaks were usually hasty, shivering affairs.

In 1953, Ó Scolaird completed Hart's Walk in 23 hours 15 minutes, faster than Hart but still behind Cronin's time

Uinseann Mac Eoin , mountaineer and a pioneer of Irish long-distance hillwalks, in 1990. JOHN MURRAY

from thirty-six years previously (see chapter 1). His companion, John O'Keeffe, dropped out at the Wicklow Gap. Later that year, on 24–25 October, Ó Scolaird, accompanied by Mac Eoin, made another attempt to beat the record, this time in competition with Michael McGarry and Larry O'Reilly, both members of a running club. This time Ó Scolaird gave up at the Wicklow Gap and the other three completed the route in a record time of 19 hours 50 minutes.[14] Mac Eoin and Quinn, with others, began the tradition of snow camps on various summits, such as Lugnaquilla and Corrán Tuathail, starting on the former in February 1952. One heard yarns of blizzard-battered tents and St Elmo's Fire. In 1956 Mac Eoin completed the traverse of seventeen of the misleadingly named Twelve Bens in 13 hours and 30 minutes.[15]

Daithi Ó Scolaird, right, in later life (1989), with Dermot Gunn. GARETH JONES

Gradually, Dublin working-class youth hostellers began to join Quinn on his more venturesome enterprises and added a new flavour to an already irreverent approach to what conventional society would then have regarded as a fairly irresponsible activity. (There are accounts from this time and even later of walkers and climbers waiting until they had cleared their neighbourhood before changing into appropriate gear.[16]) Art O'Neill's Walk was repeated several times, once by a newly researched eastern route as described in this book's prologue, as was the Lug Walk.

There were working-class climbers in the Dublin Section of the IMC almost from the beginning but these were few and were hardly identified as such in a club which, for the most part, eschewed overt class distinction. Frank Butler, a carpenter, was a club stalwart and sound mountaineer who had joined in 1949, and there were several other tradesmen and junior clerks. Many, if not most, of the Irish middle classes of the time were of rural origin, not long removed from the poverty of the nineteenth century. The Anglo-Irish aristocracy had almost entirely vanished, there was little of the conspicuous wealth which came later, and distinctions of status depended, in the cities, on education and to a certain extent on accents which would later become associated with places such as Dublin 4 (although they were then known as Rathgar accents). That status and those accents were much associated with middle-grade employees of established firms such as Guinness, Jacob's and the banks. Pat McMahon, who was then a schoolteacher, has described how, on joining the IMC in the early 1950s, he was initially intimidated by the middle-class atmosphere and tones, as was Noel Brown.[17] Those accents, in a country where many senior civil servants and government ministers now spoke with a rural lilt, inhibited relations between the club and organisations such as An Óige and probably stymied the founders' ambitions to set up new Sections around the country along the lines of continental national clubs. From a 21st-century perspective the holding of 'lantern talks' rather than slide shows,[18] is simply quaint, as was the addressing of people by their surnames in correspondence as Lynam did in his early years in Ireland, writing 'Dear Coleman' to his good friend.[19] The question of class – which does not carry the same weight as it does in some other countries – did not, according to Gribbon, arise in the Belfast Section during the first decade of its existence, given that the membership was more homogenous and white-collar, although McMurray 'had a very non-middle class background'.[20]

There was some petty snobbery and a degree of unintentional condescension in the Dublin-based part of the club as there would be in any organisation of that era, but that did not much affect the half-dozen or so young men who had been inducted to the club by Kenny and who for some years were referred to as An Óige climbers even when they had been in the club for some time.[21] As one might expect there was a degree of mutual class stereotyping. Although they received encouragement from the top climbers, they were left much to their own devices as Kenny and Winder became involved in their respective careers and, now that they could afford private transport, in forays to Donegal and Connemara, while Sean Rothery, on the heels of Perrott, Morrison, Moss and others, was about to emigrate.

It took some time for the small working-class group to expand and for some climbing talent to emerge. Its members had to start almost from scratch, initially without guidebooks to either Glendalough or Dalkey. There was a lack of transport and they still devoted much of their time to hillwalking.

From that An Óige group, Noel Lynch and Paddy O'Leary did the Lug Walk in a time of 13 hours 30 minutes in June 1956. On the following weekend Lynch led a group including the first two women, Maureen Cronin and Eileen Brennan, to complete the walk, while O'Leary, meeting Lynch on the way, brought the time for the outward trip down to 9 hours 30 minutes in completing the first return journey Bohenabreena–Lugnaquilla–Bohenabreena in a time of 29 hours 30 minutes.[22] (O'Leary had wandered around in a sleep-deprived, hallucinatory haze on the home journey, finding himself returning to a mist-covered summit several hours after he had left it.) In either 1956 or 1957 Bob Lawler, another of the tradesman climbers, riding a motorbike with Joe Brennan on the pillion, completed the ascent of the highest peak in each of the four provinces between a Saturday morning and Sunday night. Bob was on the driving seat all the way.[23] Their ride started yet another trend which they, along with the originators of other such walking ventures, may have rued had they envisaged their eventual damaging popularisation (as described in chapter 11).

Mourne

The Mournes, although more rugged than most of Wicklow, are compact, criss-crossed with well-made paths and have a large portion enclosed by the Mourne Wall, so the range does not lend itself in quite the same way to the long, wild traverses feasible in other parts. Nevertheless, even here an endurance test across a number of summit crests which were linked by the Water Commissioners' boundary wall had become a test of fitness. In 1953, seven members of the Belfast Section of the IMC completed the 22-mile (35km) circuit; the fastest time, 6 hours 30 minutes, being recorded by Roy Johnston.[24] A 'challenge walk', Ireland's first organised one, was instituted in July 1957 when the first Mourne Wall Walk was conducted by YHANI. The walk, which followed the route along the wall as completed by Charlie Brims in 1935, was not meant to be competitive but, probably inevitably, some walkers aspired to fast times and thus attracted such people as Larry O'Reilly (record-breaker on Hart's Walk) who did the fastest time.[25] The organisers were not to know that their example would be followed in other hill areas with consequences for the environment and mountaineering ethics which would eventually become controversial.

Rock Climbing

As the intensity of Kenny's input diminished from 1955 onwards – except for his continuing interest in Glen Inagh where the IMC had developed excellent relations with the sheep-grazing Bodkins family – and Winder concentrated his main effort in Donegal, it was left to the so-called An Óige climbers to nudge the standard up a little in Dalkey.

In 1957, they put up Gargoyle Groove, which would remain the hardest climb in the quarry for more than a decade, followed by Great Eastern on which one point of aid was used. The former climb was done in boots and without protection except for a sling around a flimsy gorse bush. (In a blue-collar variation of the earlier dominance of physicists and architects, the three ascensionists on these routes – O'Leary, Sé Harmey and Joe Flynn – were electricians, as were the Lawler brothers with whom O'Leary climbed High Tension in Glen Inagh in the same year.) But, apart from a few isolated endeavours such as these, there was a definite falling-off of intensity and exploratory vigour in Wicklow for several years. With so many of the top climbers gone, dead or easing down it would take until the early 1960s for someone of the stature of Kenny or Winder to emerge and longer still for the kind of numbers necessary to sustain the kind of support and, yes,

IMC members with Bodkins family of Glen Inagh 1950s. *(L–r)* Dan O'Shea, Joan Birthistle, Thomas Bodkin, Mona Monahan, Nora Bodkin, Peter Kenny with unknown girl in front, Eddie Bodkin and two unnamed women climbers. IMC ARCHIVE

rivalry which leads to greater things. The mainly working-class group ran a number of well-attended weekend beginners' courses under informal An Óige auspices over the next few years.[26] No outstanding talent emerged, except perhaps for Bríd Boyle, a fifteen-year-old whose latent talent was not spotted and who eventually, as Brede Arkless, became one of Britain's earliest and ablest mountain guides. The courses did lead to an increase in female participation in the IMC, some as rock-climbing leaders. Although they continued to hillwalk, there was for these young men little that was new or venturesome remaining in such outings. In an increasingly prosperous and recreation-conscious Ireland any initiative in that aspect of mountaineering would be confined mainly to beating records on 'challenge' walks which would soon show signs of overuse.

Donegal

While progress in Wicklow and Mourne hung fire, there was a shift in interest to the granite of the Derryveagh Mountains in Donegal, mainly led by Winder and a small number of English climbers. Winder had been responsible for Byzantium (Yeats again!), one of the earliest climbs at Lough Belshade in the Bluestacks, most of it climbed in nailed boots.[27] As Kenny's part in the very successful pioneering period neared its end, apart from some yet-to-come long, exposed routes in Glen Inagh, he completed a troika of climbs on the clean, airy Delta Face at Lough Barra, east of Slieve Snaght, in the autumn of 1955. At about the same time, one of the classics of the crag and the best at its grade, Tarquin's Groove, was put up by Winder and Harold Drasdo. Drasdo, attracted to Ireland following his meeting with Irish climbers in Chamonix, had first visited Donegal with his brother in 1954 and 'fell deeply, blindly, helplessly under the spell of [the county]'.[28] The brothers had tinkered about a little in nearby Poisoned Glen but Tarquin's Groove was a big step forward and one of several significant routes Harold was to complete with Winder during this balmy autumn. Here in Lough Barra he also did Balor with Winder, while Surplomb Grise with its tricky start fell to Winder and B. Ball. In the Poisoned Glen, Winder, Elizabeth Healy and Drasdo did Ulysses and Finnegan's Rake, the first two of a trio of Joycean-tagged climbs on The Castle at the head of the glen. More will be heard of Healy, the country's leading woman climber for many years and pioneer of some fine routes.

While some routes in the Glen and Lough Barra were opened up by Winder during the next few years, it says much of the state of Irish climbing at that time that, for four years until 1960, all the other important routes in Donegal were pioneered by British climbers. In the Poisoned Glen the absence of native initiative was to last even longer. Drasdo's name is associated with a number of climbs. With his brother Neville and later with some well-known compatriots, including Eric Langmuir, Geoff Sutton and Andrew Maxfield, he helped to develop West Buttress as well as Bearnas Buttress, the largest of the crags in the Glen, where Route Major was his main contribution. But the best routes of this period fell to Allan Austin and Brian Evans (later co-founder of Cicerone Press) who together changed the virgin status of Bearnas Buttress in

August 1957. They did Slanting Grooves and next day managed what was undoubtedly the coup of the decade in Donegal when they climbed Nightshade, a fine route on West Buttress with some sensational situations, which, together with an almost Alpine ambience, makes it one of the very best of Ireland's mountain routes. Drasdo and Langmuir, in April 1959, also did the first climb in Glen Veagh, a typical 'feeler' called Catriona which avoided the main crag. This was followed in August of that year by Empathy on the left flank of the main crag in this lovely lake-enhanced valley, which succumbed to Maxfield and R. Fryer.

Wicklow again

British influence was also felt in Wicklow when Austin and Evans managed the second complete ascent of Spillikin Ridge in August 1957. Drasdo and Bob Downes, a leading UK climber of the period, had made a previous attempt, but only the lower part of the crux pitch was climbed.[29] Then, in August 1959, Vivian Stevenson and Zeke Deacon, two of a party of Royal Marines who had been climbing in the Poisoned Glen, put up a route, Spearhead, at Luggala, which had been suggested to them by Winder who joined them on the climb. Deacon, in boots, led the finger traverse and corner which breached for the first time the great roofs, some extending out for 3m or so, on what came to be called the Main Face. Having gone back and forth cleaning out moss on a hand traverse with small holds, and having suffered several falls, Deacon launched himself along the traverse, 'his feet swinging into space and then with a vicious swing moved around the corner, looking as if he was riding a horse. He was up if he could muster enough strength in his fingers to climb the next forty feet. Then he managed to pull up with his last remaining bit of strength.'[30] Although it receives no special mention in modern guidebooks, Spearhead was a major and imaginative breakthrough. With one modest exception it would be another ten years before Irish climbers succeeded on other routes in Luggala and a year following that before another climb made its way through the Main Face overhangs.

On the day following their Luggala success, Deacon and

First ascent of Spearhead, Luggala, in 1959. Zeke Deacon leading, and Vivian Stevenson. Note boots, piton hammers, rope tied at waist, belay method. F. WINDER, IMC ARCHIVE

Stevenson (not Stephenson, as given in Wicklow guides) demonstrated their route-finding flair as well as considerable ability by climbing Cornish Rhapsody on the Upper Cliffs at Glendalough, a 'minor masterpiece' according to the 2009 guidebook, which again found a way through an apparently impregnable overhang.

And the Irish? The period 1954/55 to 1960 is generally regarded as a fallow period in the development of Irish mountaineering. The reasons for the slow-down in the discovery of new crags and creation of new routes will be dealt with below, but it may be useful first to examine what else was happening in the small world of Irish climbing.

In 1954 the Tralee Mountaineering Club was formed, followed by the North-West Mountaineering Club (NWMC) which was established in 1955 in Derry (or Londonderry, as the founders preferred). The former was almost entirely a hillwalking club while the latter, although much smaller – it had a membership of twenty in 1956 – was involved in the exploration of possible climbing crags in a number of areas in Donegal. Joey Glover has left us with some vague descriptions of new climbs done by club members at Lough Belshade and elsewhere in the Bluestack region as well as in Barnesmore Gap during 1956,[31] but the main contribution of NWMC at this time lies in the long hill walks initiated by Glover as mentioned above, particularly the traverse of Muckish, Aghla More, Aghla Beg and Errigal that would one day be named after him.[32]

In 1955 the IMC opened a new hut at Glendasan, a tributary valley of Glendalough, which replaced a poorly situated rented premises in lower Glenmalure. The new hut became the climbing and social centre for the Dublin Section and for other clubs as they were formed. It was well filled on most weekends for the next two decades. While a handful of new routes was found at Camaderry, most of the activity there for the next few years was confined to repeating routes put up by the pioneers; further development was hindered because, in the absence of a guidebook, fresh blood was

IMC hut opening at Glendasan 1955. *(L–r)* Peter Kenny, Noel Brown, Mona Monahan, Mary Gahan, Aleck Crichton, Hilary Quinlan, Sir Charles Harvey, Dan O'Shea, Elizabeth Healy, Brian McCall and Frank Winder. IMC ARCHIVE

unaware of all that had already been climbed and what remained to be done.

Distant Kerry was subject to further tentative exploration. Elizabeth Healy, who had joined the IMC in 1954, partnered Winder in August of that year in crag exploration in the south-west, notably at Adrigole, and at Cumeengadhra near the Healy Pass, and put up a 330m line at Coomanassig just to the left of the gully down which Winder had fallen while botanising years previously. They named the climb The Bastille but, remembering Winder's previous escapade, it should probably have been called Catharsis. At Easter 1956 – having hitch-hiked from Killarney – O'Leary, Lynch and Brendan Henshaw put up what Winder called a challenging line,[33] Primus, to the right of Bastille in the centre of the face and another route in nearby and previously untouched Coomnacronia. They then walked 25 miles (40km) from their campsite to catch the train home from Killarney. There would be similar episodes in other locations. Winder and promising newcomer Brian McCall did Luicin in Coomanassig later in 1956, and they also were involved, in 1957, in exploration of the excellent sea cliffs at Sybil Head and Ballydavid Head at the tip of the Dingle Peninsula.[34] No record of their few climbs there seems to have survived.

In March 1958, Dan Turner and Sean Ryan, both from Cork, did a roped ascent of the broken ground which separates the north face of Corrán Tuathail from the north-east face.[35] Sean has said this may be the route later called Primroses.

(Winder's activities in Kerry did not go unnoticed. In about 1999, Winder and O'Leary returned to Coomanassig and came across a man driving a tractor on a track which had not existed on their previous visits. On being told that Frank had first visited the coom fifty years previously the man, who was in his forties, declared 'Ah, you're the fella that fell down the clift!' [sic].)

Kenny was fairly active in Connemara until 1958 and insisted that Glen Inagh was a better rock-climbing location than was Donegal, a short-sightedness no doubt affected by what he saw as rivalry with Winder. He put up a number of long, sparsely protected routes in Glen Inagh, some of which he himself regarded as of little character,[36] but which also included Mona Lisa, which was also climbed on that October day of 1958 by a second party with Noel Brown to the fore. The Dublin University Climbing Club (DUCC) was formed at Trinity College Dublin in 1958 with Ronnie Wathen as President. That club, like the university itself, would remain a little exclusive and largely Anglocentric, besides being all-male, well into the 1960s.[37]

As can probably be gleaned from preceding paragraphs the lack of transport which Winder had bemoaned in earlier years now affected younger climbers, some of them earning apprentices' wages, who limited their outings outside of Wicklow to holiday weekends when cars were sometimes rented or a resort was made to hitch-hiking. Most of the crags in Donegal, Kerry and Connemara were not accessible by public transport. Gibbons' barn at Lough Barra in County Donegal, built in the late 1950s and in which climbers were warmly welcomed to stay, was a five-hour drive from Dublin and often longer on bad roads as there was a reluctance to drive the shorter route through Northern Ireland because of possible late-

Gibbons' barn, Lough Barra, c. 1960. GARETH JONES

night encounters with the B Specials (auxiliary police force) who were active and touchy due to the 1950s IRA campaign.

Snowdonia was easier to reach if one did not have a car so, as the mail train then stopped at Bangor, Dublin climbers could be frequently found on crags in north Wales. Trips abroad had to be squeezed into a fortnight's holiday. For several years, apart from Kenny and Winder who were increasingly involved in their careers, there was just a handful of people capable of climbing consistently at VS standard, and perhaps two or three who could manage anything more difficult. It was supposed that there was little left to be done at Glendalough, and at Luggala a similar lack of imagination and drive resulted in few visitors. The kind of protection then available was, of course, an inhibiting factor but ought not to have been decisive.

Things began to change, at least in Wicklow, in May 1959 when Winder and Healy completed a traverse of the Main Face at Luggala just below the big roofs (was this when they saw the possibility of breaching the overhangs which Zeke Deacon and Stevenson later exploited?). Kevin Shelley and O'Leary did this traverse in the opposite direction in the following year. Also in 1959, Tony Kavanagh and O'Leary made the second Irish ascent of Spillikin Ridge; P. Gordon and Glyn Cochrane of DUCC followed later that year.[38] Healy, Brian MacCall and Sean Rothery (newly returned from Africa) managed the second ascent of the marines' Cornish Rhapsody, while Rothery led Winder and Kenny up Spearhead not long after its first ascent,[39] confirming that it was not lack of climbing ability alone which had inhibited progress. Guide books were produced for Wicklow (1957, Kenny and Winder), Mournes (1957, Gribbon) and Dalkey (1959, Kenny and Mona Monahan), the latter two books being produced by newly departed emigrants, Gribbon writing his as he sailed to Canada.[40] Also emigrating were those two fine mountaineers who climbed the middle grades, Frank Butler and Charlie McCormack. Charlie is generally supposed to have been the first Irish professional mountaineering instructor and would work at the renowned Hafod Meurig in Wales for a number of years.

The Mournes in the late 1950s hardly warrant a section to themselves as so many activists emigrated and the pace of development slowed, with only the doings of P. Wilson on Hen Mountain being recorded in club notes and guidebooks. A short-lived rock-climbing club was revived in YHANI in the mid-1950s and a number of transitory groups formed in the various army and air-force units stationed in the province. In 1959, that Derry stalwart Joey Glover completed what was probably the first traverse of the Nephin Beg range from Bangor Erris to Mulrany, Pat McMahon having almost succeeded some time before.[41]

As a fitting endnote to a quiescent period, besides a harbinger of things to come, Emmett Goulding's name is associated for the first time with a new climb, Borstal Boy on Ariel Buttress in the Comeraghs in County Waterford, which he did with Barry O'Flynn in 1959.

Abroad

Speculation about the possible causes of the fairly static period in Irish climbing during the latter half of the 1950s, particularly in Wicklow and the Mournes, becomes especially intriguing when one considers the purposeful, if relatively modest, doings of Irish mountaineers abroad. Some of these doings were those of emigrants who otherwise might have helped to maintain progress at home. Harder rock routes in the Alps were neglected in 1955 and 1956 as attention was focused on classic mixed ascents particularly in the Zermatt area. Gwynn Stephenson and Lynam, who was now working in the Lake District, stretched themselves in 1955 on the Rothorngrat, a route that they felt was outside their comfort zone. Monte Rosa was also climbed by club members, as were the Weisshorn and Dom.[42] Similar routes were completed in the following year, by far the best being a traverse of Monte Rosa in poor conditions by Healy, Butler and Brown.[43] Austria, the eastern portion of which was still under Soviet occupation in 1955, was a popular choice for Irish climbers because it was then one of the least expensive countries in Europe, with good cheap *Bergsteigeressen* ('mountaineer food') available in the huts, and the chance of having your lunch sandwich made of a slice of bread between two slices of Emmental-style cheese.

Further afield John Morrison anticipated the wide-ranging, backpacking style of the hippy 1960s as he climbed Mexican volcanoes Orizaba (5,699m) and Popocatapetl (5,452m), besides tackling South Dakotan spires in 1955 before struggling mightily through the Horsethief Range and Bugaboos to reach first ascents in the Scotch Peaks of the Purcell range of British Columbia. There the party of about six completed the entire summit ridge of Scotch Peaks (2,755m), in four hours.[44] In 1958, having come from Mount Cook in New Zealand, he was defeated by heavy snow in attempting Indrasan in the Kulu region of the Indian Himalaya with Britisher Bob Pettigrew and others,[45] and then went on to climb Demavend in Iran.[46] Sean Rothery, who had emigrated temporarily to Uganda, climbed several peaks close to 5,000m altitude in the glaciated Ruwenzori ('Mountains of the Moon') in 1957, including Edward Peak (the highest point of Mount Baker), Alexandra (the second highest peak of Mount Stanley), and Mount Speke. Rothery, who had been involved in almost all of the important climbing initiatives in Ireland and abroad in the early 1950s, has tended to be neglected in accounts of that era, probably because of the dominance of Kenny and Winder. Initially encouraged to take up climbing by his fellow-architect Fred Maguire, Sean was slight in build as were so many of his climbing contemporaries; he was highly competitive and contagiously enthusiastic, besides being more socially engaging than his two better-known friends. He remained active when most of his contemporaries had hung up their boots and ambitions.

Also in 1957, Ronnie Wathen was a member of a Cambridge University team who completed the difficult first ascent of Pumasillo which was thought to be the highest unclimbed peak in the Peruvian Andes.[47] In 1958, Peter Robson, Brian Kennedy and Keith Millar of the Belfast Section and QUBMC were on a college expedition to Spitzbergen, of which Robson was deputy leader, where climbs included the first ascent of Vasa.[48] These various ventures may be seen to vie with each other to be considered as the first Irish expeditions to distant ranges. In the Spiti-Lahul area of India, which was not at all easy of access in those days, Lynam and Stephenson were members of a Sherborne Expedition (Sherborne is an English public school) which succeeded in penetrating a gorge to the virtually unknown Gyundi glacier and managed to link this across a high pass with the extensive Bara Shigri glacier. They also climbed two virgin peaks of over 6,000m and two others of about 5,800m, besides completing a plane table survey which filled a large blank on the existing map.[49]

During the following year reports filtered back from Canada about the doings of a combined Dublin and Belfast emigrant contingent, which included Millar, Doug Sloan, Brian Rothery (Sean's brother) and omnipresent John Morrison, which was active in Quebec and upper New York State, putting up new routes up to HVS standard, and discovering new crags, as at Bon Echo.[50] One of these exiles, Phil Gribbon, predictably went further afield, and with an English friend did the second ascent of the worthwhile North Face Ridge on Mount Baker in Washington State in poor conditions.[51]

The Alps

What was remarkable in the latter half of the 1950s was the absence of continuity, the entire absence of previously outstanding performers from Irish Alpine ascents. Links were so weak that routes were being repeated without knowledge of previous Irish ascents. Short duration of holidays was an inhibiting factor, usually shorter than the three weeks which Kirkpatrick, a man of leisure, had considered too short. The more active climbers were not academics or students. A journey to the Alps entailed two ferry crossings, races between stations in London and in Paris, and multiple train changes over the course of a hectic minimum of 36 hours. The cost of air travel was prohibitive and there were no direct ferries to the continent.

From this time on the numbers of climbers and clubs would gradually increase to the extent that accounts must be selective. Almost all Alpine routes mentioned here in this chapter will be first Irish ascents unless otherwise made clear.

In 1958, taking advantage of a post-apprenticeship break and some experience acquired on two previous trips, O'Leary hitch-hiked to Switzerland, and, mainly with Brian McCall, had the most satisfying Irish Alpine season to date, reaching twelve 4,000m summits in the Zermatt area. The routes followed included a traverse intégrale of Monte Rosa, Lyskamm, Castor and Pollux; and of the Matterhorn by way of the Z'mutt Ridge and the Italian Ridge. As the Irish pair tackled a steep ascent to reach the Matterhorn glacier on the traverse from the Hörnli, two Germans intent on the Nordwand (north wall or face) front-pointed speedily past them, wearing helmets and wielding a pair of ice axes each – the first the Irish pair had ever seen of climbing helmets, the use of an axe in either hand or continuous front-pointing. Indeed, they had been amused on seeing the helmets when they previously saw the pair in Zermatt's main street.

Later, in Chamonix, O'Leary met Wathen at the end of the latter's successful season in the company of Chris Bonington and the likes of Don Whillans on routes such as the East Face of the Grand Capucin and the West Face of the Petites Jorasses.[52] Wathen inveigled his Irish friend into a farcically unsuccessful attempt on the West Face of the Aiguille du Dru which did not even get across the initial marginal crevasse. This was a fleeting stay in that area on O'Leary's way home and was the only recorded visit to Chamonix by an Irish climber in that year.

In the following year the first recorded Irish female Alpine team of Sylvia Yates and Mary Gahan climbed the Trifthorn from the Rothorn hut and the Dom via the Festigrat. George Narramore and Mike Lunt, both fine mountain photographers, were probably the first unguided Irishmen since Kirkpatrick in 1903 to reach the summit of Dent Blanche, the best of their climbs that year. In Chamonix, McCall and Healy climbed a number of Difficile routes in the Aiguilles, while Eamonn Gallagher and Tom Cullen managed easier climbs. Tony Kavanagh and O'Leary, from their tent on the Plan de l'Aiguille above Chamonix, concentrated on TD routes including the Chamonix Face of the Peigne, not knowing it had already been done by Kenny and friends, and then enjoyed the south-west ridge of the Fou and what they wrongly thought was the first Irish ascent of the Mer de Glace face of the Grépon. Winder, Kopczynski and Kenny had climbed it some seven years previously.[53] (In retrospect, it seems extraordinary that just Kavanagh and O'Leary were climbing at this level in 1959.) The same pair had another Alpine trip (c. 1960) but neither remembers anything but bad weather and being confined for several days in the Estellette bivouac shelter. Although in no way remarkable in regard to technical difficulty, the level of activity outlined above was an indication of the IMC's growing maturity and of the settling into a pattern familiar to ordinary clubs worldwide.

Kavanagh, McCall and O'Leary had failed to build on the experience and expertise acquired during the previous seasons, especially on the bigger, albeit middle-grade, routes, and had, in the last year of the decade, confined themselves to the Chamonix Aiguilles and the sort of rock routes which were, in essence, their Irish experiences writ large and on which they were never seriously stretched. Enjoyable, yes, but in common with many of the Irish who followed them, they missed out on the opportunities to commit themselves further on harder routes or to venture onto some of the area's grander courses with their testing mix of steep ice, rock, snow.

Those opportunities would soon be seized upon by Emmett Goulding, who, in 1959, made his up-and-coming presence felt by completing, with Barry O'Flynn, a traverse of Maurerkeeskopf, Simonyspitze and Dreiherrenspitze in Austria.[54]

4

West Face of the Dru

One August morning in 1961 two Irish climbers in their mid-twenties arrived heavily laden at the marginal crevasse, or rimaye, at the foot of the shallow couloir, or gully, which leads to the West Face of Chamonix's Petit Dru. The ascent of the West Face of this enormous, rough-hewn obelisk was regarded as perhaps the most important breakthrough of the post-war era in the Alps when it was first climbed by a French team nine years previously. Its first British ascent by the extraordinarily tough and talented Joe Brown and Don Whillans had taken place in 1954. Standards had been improving rapidly in the intervening years, most relevantly amongst a small group of British climbers who followed the example of their continental counterparts by moving on to harder things, such as the Bonatti Pillar – also on the Dru – and the Walker Spur of the Grandes Jorasses. But the West Face was still among the very hardest of alpine endeavours.[1]

The Irish pair crossed the rimaye and climbed a crack in the steep wall leading to the wide couloir, down which falling stones whined and clattered. A few rope lengths of easy climbing led to ice-covered rocks which obliged them, as they had no ice-climbing

West Face of Petit Dru.
HARRY O'BRIEN

gear, to climb for about a hundred metres using a piton hammer to cut minute steps, and a rock peg as a substitute ice piton. Their determination and skill were further displayed throughout their three-day ascent of the face in bad weather. They suffered several falls and encountered steep pitches down which water cascaded, soaking their clothes prior to freezing bivouacs on narrow ledges, the last night being without drinks or hot food due to saturated matches. Then, roped cooperatively with an Austrian pair with whom they had exchanged leads several times on the face, they completed a final desperate traverse to the top of the Bonatti Route which they followed to the summit.[2] The ascent was by far the hardest completed by Irishmen until then and the two climbers, Emmett Goulding and Tony Ingram, were setting new standards and displaying a level of skill which was unprecedented in Irish climbing in the Alps and at home.

Goulding, a house painter, and Ingram, a carpenter, were the leading exponents of a new approach, which reflected a new dynamism in Ireland of the 1960s. Remarkable in view of their performance on the Dru was their relative inexperience of hard Alpine climbing. In 1959, Goulding had been to Austria, and in 1960 had climbed several worthwhile mixed routes in the Zermatt area but none that would indicate that he was ready to tackle one of the Alps' hardest rock climbs. Ingram, whose physical strength was well known in the building trade, had even less experience, having been to Austria once on a mountaineering course.[3]

But neither was a neophyte in this game of testing their limits. They had developed their craft at home, using skill, resourcefulness and artisans' strength to establish themselves as Ireland's leading rock climbers over the course of the previous two years. They would be largely responsible for a change in attitude, one result of which would be the ascent by a few of their young followers of some of the hardest climbs in Ireland in the bendy walking boots which were all that the youngsters could afford.

The socially and economically transformative decade of the 1960s would have its impact on the development of Irish mountaineering. Emigration dropped sharply in both Northern Ireland and the Republic as the economies improved, and the outflow of enterprising climbers, which had affected both Sections of the IMC in the late 1950s, was much diminished. Better employment prospects and higher incomes meant that places like Donegal, and later Fair Head, could be reached by newly acquired motorbikes and cars, albeit usually second-hand and subject to the prevailing unreliability. Changing social attitudes led to greater egalitarianism in mountaineering circles, an acceptance among the general public of what had been seen as an eccentric activity – and to better music in the pubs frequented by climbers. Towards the end of the decade the political situation in Northern Ireland and the consequent Troubles would affect cross-border and internal travel, and would place severe restrictions on access to some hill areas.

Goulding's impact on standards, and his Alpine performances would not be emulated and improved upon until a new decade had come. An important feature of the 1960s would be the increased interest in ventures into distant ranges and the first Irish team ascents of remote peaks. Other factors which would influence Irish mountaineering were the establishment of the Spillikin Club in 1965, that club's ties to the Glenfoffany Climbing Club in Northern Ireland, and the consequent initial development of Fair Head. An interesting element was the emergence of women who led and put up climbs at the harder grades.

Home

O'Leary and Goulding were in almost at the start of a thrilling period, and the end of British dominance in Donegal when, still using a hawser-laid nylon rope, they finished a climb which they named Aiséirí at Lough Barra in June 1960, a climb on which Bob Lawler and O'Leary had been washed off in heavy rain in 1959. During 1960, sixteen new climbs were put up at Lough Barra while Rothery was the first to venture onto the central wall of the main face at Glenveagh when he led a new route called Sinn Féin, with Brown and Butler in support. Other fresh names are recorded at Lough Barra that year, among them Kevin Shelley and Padraic O'Halpin. The latter would soon form a potent pairing with Elizabeth (Betty) Healy who in this year would emerge from Winder's shadow when she led Fomorian, also at Lough Barra.

Lough Barra 1960. *(L–r)*: Paul Power, Paddy O'Leary, Emmet Goulding and Barry O'Flynn. IMC ARCHIVE

McCall, Sylvia Yates and O'Leary emigrated that year so they were to miss out on the next two important years. Ingram, who had been introduced to climbing by Barry O'Flynn in about 1958, and Goulding who came to climbing through hillwalking with the scouts and An Óige, formed a partnership which in a very short time during 1960 and early 1961 completed all the harder routes in Dalkey and

Wicklow. In May 1961 they put up the first hard route completed for five or six years by Irish climbers at Glendalough's Twin Buttress when they forced Sarcophagus, a tricky corner to the right of Spillikin. The crux pitch was led by Goulding wearing stiff-soled boots and using just one point of protection, a sling over a rock spike. Graded initially at XS, the highest grade then in existence, the climb had a greater significance than its present somewhat easier status would suggest, in that it confirmed in their own minds the capabilities of the talented pair and persuaded them that they were ready for the West Face of the Dru and all that followed.[4]

On the same day as the Sarcophagus ascent, Land's End was put up in the Upper Cliffs at Glendalough by a DUCC pair, G. Bergess and Cochrane. Not long afterwards, in July, Elizabeth Healy and Sean Rothery completed a 325m girdle traverse of Twin Buttress. Healy consolidated her reputation the following September as one of the country's foremost climbers by leading Winder and Rothery up Sebastian, a hard route with several points of aid. Elizabeth had earlier shared a first ascent, Ploughshare, at Lough Barra in Donegal with rising newcomer Padraic O'Halpin. Another waxing star, Eddie Gaffney, extracted a new route, Lassitude, at the Expectancy slab on the extreme left of Twin Buttress. Eddie was one of those newcomers – Pat Higgins was another – of whom Frank Winder remarked that they raised standards 'by sheer climbing ability, not by the new technology which caught on only later; they usually climbed in boots and were far from lavish in their use of protection'.[5] Gaffney, then a post and telegraph technician, was small, and acrobatic to an extraordinary degree, as was demonstrated on a subsequent ascent of Lassitude when he fell from the top and tumbled the length of the 20m slab and into the gully below before standing up unhurt.[6]

Ingram brought a successful year for Dublin climbers to a close when, in November, he and Kevin Shelley climbed Praxis, a route on Lower Cove in the Mournes which would remain the hardest in that area for the next five years.

Other climbs in the Mournes were completed by Belfast climbers in 1961, with the names of George Garrett, Ivan Firth, C.

Tony Ingram and Eddie Gaffney, c. 1962. GARETH JONES

Leeke, J. Sloan, Eric Wilkinson, Phil Grindley and Harry Elwood recurring on a variety of crags. The overdue break-through to the higher grades was just around the corner, but the turn had not yet been made.

In Donegal in 1961, in addition to Healy and O'Halpin's Ploughshare, the year had seen Sean Rothery doing Firbolg on Lough Barra's main face in April (not in 1959 as recorded in several guidebooks) with O'Halpin and Wilkinson.[7] But the climb which caused a sensation at Easter was the ascent by Britons Hugh Banner and J. O'Neill of a climb they called Rule Britannia – originally much over-graded – which started to the right of Surplomb Grise and veered off to the left to join that climb higher up. Goulding and Ingram were at Lough Barra that weekend and were incensed by what they saw as a deliberately provocative epithet and they determined to respond, as they did in 1962 by straightening out the poor line of Rule Britannia and making a much better climb which they called – what else? – Erin-go-Bragh. (Many years later Hugh Banner, who was a more genial man than expected, told O'Leary that the name had been given quite innocently with no intention to provoke or insult.)

In early 1962 O'Leary travelled up from London to meet Goulding in what was then the quiet backwater of Fort William in Scotland. With only one small shop open in the evening they barely managed to get enough supplies to last them a week at the CIC hut (the Charles Inglis Clark Memorial Hut) under the great north-east face of Ben Nevis. On this, their first experience of winter in Scotland, they were lucky in a way which seems remarkable in the twenty-first century to find that, following a heavy snowfall and freeze, they were the first climbers on each route they did. All traces of other ascents had been wiped out and they encountered no other climbers on their chosen routes. They learned a great deal as they moved from easier climbs to delightful tests on the likes of Glovers Chimney, Comb and Green Gullies, hard routes at the time, and repeatedly raced across a deserted summit plateau to escape benightment.[8] They were still using long, wooden-shafted axes with which they cut steps on ice, and a long blade as their one effective ice peg. (They had a few ice corkscrews which were as ineffective as they sound.) The insecurity associated with using such tools was apparent when they failed to construct a safe belay in deep unstable snow as Goulding struggled to breach a large cornice while exiting Green Gully. The immediately previous attempt had resulted in a long fall from the same spot and the death of one of the climbers. There is no record of Irish climbers having previously tackled Scottish winter climbs although it is possible that there were prior visits.

At Lough Barra, Gaffney, Gerry Moore and Gerry Cairns got the 1962 season started with their ascent of Gaffney's Climb, the crux on the second pitch being done mistakenly for Surplomb Grise.[9] Erin-go-Bragh was put up at about the same time in May, as was Kestrel, which featured Goulding and O'Halpin as leaders. This latter pair had climbed Ariel, HVS, in Glenveagh the previous day. O'Halpin, who had been born and gone to school in nearby Letterkenny and had come to climbing late at the age of thirty-eight, was a clever, sensitive man, an engineer given to self-analysis and one of the finest writers in a surprisingly ordinary collection of Irish mountaineering literature. He composed poetry privately. His self-deprecation is exemplified in his description of a pitch on Ariel:

To follow Emmett up a climb is not always possible. Although I had led part of this pitch before I was by no means certain that I could follow it now. The rope on such climbs does not always help. It is the trauma one fears, not the fall. Assured by now of insecurity – slowly with poison the whole blood-stream fills – I too swung strenuously out on the rib into the unfair complex of delicacy and muscle. I forced a way up the rock with all the ways I had in me; the knob came into sight and then to hand. It was my secret hope to hang a long sling on it (where I was invisible to Emmett under the overhang), sit in it in relative comfort and rest. This I eventually did, reflecting that on the last occasion, perhaps because I was so clearly visible to those below, I had not taken this pendulous rest and would perhaps have been ashamed of it. So does technique advance.[10]

But Padraic probably underestimated his own abilities, especially when he was not subjected to Goulding's all-too-knowing eye, as he had already that year led Setanta, HVS, in Glendalough and would lead or share leads on several other climbs at Lough Barra with various partners. In 1963, he and Healy did the lengthy Dolphin at Glenveagh. Healy's name would feature for almost the last time in guidebooks in 1965 when she and O'Halpin shared leads on Toraigh at Lough Barra, with Sean Rothery and O'Leary following on a separate rope.

Padraic O'Halpin, rock-climbing activist of the 1960s, in his native Donegal.
ELIZABETH HEALY

There had been other able female climbing leaders, notably Sylvia Yates, Ruth Ohrtmann, Ingrid Masterson and Jill Rowe. Then there was the brilliant English woman Anthea Peel of DUCC who led Cenotaph Corner at Llanberis when it was still of fierce repute, having already led the hardest Glendalough routes.[11] Elizabeth Healy was in a class of her own, first as an impressionable and keen junior partner to such as Winder, Kenny and Rothery, and then as a talented co-leader with O'Halpin. Initially a copywriter, she was to become editor of the respected *Ireland of the Welcomes* and then an author, but wrote little of her climbing experiences. Originally from Cork and never losing that striking accent, her Dublin experience and her own self-expression truly came to life when she discovered climbing and encountered 'people who read books and listened to music as well as doing this wonderful activity'.[12] She recalls the first time she climbed Nightmare at Glendalough about six months after she had started climbing when, after leaving Nightmare Ledge and traversing to the exposed ridge where space, the waterfall and the entire valley came abruptly into view: 'I remember stepping around the corner up above and . . .

screaming for delight and excitement and saying what a fabulous place. That is my most memorable experience and I don't remember being frightened or anything'.[13] Rather suddenly, about twelve years after she had taken to the activity, she stopped climbing at an advanced level or indeed at any level except for a few nostalgic trips to Donegal, and outings to Dalkey in the early 1990s with some of her ageing friends from the early days. In a remark which must prompt much head-nodding, she

Elizabeth Healy, outstanding rock-climbing leader of the 1960s. HEALY COLLECTION

notes that, 'I don't think you can combine too many things in your life with climbing . . . Once anything else starts to take over in importance that's the end of it, that's the end of high standards anyway.'[14]

The doings of Healy, O'Halpin and Rothery were an essential element of Irish climbing in the first half of the 1960s. While there seem to have been more leaders than before at Glendalough and in Donegal, most attention was focused on the group which formed around Goulding: Ingram and Shelley at first, and then Gaffney with Pat Higgins and others. The latter pair led Jackey at Camaderry in Wicklow in 1963 and followed Goulding up adjacent Celia and other harder routes. When O'Leary returned from London, a parent, in 1962, form and ambition blunted, he was impressed by the natural abilities of this new breed of mainly working-class climbers but somewhat dismayed to find himself sometimes in an unaccustomed supporting role to some talented cragsmen. New routes at Glendalough and elsewhere demanded strengths, physical but also of purpose and imagination new to Ireland, or perhaps re-emergent following a long period of somnolence.

Mourne

In the Mournes, Calvert Moore and Frank Devlin eased into the guidebook in 1962 with Starlight on Eagle Rocks and Sunset on Hen Mountain, a tentative beginning to careers which would leave more emphatic marks on that area. Most of the climbers mentioned above in relation to the Mournes continued their endeavours. Moore, along with Davy Dick, would venture experimentally, and not very fruitfully, onto hitherto neglected and somewhat distant Eagle Mountain with their Funk in 1963, and more successfully with several climbs on Eagle Rocks where Devlin and J. Brown also featured. In 1964 the first definite signs of a new and exciting period would appear. In that year Frank Devlin would second a Dubliner, Pat Kavanagh, on Dot's Delight, a congenial gem on Lower Cove. Moore with Geoff Earnshaw made the first significant breakthrough on Eagle Mountain with their Sammy Higgins, besides putting up the excellent Stratocumulus and other routes at

Eagle Rocks. Earnshaw was also responsible for a hard route on Spellack, a steep and readily accessible crag rising above the much-used Trassey Track, while many of the people mentioned in preceding paragraphs would feature on a number of routes spread throughout the Mournes.

New clubs

At about this time dissatisfaction with both the Belfast and Dublin Sections of the IMC, combined with the new energy apparent among working-class climbers, led to the setting up of new clubs, and a subsequent rise in general climbing standards. Such events were probably inevitable given that the IMC was past its youthful flush and that the influence of the early activists had waned. According to Ian Rea, writing about the Belfast Section:

> There were those to whom the stuffy middle-class, professional atmosphere of the IMC was not amenable and as a result Glenfoffany Climbing Club was formed by Calvert Moore and friends in 1962. This was rumbustious, proletarian and full of life and from its foundation until the end of the sixties it was the main force in northern climbing.[15]

While this statement is inconsistent with the continued presence in the Belfast Section of some working-class climbers such as Garrett, Brown, Jim Milligan, Sloan and of Calvert Moore's good friend Frank Devlin, it reflects a widespread view among activists of the time. Ian Rea, who was not around at the time, stated that his attitude to the IMC was influenced by that of Calvin Torrans.[16]

In Dublin, sometime towards the end of the 1950s, there were increasing tensions as the behaviour of some working-class club members in the Glendasan hut went beyond the expected boisterousness of late arrivals from the pub. Things came to a head when a display of crass misogyny by drunken yobs on the climbing fringe led to serious fractures in the club's fellowship and to some resignations. Later, less crude dissension within the Section led to a leaking away from the club of some active climbers which stemmed partly from a lack of rapport between those activists, who happened to be working class, and a few of the more conservative established committee members. There was also ill feeling between Goulding and O'Flynn which somehow permeated much of the club's social interchange. As the author was involved to a degree in the later stages of this conflict he must rely on the comments of others. There was a certain friction between the craftsmen and those described as being interested, perhaps too ostentatiously, in 'poems, operas, fine wines and things like that',[17] but this hardly impinged on climbing friendships in a club and general society which had hazy and shifting class boundaries. Niall Rice disputes Joss Lynam's view that there was an underlying class element, and there was but little generational motivation in the breakaway, although Niall does mention an unwelcoming atmosphere at the hut for activists like him.[18] Perhaps Joss, not fully in touch following a long absence in India, misunderstood several heated but rather petty wrangles and in subsequent accounts conflated these with the earlier nasty rows. It is true that those who gradually trickled from the club – with Goulding making a thing of formally resigning[19] – all happened to be tradesmen but motivations varied. Rows continued, and even worsened, after the few had left.[20] The departing group became the core of the Spillikin Club which was formed in late 1965.

This question of class was to arise again in the 1970s and there would be suggestions that the keenness of working-class activists was blunted by association with middle-class conservatives and that it was necessary for such activists to strike out on their own to reach their full potential. But, reverting to the author's own opinions, it is not seen quite like that. Differences arose which had nothing to do with class and were much related to a clash of views on what a mountaineering club should be. When these differences were centred around strong personalities people were inclined to take sides. There were always those mountaineers who just got on with climbing at various degrees of difficulty and avoided controversy.

Spillikin Club was formed in order to provide a focus for all or most of those climbing at higher grades in Ireland and to counter the hitherto all-too-common situation where capable but isolated individuals in a small climbing community gave up or lowered their sights because of a scarcity of partners. It was constituted in a way that obliged members to continually seek out new climbs. It was not set up as a climbing elite in order to exclude 'hangers on' as Torrans has suggested,[21] and the cars which headed for crags at weekends continued to consist of old friends of mixed abilities. Loosely knit, the club's membership included activists of various social classes from other clubs such as DUCC; the Cavern, Rock and Fell Club (CRCC, which was centred in The Royal College of Surgeons in Ireland); QUBMC; the IMC; and Glenfoffany, as well as otherwise unattached individuals.[22] In a little over a year the club had twenty members, which constituted the majority of the country's small number of strong climbers. Healy was winding down when Spillikin was formed so the club never had a woman member. The connection with Glenfoffany was particularly fruitful and led to an unprecedented mixing and matching of climbing partnerships and friendships, as well as to a warm appreciation of that passion fostered by Moore who was a big man with an even larger personality. It was understandable that the formation, separately, of Glenfoffany, Spillikin and another club, Slievadore, was seen, wrongly, as being anti-IMC rather than pro-climbing, and it did not help that the new clubs were none too tactful in their defensiveness.

In 1965 Frank Devlin, Dorothy Devlin and Des Agnew began the development of a crag at Ballygally on the Antrim coast road. Bruce Rodgers and his friends from Portora School and DUCC opened up the small crag at Monastir Sink in Fermanagh.[23]

By this time routes of some quality were being put up all over the Mournes and the rate at which they were being done would intensify during the next few years. Moore, a relative newcomer with a huge grin called Calvin Torrans, Devlin, Sam Crymble, Willie Jenkins, Earnshaw, Harry Porter, Ricky Cowan, Dick, and the independent climber Brian Moorhead, all contributed to varying degrees. Some routes fought hard before they succumbed, among them being Great Corner on Eagle Mountain which resisted attempts over a period of three years by a succession of attackers until finally yielding in 1967 to Jenkins, Torrans and Robin Merrick. While the standards rose steadily, there were excellent new, easier climbs such as Class Distinction (Crymble), at Pigeon Rock, and Pillar Variant (Moorhead and Stead), on Lower Cove. In 1968, the *IMC Journal* recorded that thirty new climbs had been forged in the Mournes in the previous eighteen months.

Sean Barrett in the 1990s on Great Corner, a classic climb on Eagle Mountain in the Mournes. IMC ARCHIVE

Dublin

In Dublin, an increase in activity was apparent as new talent emerged in the college-based clubs and in the IMC. In 1964 a young and dynamic group of scouts from the Walkinstown/ Crumlin area of Dublin were introduced to mountaineering and the IMC by Niall Rice and Christy Kavanagh.[24] Several of the group, particularly Paul McDermott and Shay Billane, would have an impact on the Spillikin Club when it was formed. That year of 1964 was quiet but, in the following year, routes were pioneered in Glenveagh and also at Lough Barra. In Wicklow, Goulding led one of the harder pitches in the country when he tackled, with some points of aid, the crux pitch of Spillikin Ridge which had become longer and more difficult following the collapse of the great pinnacle, the Spillikin. Also in 1965, Ken Price revived DUCC's much-frowned-upon practice of climbing college buildings and repeated a night-time ascent of the Campanile in Trinity's College Square.[25] That club had by now reversed its original ban on women members, largely due to the superior skills of Anthea Peel,[26] and also allowed a female presence in the club hut which was across the river from the IMC hut at Glendasan. Under Price's presidency, DUCC would become unambiguously embedded in the Irish climbing scene, which came about partly through his association with Spillikin.

University College Dublin (UCD) had a covert, fledgling club dating from an initiative of Denis McCarthy late in 1961: covert because of the attitude of college authorities whose opinions on such matters can be gauged from their ban on the wearing of trousers by female students.[27] (This reflected the outlook of the Catholic Archbishop of Dublin, J. C. McQuaid, who forbade the wearing of trousers or shorts by girls taking part in sport,[28] a decree which ensured that there would be no shortage of male helpers when, later in the decade, older Girl Guides in skirts attended rock-climbing courses.) According to Nuala O'Faolain, the college's president insisted that the lady dean of residence accompany the club to the quarry because of the presence of two female members.[29] It would take some years for the UCD club to receive official recognition, and its cause was not aided by the death of two students (not club members) on an icy Lugnaquilla in 1963.

In 1966 W. Dick of the IMC and DUCC added Jameson 10 in Dalkey – 'magic climbing' according to the guidebook – and Gareth Jones (CRCC) continued to add to his handful of new routes in the quarry, several of which were exposed through extensive 'gardening' (clearing vegetation to reveal clean rock). New crags were developed by the IMC at Lough Reagh near Glencar in Kerry where the names of Harry O'Brien and Frank Nugent first appear, and by the Spillikin Club at a gritstone edge of modest height called the Playground or Playbank near Glangevlin in County Cavan.[30] (At Glangevlin we camped in the grounds of a disused police station which had been built to counter the cross-border IRA campaign of the 1950s led by the brother of one of our members. The campsite was overlooked by hills across which another of our climbing friends had been chased at night by the Royal Ulster Constabulary following a cross-border raid. That kind of thing was long gone, we naively thought.) Neither Kerry nor the Playground fulfilled the need for a challenging arena which would inspire new talent and the kind of intense level of activity which was now evident in the Mournes. That need was more than amply filled by the discovery of Fair Head at the extreme north-east corner of the country. The first climb on this 4km-long stretch of dolerite was Earnshaw's Route, by Earnshaw and Moore. It is described in the 2002 guidebook as 'a dangerously loose on-sight lead and was typical of the early routes'.[31]

On 22–23 April 1967, at Moore's urging, the Spillikin Club held a meet at Fair Head, staying at a cottage near the beach in Murlough Bay.[32] The excitement at opening up a new crag was almost equalled, in one mind at least, by the pleasure and pride generated by the cordial gathering together of almost all the top climbers of the day – enthusiasts from a number of clubs, North and South – joined as members of Spillikin in the exploration of what was obviously a major new find. Nonetheless, it was hardly sensed immediately just how outstandingly important the new crag would become. Mistakes were made as some of us chose what on another crag might seem to be obvious feeler lines of lesser steepness but which proved to be dangerously loose and unworthy of the challenge presented by harder, steeper but safer lines. On the first two outings there, three ropes were cut by falling rocks,[33] and it quickly became apparent that steeper lines were sounder and safer. It was more slowly realised that it was frequently desirable to clean potential lines on abseil, a practice hitherto frowned on. The best climb in 1967 was Curser (Jenkins and Crymble) which had what was probably the country's first 5c pitch, while newcomer Paul McHugh signalled the impact he would make on Fair Head and elsewhere with his Clarion, done with his regular partner, Jim Heffernan.

Routes fell slowly and steadily during this first phase of development at Fair Head with McHugh, Heffernan, Jim McKenzie,

Fair Head, 1968. First ascent of Doldrum (now E1). Climber is Paul McHugh who was seconded by Jim Heffernan. PHOTOGRAPHER UNKNOWN

Goulding, O'Brien, Billane, McDermott and Rodgers all contributing. The period drew to a close with the ascent of Hurricane, then at the extreme edge of difficulty, by McHugh and O'Brien in June 1969, with the publication of an interim guide by the Spillikin Club, and a slackening of pace due to the Northern Irish 'Troubles'. Thereafter, Fair Head would intermittently play a momentous role in the development of Irish rock climbing to the extent that it would be tedious to list any but the most significant of new routes there. Not least of the crag's impacts was the blurring of distinctions between climbing and climbers either side of the border, a process which would gather pace as standards rose and a new club, Dal Riada, was formed in the mid-1970s.

Those sad troubles in the north, some of which bled south across the border, affected mountaineering in various ways and to an immeasurable degree. An entire generation of climbers would have to accept as commonplace certain limitations on their freedom of movement and of their choice of venues. This had occurred to a lesser extent during the 1950s IRA campaign when southern mountaineers, who probably travelled across the border much more often than the general population, tried to avoid late-night travel, especially through certain hill areas in border counties.

There, part-time 'B' Specials, some of whose members were no doubt worthy and patriotic men, could be expected to mount dimly lit roadblocks and nervously inspect travellers while wielding the notoriously tetchy sten-gun. The IRA mounted cross-border raids across hilly terrain, rendering such ranges as the Cuilcaghs and the hills of south Armagh somewhat risky to frequent.[34] Even in the peaceful early and mid-1960s one could sometimes expect police surveillance. (O'Leary's father, an ex-policeman, was at least once visited at the family home by detectives asking what his son had being doing in Donegal in the company of someone with republican connections.) During the much more serious conflict which began in the late 1960s one could rarely climb in the Mournes or Fair Head without an encounter with police or army on either side of the border. Drivers of cars with southern registrations learned to avoid certain areas and some mountain car parks in order to prevent having their vehicles selected for vandalism or theft – or perhaps worse. Even a journey from hut to pub could entail an interrogation while standing 'in the position' in darkness, followed by a bomb scare at the bar.[35] Frank Devlin, with whom we had become very friendly, was a technician in the UK diplomatic service and was instructed to stay away from us southerners. We were never again to see him or his wife and fellow climber, Dorothy.

Northern climbers were also to suffer from restrictions and not a little danger. As early as the spring of 1969 a series of explosions at water installations (carried out by 'Protestant extremists' according to historian Joe Lee),[36] caused the British army firstly to block access to the Belfast IMC's hut which was now at Dunnywater quite close to a major pipeline, and then to allow access only during daylight and under certain conditions. With the aid of publicity this restriction was also lifted although the pipe remained under army guard. Later, some members crept out under cover of darkness and made their way along a riverbed to paint BANG! on the pipe.[37]

Developments elsewhere went on apace. In 1966 Richard Maguire and P. Cremin were probably the first local climbers to

New Bloat House at Dunnywater, early 1960s. It burned down in 1989.
BRIAN KENNEDY

put up a named rock-route when they climbed on a 60m sandstone crag north-west of Torc Mountain near Killarney and they went on to do a route in the Gap of Dunloe and other lines elsewhere in the following year.[38] The Kerrymen used a rope, 'it was like something you'd use for tying down bales of hay' bought in a local hardware shop.[39] In 1967 the IMC brought out stencilled guides to Bencorr at Glen Inagh and to Luggala, while the Spillikin Club produced a similar guide to the Playground and Ballygally. Some climbs were done on Bencorr, of which Klepth, a long and serious one by Britishers Maxwell and Dixon, was the most significant. A new club, Laune Mountaineering Club, which had particular interest in mountain rescue, came into being in Killorglin, County Kerry, in

1966–67, mainly in response to several fatal accidents which had occurred in the nearby Corrán Tuathail area. Slievadore Mountaineering Club was formed in the Mournes in 1967 and UCDMC received recognition from the college authorities, with concomitant financial aid, in January 1968.[40]

New climbs were still being found in Dalkey including an awkward climb called Thrust which was led by Gareth Jones and seconded by Peter Duggan. At Glendalough, in 1969, Paul McDermott and Bruce Rodgers did two good, hard routes, Left Wall Crack which can be considered an extension of Sarcophagus, and Bruce's Corner to the left of Mica Wall. In the Comeraghs, where rare visits were usually wasted looking for hard-to-find existing routes, an IMC party put up a few routes in Coum Mahon in 1969.

In Donegal, Britishers Doug Scott, R. Shaw and D. Nicol helped to move the focus away from inland crags when they climbed Main Mast at Carrigan Head near Slieve League in 1967, using ten points of aid. They were not the first climbers on this crag rising from the sea, as Mick Curran and Phil Blake had managed to complete Flying Dutchman two months before, but the imprimatur of the highly regarded Scott, and the dramatic nature of his climb, were important. Interest in the great mountain crags had not died. Goulding and McDermott put up two hard routes, Saoirse and Obituary Corner on Bearnas Buttress in the Poisoned Glen in 1968. Andrew Maxwell and Harold Drasdo returned to scenes of past exploits, but interest had pivoted to the coast which had so long hidden its promise from various tentative, exploratory sorties.[41]

The great mountain routes, especially in the Poisoned Glen, provided challenges of route finding, speed, endurance, rope handling and partnership, a different kind of uncertainty and almost alpine scale. Although sometimes modified by having to deal with vegetation, these challenges were of a kind quite unlike those presented by the shorter, albeit sometimes technically much harder climbs which would be developed on the Donegal coast and islands.

The end of the 1960s was marked by a series of climbing fatalities and the deaths of some of the early pioneers. A newcomer, Alan Walsh, fell to his death in Snowdonia in 1969,[42] Dermot Bouchier-Hayes, a well-known IMC member, died in 1969 from injuries suffered in Austria the previous year, and McDermott and Rodgers died in an avalanche while attempting the Sentinelle Route on the Brenva Face of Mont Blanc.[43] (See p. 105.) Harold Johnson, a true and modest mountaineer, died prematurely in 1968, as did his northern counterpart Charlie Brims. They had been important pioneers and in later years generously and genially served their respective IMC Sections in various ways.[44] Earlier, in 1966, the death had occurred of John Shortell, who had been instrumental with Gribbon and others in setting up the IMC Belfast Section.[45]

The decade ended on a more optimistic note with a renewal of interest in Luggala, perhaps brought about, as so often happens, by preparations for a new guidebook. Doug Milnes, an English climber working in Dublin, led Lynam and Richards up North Buttress. McKenzie and O'Leary eliminated aid on that route not long afterwards. The route was unremarkable but it was the first shoot of a new blossoming of interest in this great crag. Development continued at Ballygally and further north on the Antrim coast at Garron Point where the first climbs were put up by McHugh, O'Brien, Curran and Phil Blake.

Hillwalking

Completion of the Lug Walk became increasingly common and the rise of new clubs in Kerry and elsewhere meant that more people were involved in the activity. In October 1964, O'Flynn organised a mass attempt on the Lug Walk from Bohernabreena to Lugnaquilla on behalf of Arnotts, the Dublin department store. In all, 115 people took part of whom 22 completed the course – figures with which the organisers were delighted at the time but which afterwards they probably rued as, over the years, the route showed all too obvious signs of traffic. Almost all the finishers were well-known mountaineers with Niall Rice doing the fastest time: 13 hours 24 minutes.[46]

Two years later Rice was to trample these times, and previous records, into the Wicklow peat hags, as he lowered the time to 7 hours. At about that time – he cannot quite remember when – he completed a traverse of twenty-two peaks, not including Diamond Hill, in the Twelve Bens range in the quite remarkable time of 9 hours.[47] The Mourne Wall Walk need not be subject to further scrutiny except to occasionally point out the continued creditable performances by mountaineers such as Denis Rankin and Jim Patterson. Summer and winter trips to Scotland were no longer a rarity.[48]

In response to Spillikin's invitation, the first meeting was held in June 1969 which would result in the setting up of a national body for Irish mountaineering, and the cumbersome name was agreed by which this body would be known for the first twenty years of its existence: the Federation of Mountaineering Clubs of Ireland (FMCI).[49]

5

Distant Ranges and Domestic Strife

In 1960, the year before Goulding and Ingram achieved the breakthrough on the Dru, Firth, Wilson, Carew and Leeke began a trend which would see Belfast climbers concentrating most of their efforts during the decade on the more frequently climbed routes on Zermatt's 4,000m peaks, with occasional forays to the Dolomites. Goulding and O'Flynn pushed a bit harder, with the Cresta Rey on Monte Rosa's Dufourspitze and the impressive Triftigrat on the Breithorn being among their routes. George Narramore and Frank Cochrane had an energetic few weeks around Mont Blanc.[1]

Having completed the East Ridge of Mont Dolent with friends, O'Leary and Sam Payne climbed the Dent du Géant by the North Ridge and North Face route which was even more iced-up than their loose-leaved guidebook had predicted – and which the later Alpine Club guidebook was to describe, somewhat dementedly, as sometimes being impossible in these conditions. They were caught in bad weather and had a fight on their hands which involved two bivouacs, the second in thick mist after they got off the mountain, as well as Sam's touch of frostbite and a thunderstorm that sizzlingly harassed their descent.[2] The guide-book time for the climb was six hours from the Torino Hut! (To their eternal embarrassment, their friends sent out guides who met the pair on their way back. Fortunately, the guides were Italian and easy-going.) The rest of the party did the Rochefort Ridge, and Mont Blanc from the Gonella Hut.

Before doing the Dru West Face in 1961, Goulding with Kevin Shelley, besides repeating a few routes previously done by Irish climbers, also completed the North-West Ridge of the Blaitière. Then Ingram appeared on his short fortnight's holiday and managed, with Goulding, to squeeze in the Ménégaux route on the Aiguille de l'M before tackling the Dru. O'Flynn's most notable climb that year was the North Face of the Aiguille de Bionnassay which he did with IMC veteran Peter Healy.[3] Glyn Cochrane, an English member of DUCC, did the Cassin Route on Piz Badile, incorrectly claiming it to be the first *British* ascent and, according to the club's minute book, reached the ice hose (a narrow funnel of ice) between the first and second ice fields on the Eiger's north face.[4] (The first British ascent of the Cassin Route had been done in the mid-1950s.[5]) Eamonn Gallagher, obviously enjoying himself, added to his inventory of worthwhile rock routes. Pete Grindley of Belfast was on the Via Fehrmann on Campanile Basso in the Dolomites while Challoner did the Preuss Wall on the same peak.[6]

Weather predictions were not then very reliable or accessible in any of the Alpine areas so speed was essential, as it always has been, to avoid being caught by unexpected storms. A fast and rope-wise companion was essential for enjoyment as well as safety, a circumstance not often achieved on harder routes due to the smallness of the community from which choices were made. Many routes had pitons *in situ* but most parties carried an ample armoury of these, as climbers, especially those from the eastern Alps, were apt to strip more popular climbs of their ironmongery. The use of metal wedges and wired nuts was something which was just being experimented with in the UK, and camming devices were a long way off. By 1965, stiff-soled and well-made alpine boots had become available in Dublin with Fitzpatrick's of Henry Street advertising Toni Egger boots at £10 10s a pair.[7] Earlier, in the very late 1950s, it was possible as one passed through Paris to buy the precursor to the modern rock-climbing shoe, tight-fitting with rubber rand, which had recently been developed by the great French climber Pierre Allain. At that time also, a few of us used excellent cagoules – thigh-length hooded anoraks – which Tony Kavanagh had made up by someone in Dublin and which served us for a number of years. In Chamonix we camped, without toilets or running water, in woods near the cogged rack railway which led up to Montenvers. The police later cleared the place. Higher up, it was still possible in the late 1950s to leave tents and gear safely near the little lake at the foot of the Aiguille du Peigne or in a shack cheekily called Chalet Austria near Montenvers. This writer cannot remember ever having used any of the téléphériques (gondola lift systems). On the mountains, before we could afford the tent-like Zdarsky sacks, we used makeshift bivouac shelters made of proofed nylon sheets.

In 1962, Goulding and Ingram did the Charmoz-Grépon traverse and the East Face of the Grand Capucin, a TD Sup. route first completed in 1951 by the brilliant Walter Bonatti. Ingram had used oak to make the steps of their etriers (sets of stirrups or short rope ladders with three to four steps each, which can be clipped to a piton) to deal with this impending face which was then an almost continuous aided climb. Shortly after launching up the first difficult groove, they found that the steps of the etriers began to break one by one so that at one point Ingram was left standing on the very last creaking rung. They nonetheless completed the climb and then, despite Ingram's short leave, confirmed their Alpine credentials by climbing a variant on the formidable North Face of the Grands Charmoz, an icy facet much favoured by climbers from the eastern Alps. They benefited from advice proffered by Hans Lobenhofer of Nanga Parbat renown who was at that time a member of the IMC working in Ireland. They also climbed the East Face of the Aiguille de Roc. They aborted an attempt on the Walker Spur of the Grandes Jorasses because of bad weather.[8] O'Flynn did the Old Brenva Route, probably the first Irish person in the modern era to venture on to that flank of Mont Blanc. Shelley and Aubrey Flegg completed the traverse of the Drus, while O'Halpin and O'Leary did, among other things, the Charmoz-Grépon traverse already done by Goulding and Ingram, encountering a thunderstorm during which they were knocked unconscious twice by lightning strikes. Neither of them ever forgot the experience. Other IMC members were in the Dolomites.[9]

Sloan and Milligan, and Garrett and Wilkinson of the Belfast Section were in Zermatt where the former pair completed many of the ordinary routes on the area's four thousanders, as did DUCC members Oakley, Frank Cochrane and Clarke. The DUCC party seemed unaware of the 1958 ascent of the Rotgrat on the Alphubel by McCall and O'Leary, and indeed of the fact that the route was first climbed by a guided Briton in 1889, and claimed the first British ascent of that route.[10]

Goulding further developed his practice of climbing in turn with a succession of partners coming to Chamonix on short holidays, and raising the standard of his climbs as the season progressed. In 1963 he began with O'Leary when they completed, without untoward incident, the North Ridge of the Peigne, the Frontier Ridge of Mont Maudit and the North Face of the Plan, all first Irish ascents. They were foiled by bad weather on an attempt to complete a traverse of the Chamonix Aiguilles from the Tour Rouge Hut, having crossed the Charmoz, Grépon, Blaitière and Fou, past the Lepinay and Chevalier to the Col du Caiman in what they were told was the fastest time yet of the very few previous attempts. Elizabeth Healy joined Goulding to do the Mer de Glace face of the Grépon (probably the first ascent by an Irishwoman) and was followed by Eddie Gaffney who went straight from the train station in Chamonix to join Goulding on an ascent of the North Face of the Dru, which was followed by the South Face of the Midi and other TDs. DUCC climbed in Chamonix, Zermatt and other venues but details are not recorded.[11]

By the mid-1960s, trips to the Alps, mostly fitted into short holidays, were commonplace with most Irish climbers sticking to well-tried favourites in Austria and around Zermatt. In 1965

Mac Eoin, Niall Rice and Jem Tobin were members of a sizable party which completed the Haute Route from Chamonix to Zermatt, probably the first Irish effort on this traverse. Chamonix was left largely to those interested in harder routes with Goulding doing the Bonatti Pillar of the Dru with a Scottish friend – Brian Wakefield – making Goulding one of the very first climbers to complete all three of the then hardest climbs on the Dru.[12]

The group of youngsters recruited to the IMC by Niall Rice (see p. 88) moved to the Dolomites from Austrian Stubai where they had climbed Zuckerhütl, Wilderpfaff and the Stubai Wildspitze. In Italy their ascents included the North-East Ridge of the Cima Grande de Lavaredo, the Yellow Edge of the Cima Piccolo and the Preuss Route on Cime Piccolissima.[13] On all these, the main climbing leader was eighteen-year-old Paul McDermott who would make a name for himself in the coming years, as would Shay Billane, while Shay Nolan would take full part in a number of expeditions over a long climbing career.

DUCC members were active in Nepal and in the Dolomites, although details are lacking, and one of its members, Harry Jacques, was killed while climbing in Corsica.[14]

There was a large Irish party on the Grossglockner in Austria in 1966 and Jim McKenzie had his Alpine debut while climbing with Dermot Bouchier-Hayes in Zillertal. Ingrid Masterson, a seasoned skier and very active climber, completed guided ascents in the Bernina of Piz Morteratsch, Piz Rozegg and Piz Palu, and did a traverse of Piz Bernina via the Biancograt and the Spalagrat. Goulding and O'Leary joined with McDermott and Billane on an ascent of Aiguille Mummery, the former pair going on to combine this with a traverse of Aiguille Ravanel. Bad weather foiled further attempts by both pairs.[15] It is worth recounting what occurred on an attempt by the two older climbers to complete the traverse intégrale of the Aiguilles Noire and Blanche de Peuterey to Mont Blanc, partly because it presents an opportunity to delve a little into the character of Goulding, and perhaps to appreciate what it is that makes an eminent mountaineer.

Described by Calvin Torrans as Ireland's most outstanding

alpinist,[16] and by Jim Perrin, the British mountaineering writer, as at one time 'being highly regarded in the UK as being the best technical climber in these islands',[17] Emmett Goulding dominated Irish climbing, at home and abroad, throughout the 1960s and had an effect on Irish alpinism well beyond that decade. In addition to the routes already mentioned he had, by now, with Brian Wakefield, also completed the Route Major on Mont Blanc's Brenva Face, and the Brown-Patey Route on the West Face of the Aiguille du Plan (probably the second ascent of this fine route). He came from a family whose republican credentials, in both Irish meanings of that term, went back over three generations and could hardly be bettered. Emmett was not a 'by-force' activist. His involvement with the family business – painting and decorating – facilitated his lengthy sojourns in the Alps. Quietly spoken, modest in normal intercourse and about his own achievements, he had an engaging sense of humour. He could be steamy about climbing politics, and his impatience on long routes was legendary among his regular partners – and a cause of amused embarrassment when he 'lost it' on a crowded Welsh crag.[18] This impatience made for speedy Alpine ascents, which suited O'Leary well, especially on mixed going, although it sometimes meant yielding to Goulding's testiness and superior skills on difficult pitches. But he was otherwise very easy to get along with; one just had to be aware of a fierce dynamism, especially *in extremis*. Goulding, no doubt frustrated with the lack of home talent to equal his own, twice went to work and climb in the UK where his reputation was soon secured. However, he was justifiably irked by the rejection of his application to be admitted to the high-powered Alpine Climbing Group.

From the tiny Noire Hut the Irish pair started on the South Ridge of the Aiguille Noire de Peuterey early enough to overtake several British parties who had bivouacked low down on the ridge; they were gaining on the leading English pair and not far from the summit when they were hit by a storm of some intensity. In heavy snowfall and assailed by nearby lightning strikes they got off the ridge crest and hunkered down to wait for a break. All those behind had retreated earlier. The storm continued throughout the day and into night. Snow was still falling heavily the next morning so it was decided, not too wisely, to abseil more than 1,000m down the south-east face rather than try for the exposed summit or to climb back over Pointe Bich – or perhaps it was Pointe Brendel? – and the difficult Pointe Welzenbach. At one point, well down the face and trying to see clearly through densely falling snowflakes, they abseiled over a considerable overhang and with difficulty gained a ledge where they found that despite strenuous efforts, including an attempt to break the anchor loop by force, the rope could not be retrieved. With almost no hesitation and not giving his companion time to brood about dire possibilities or unlikely solutions, Goulding attached Prusik loops to the rope, stepped into them and dropped about three metres due to rope stretch. He mentioned later that he had never before climbed using Prusik loops (slings attached to the rope by friction knots which slide easily upwards but lock when weighted). As he moved up past his partner he was about 3m out from the rock and was using only a pair of poorly adjusted foot loops, which meant that he had to cling to the wet rope with one hand, or to hold it in the crook of his arm, when he moved the loops upward. Sit harnesses were not yet then in use. Despite urging by O'Leary to attach an underarm or chest loop he just grimly continued up, gyrating slowly in the misty void. There and then, any fears which O'Leary had in relation to the abseil anchor loop snapping or Goulding's arms tiring were entirely overwhelmed by the realisation that he (O'Leary) was very much the junior partner. The rope-climbing manoeuvre was remarkable in itself, but what he was now witnessing was a fatalistic – or was it the opposite? – intensity of purpose and strength, a calm certainty which was beyond his reach or, he guessed, that of all but a very few. Having reached the abseil anchor where the rope had become embedded and immovable in the rapidly falling snow, Goulding swept it clear of snow and came down quickly in order to pull the rope in before it became stuck again. (In retrospect, Emmett's feat seemed unlikely but when questioned during the writing of this book, he confirmed that the author's memory was correct.) The duo reached the foot of the face the next morning following another miserable bivouac, having run out of slings and pegs. Despite their travails they realised that they had made the right decision when they learned that the pair who had been ahead of them near the summit had not yet made their way down, and seemed unlikely to do so until the following day.

Goulding went on that year to do the Sentinelle Route on Mont Blanc's Brenva Face, and the North-East Face of Les Courtes, two fine mixed rock and ice routes, with Brian Wakefield who would be his partner on other hard routes. Jem Tobin of the Spillikin Club did the Bonatti

(L–r): Calvin Torrans and Sam Crymble in the Alps in 1957. SHERIDAN COLLECTION

Pillar on the Petit Dru with the English climber John Fullalove, known as Daniel Boone.[19]

There was a flurry of Irish activity in the Alps in 1967 with groups from North and South coming to Zermatt and Chamonix in unprecedented numbers. Calvin Torrans and Sam Crymble, in line with their doings in the Mournes, raised the standard of alpinism of northern climbers when, having completed some ordinary routes in Zermatt, they repeated the North Ridge of the Peigne in the Chamonix Aiguilles and also a route on Pointe Albert, presumably the Leininger line. Billane and McDermott also climbed the North Ridge of the Peigne and the Leininger route on Albert (a common bad-weather option), besides the South-West Ridge of the Moine and yet another Irish traverse of the Charmoz-Grépon. Harry O'Brien and Frank Nugent were also in Chamonix, as were Rankin and Joe McGrath. Four Belfast members of the IMC – Armstrong, McEvoy, Dave Wilson and Geoff Wynne – did various routes on the Sella and Vajolet Towers in the Dolomites.[20]

The most dramatic happening in this year occurred on the

notoriously loose Rotgrat on Zermatt's Alphubel when Sean Rothery had his femur smashed by a large falling rock dislodged by an inexperienced climber. With his left leg turned around horribly, Sean was carried to a safer ledge by Peter Shortt and had his leg crudely splinted by Frank Doherty who had held him on the rope when he was torn from his holds. He endured eight hours of pain as they waited for help which was to be summoned by their friend Pat Colleran and the partner of the unfortunate novice who had dislodged the rock. Vividly described by Rothery in his book *A Long Walk South,* his rescue by helicopter involved plucking him at an angle from a small ledge and a terrifying pendulum many hundreds of metres above glaciers. It was to be three years before Rothery could walk again without a stick but he was back again in Zermatt six years after the accident as a member of a Tiglin group, when he reached summits on several occasions. (Tiglin was the National Adventure Centre.)

In 1968 IMC Belfast Section members were in Zermatt and Chamonix.[21] There is no information available on Dublin Section doings, probably due to what a 1969 IMC newsletter described as the apathy of club officials which, in turn, led to low morale of ordinary members.[22]

In 1969, northern climbers were out in force in Zermatt where many 4,000m peaks were done and attempts on the Weisshorn and Dent Blanche were repulsed. Almost all the northern climbers mentioned above were involved, including Wilson and Armstrong who had been on QUBMC's Taurus trip (see p. 116). The names of John Forsythe and Robin Merrick appear for the first time in an Alpine context.[23]

Bruce Rodgers and Paul McDermott were killed by an avalanche while attempting the Sentinelle Route on Mont Blanc in August 1969. McDermott, who was about to graduate as a telecommunications engineer at twenty-two years of age, was the most driven of the 1968 Irish Andes expedition (see p. 112). He had displayed this quality in abundance, along with his cheerful and outgoing personality, since he had taken up climbing just a few years previously. These traits enabled him to push himself to achieve more than some more stylish climbers had done, and it was generally felt that he would become an outstanding mountaineer. Rodgers, who was quieter and competent, had married just a few months before his death. Before their accident the pair had climbed the Frendo Spur (a relatively new climb then) in bad conditions and, it is thought, the Gervasutti Pillar on Mont Blanc du Tacul, an ED route and one of the finest rock climbs in the Mont Blanc area.[24]

Distant Ranges

In 1960, temporary emigrants Phil Gribbon and Brian Rothery somehow convinced Canadian authorities to allow them to fly to Baffin Island to carry out a scientific and mountaineering expedition. The first mountaineering expedition to the area had taken place just a few years previously and access to the island was officially discouraged, partly because of work in progress on the chain of Cold War radar stations (the Dew Line) which ranged across all of northern Canada. They had to bluff their way past the construction camp boss at a Dew Line station before spending some glorious if sometimes uncomfortably cold weeks climbing six virgin peaks, including their highest, Mount Gilbert (1,551m). They made attempts to maintain scientific respectability by collecting the occasional geological or botanical specimen.[25] The story of how they escaped from being trapped in isolation by a series of river estuaries is vividly described, in fictional form, in Rothery's novel *The Crossing*. The experience fired Gribbon's imagination and he was to lead seven further Arctic trips, all to Greenland. Another emigrant, Mona Monahan, climbed the Durrance Route on Wyoming's Devil's Tower with American friends.[26]

Further afield, Joss Lynam was again in Spiti in 1961 with Gwynn Stephenson, this time as leader of a four-man, mainly English, team. They made their way up the Bara Shigri glacier, taking five strenuous days on the tangled ice mass to reach Concordia, their base. Inner Line restrictions (operative within a certain distance from the Tibetan border) prevented them from exploring into the Parahio basin as they had hoped to do. From Base

Shigri Parbat *(centre right)*, the highest peak climbed by Joss Lynam in 1961. The area and peaks nearer camera were climbed and explored by several Irish teams from 1999 onwards. (Photo taken by Gerry Galligan during the first ascent of Ramabang, 2008.) GERRY GALLIGAN

Camp they did a little surveying and some exploratory trips but their main objective was to make a first ascent of a 6,644m peak, later called Shigri Parbat. All four succeeded in reaching the summit along with two of their porters, despite having much trouble with freezing feet.[27] Joss suffered from frostbite which, although not too serious, was to hinder him on later high-altitude ventures.

In early 1962 an Anglo-Irish expedition to Patagonia, partially supported by Guinness, succeeded in making the first ascent of Aiguille Poincenot (named after a French climber who had drowned crossing a nearby river in 1952). Organised by George Narramore of the IMC, with Frank Cochrane of DUCC as leader, the team was made up of three English DUCC members – Cochrane, Francis Beloe and Clive Burland – two IMC members – George Narramore and Tony Kavanagh, both of whom, not by coincidence, were Guinness employees – and Don Whillans, the brilliant and rough-cut Lancashire cragsman as climbing leader. Coping with the typically fierce storms of the region by living in snow caves, Whillans and Kavanagh managed to fix ropes on the icy approaches to The Ramp, itself a steep icy slope, by which they hoped to reach the South-East Ridge which led to the summit. A storm which piled what was reckoned to be more than 5m of snow in one night on one of the snow caves, cutting off oxygen and almost causing a cave-in, led to the abandonment of the cave and, apparently, their efforts. However, a clearance in the weather enabled Whillans and Cochrane to mount a last-minute successful summit bid on the last day of January.[28]

Cerro Poincenot, 1961. The Irish expedition's top camp was in a snow hole on a big snowfield at half-height. From there the route went up the ramp on the left to the skyline and thence to the summit. G. NARRAMORE

In 1963 Gribbon was in the Angmassilik region of East Greenland where he and fellow members of a Scottish team made twenty-one first ascents. Also in Greenland, Chris Oakley of DUCC was climbing leader of a TCD scientific expedition. John Morrison continued his Homeric wanderings, making ascents from the Ugandan side of Mount Speke and the East Ridge of Marghereta Peak in the Mountains of the Moon (Ruwenzori). There were others venturing off the beaten track with Geoff Earnshaw making periodic excursions in the Atlas Mountains (where he had made a winter ascent of Toubkal in 1962), and Brian Farrington writing enticingly of his wanderings in the then relatively unspoiled Pyrenees, a range poorly mapped, with few of the amenities and tourist developments of the Alps and with frontier restrictions imposed by the Franco regime.[29]

In 1964, an IMC expedition to the Himalaya was the first such Irish venture in the region (although the individual efforts of Lynam and Morrison, as detailed above, should be borne in mind). The IMC team (Garrett, Goulding, T. Kavanagh, Lynam, O'Flynn, O'Leary and Payne) mounted an attempt on the North-West Ridge of Rakaposhi (7,788m), a peak in the Karakoram range in Pakistan. It was a bad time to travel to the Himalaya, India having fought a high-altitude war with China in 1962; it would be involved in another with Pakistan in 1965 and there were constant skirmishes on shared borders with these countries. There was an ongoing, though low-key, guerrilla conflict in Tibet. Nepal was still difficult to access, indeed it was to ban foreign expeditions for some time.[30] Permission to climb was tricky to negotiate and subject to severe restrictions. It was not intended by the IMC, which launched the expedition in response to Noel Kavanagh's proposal, that the Irish team would tackle anything as high as Rakaposhi which had already been climbed by another ridge. All the preparations over a two-year period were made on the under-standing that a lower peak would be attempted. Kampire Dior, a fine peak, was chosen and Pakistan's government permission seemed to extend to this. But shortly before the team left Ireland, Pakistan's military regime redirected the team to Rakaposhi for which its resources were hardly adequate. The expedition failed, turning back somewhere about 6,200m, partly because of an early monsoon and also because of dangerous snow conditions on the lengthy and difficult North-West Ridge. A camp was destroyed by an avalanche which also put one of the team out of action.[31] The ridge had already been attempted three times and it would be another fifteen years before an ascent by this avalanche-prone route was successful.[32] Understandably, it would be twenty years before an Irish team would again attempt a 7,000m peak.

Emmett Goulding at Camp III, Rakaposhi, 1964. The South-West Ridge is in the background.

Rakaposhi team and Hunza porters. Back row *(L–r)*: Paddy O'Leary, Joss Lynam, George Garrett, Tony Kavanagh, mail runner, Emmett Goulding and Barry O'Flynn. (Sam Payne in hospital). Front row *(L–r)*: Habibullah, Ayub, Sagai and Wapai, local Hunza porters. AUTHOR'S COLLECTION

Mistakes were made due to the club's inexperience, and to O'Leary's as leader of the venture, but we learned a great deal about great range climbing as well as logistics, fund-raising, equipment and particularly about the pitfalls associated with mounting an official club expedition. Although the term 'expedition' has become much debased, ours was accurately described as such at that time, with equipment being sent by sea, then transported by train from Karachi to Rawalpindi, by unpressurised plane across high passes to Gilgit, then by jeep to Nomal where a raft composed of inflated ox skins and pieces of driftwood and bamboo brought it across the wide and turbulent Hunza River before being carried by a gang of porters for three days to base camp. Shortage of funds, mainly arising from the change of our objective, meant that four members had to drive out in an old Chevrolet van donated by Harold Johnson (which he never got back), while the remainder utilised free or reduced travel costs available through their employments. As has been the case with many such endeavours, for the organiser the hardest part, or perhaps the least pleasant, seemed over once we had reached our base camp.

Almost at the same time a CCPR (Central Council for Physical Recreation) expedition to the Taurus mountains of south-eastern Turkey, involving a number of teenagers as well as a suitable contingent of adults, was launched from Northern Ireland. The team of mountaineers and scientists, including sixteen IMC members, was led by an ex-military man, Jack Quan, and also featured Bert Slader and John Wheatley who were to become well known in Irish outdoor circles and further afield. Altogether, the group climbed twenty peaks varying between 3,350m and approximately 4,000m in height, including one first ascent.[33] From what can be gleaned from journals this was the year Calvert Moore went to Lyngen Alps in Arctic Norway with Eric Wilkinson, Kurt Muller, Denis Baird, David Dick, Jim Armstrong, Ivor McDonald and Ian Campbell.[34]

In 1965, Phil Gribbon, who was now a lecturer at St Andrews University in Scotland, was on a college expedition to the Sukkertoppen region of west Greenland.[35] He was back again in 1967, when he led a St Andrew's team to Upernivik Island.

Two expeditions left Ireland in 1968, one to Greenland led by Joss Lynam and the other to the Peruvian Andes led by O'Leary. Neither was an official club venture and it is worth noting that the politically shrewd Lynam, who would play a leading role on quite a number of subsequent such trips, never led a club expedition. He may have been influenced, as others were, by some of the less savoury aspects of club wrangles associated with the IMC's Rakaposhi venture. The team to Peru more or less picked itself and consisted of Goulding, McDermott, Billane, Ingram, Niall Rice and O'Leary, with Mike Lunt as cameraman. It was a happy and successful trip, the recounting of which would be flat due to the way in which our plans went without a major hitch. Again, equipment and pre-packed rations were sent by sea (although it transpired that most food items were available

Irish team in Peru in 1968 *(no photo of Mike Lunt)* AUTHOR'S COLLECTION

Niall Rice

Paul McDermott

Shay Billane

Emmett Goulding

Tony Ingram

Paddy O'Leary

in larger Peruvian towns) but internal travel was easier, as was dealing with light-handed bureaucracy. We made two first ascents of 5,000m peaks in the Cordillera Urubamba. Punta Rosaleen was climbed by Rice and Billane who also ascended two previously climbed peaks. Our main objective, Chainapuerto (5,788m), was climbed by Ingram and O'Leary, followed a few days later by Goulding and McDermott who had previously prepared most of the route for their teammates. Three other 5,000m peaks, one of them a first ascent, were also climbed in the region of Padre Eterno.[36]

A gratifying feature was the ease with which we raised funds and sponsorship in an increasingly prosperous Ireland. Lessons learned in 1964 enabled us to raise all the support we needed very quickly and to the extent that the individual cost to team members was very much less than what it had been on the Rakaposhi venture.

Chainapuerto first ascent, 1968. The route skirts to the right of the minor peak and follows an arête separating the sunlit slope from the shadowed face. AUTHOR'S COLLECTION

Lynam's team venture to the Cape Farewell region of Greenland (Joss Lynam, Noel Lynch, Ken Price, Paul Hill, Joe Bent, Frank Doherty and Doug Milnes) was held up for two weeks by pack ice on the boat trip along the Greenland coast from the airstrip at

Narssarssuaq to its base at Tasermuit Fjord and was then bedevilled by bad weather. Nonetheless, the group succeeded in making four first ascents, including that of Cathedral (2,130m) the highest peak in their area. This was climbed by Price and Lynch and included rock pitches of grade V. They also carried out botanical, geological and physiological research and produced a 1:50,000 watershed map.[37]

Minster attempted by Irish South Greenland expedition in 1968. The first ascent by an Irish team was in 1971. JOSS LYNAM

Tasermuit Fjord. JOSS LYNAM

In 1969 Gribbon, well on his way to earning an eventual Polar Medal, was back again in Greenland with a St Andrews team. He had a successful few weeks on Upernivik Island, and then transferred attention to the nearby mainland where twenty-four hours of Arctic daylight and of continuous hard climbing on a 1,500m ridge got them to the summit of a peak called Qioqe Qioqe. 'The hardest and most sustained climbing I have ever enjoyed,' Gribbon remarked.[38]

Phil Gribbon on Upernivik Island in Greenland in 1969. GRIBBON COLLECTION

QUBMC mounted a climbing trip to the Taurus mountains of eastern Turkey where many peaks were climbed. In that same year Eric Lawther was probably the first Irish climber to visit Yosemite where he was with the London Mountaineering Club but there is no record of what was climbed.[39]

6

Fianna Warriors and Hillwalking Challenges

A new confidence was evident in Ireland's small climbing world as the 1970s began. In June 1970 Billane and McHugh succeeded in 'establishing a new order of climbing difficulty'[1] when they put up Soyuz Ten at Luggala, a sensationally exposed 70m route on the Main Face. Initially graded Extreme (XS) as numerical E grades had not yet come into being, the climb had three points of aid, a precedent which would be followed in years to come and which decisively shattered a long-established taboo – the use of aids – which is not to say that, previously, the taboo had not occasionally been breached. Aid would be eliminated on that route over the next ten years or so resulting in a harder grading, an ethical progression which would mark much of what happened here and elsewhere as techniques and confidence improved, as did developments in gear and its placement. Progress would not have been made so rapidly at this and other crags if some of the more able climbers had not possessed the imagination to envisage the routes, to realise that aid was necessary on some new, uncleaned lines and had the knowledge and good sense to know when overuse of aid demeaned the climb and themselves. The trick, of course, was to strike the correct balance, an obligation not always observed but usually subject to the corrective influence of peer pressure.

McHugh and Billane had already established themselves as a formidable pair at Fair Head, while McHugh also pioneered the strenuous Bushmills in Dalkey. In 1971, the same pair put up the excellent Equinox at Fair Head. The partnership was formed of two very contrasting personalities. McHugh, a plumber who would later spend some years as a sculptor, was mercurial, a naturally gifted climber who was physically supple to a remarkable degree, given to nettling those less gifted, always ready to be perverse in argument – a disposition easily adopted in a climbing fellowship given to contrariness. Beginning in the 1960s, his spirited approach extended to heart-stopping journeys to distant crags in a rapidly changing series of battered bangers, particularly a pair of Renault Dauphines, one of which he wrote off on a bad bend outside Annamoe in County Wicklow. His abilities at home and in the Alps were of a very high order and he would probably have featured prominently on the international stage had he continued to climb. His name ceases to appear as a lead climber in guidebooks from 1972. Billane was easy-going, boyishly likeable as will be described later, with unusually strong hands which may have come from his being a silversmith. He would be at the centre of Irish climbing for the next few years.

That assertiveness at Luggala reflected the country's growing self-assurance brought about by a 50 per cent rise in living standards in the 1960s.[2] This in turn led to a surge in car ownership in the early 1970s an improvement in reliability which allowed for more frequent trips to distant crags.[3] The introduction of free secondary education south of the border in 1967 meant that many more third-level students would avail of long leisure periods and the support of college-based clubs.[4] A shorter working week freed climbers to take advantage of new affluence and enhanced mobility. But these factors also led to a decline in the use of the IMC's Glendasan hut and the loosening of club bonds as it became normal practice to return home after driving down for a day's climbing. The dynamic was somewhat different in Belfast because of the Troubles-induced imperative to get out of town at weekends.

Other changes would occur at an accelerating rate. At least one woman, Clare Sheridan, would outstrip Elizabeth Healy's achievements and perform on equal terms with men at home and abroad. Improvements in gear, particularly the invention of spring-operated camming devices ('friends') and wired metal wedges, would improve safety later in the decade. New training methods akin to those of competitive athletes would dramatically raise rock-climbing standards worldwide and the Irish would strain to keep within somewhat distant reach. The national representative body for mountaineering was established on firmer footing, as were a number of new clubs, all backed by government money initially made available by an imaginative but flawed politician. (See chapter 11.) There were less welcome manifestations of a changing Ireland and of the climbing world at large. The elitism now apparent in clubs such as Spillikin and its successor, Dal Riada, would acquire an unwonted edge at variance with the affability favoured by most climbers. There was a vanishing innocence, an awareness that one's belongings could no longer be just dumped at 'base camp' under D Route at Dalkey, or left beside the lake at Glendalough while one went off blithely to climb all day without worrying about theft. (It would be another decade before theft from cars became common.)

This historian's direct connection with what was happening at the forefront of Irish mountaineering (apart from events described in chapter 11) became increasingly tenuous as the decade rolled on so there is greater reliance on the accounts and opinions of those at 'the sharp end of the rope'.

Luggala displaced Glendalough as the focus of Dublin's top climbers as it gradually revealed its complexity, its considerable extent, its ways around or through striking overhangs and its remarkably beautiful setting. Closer to the city than Glendalough, although more difficult to reach for those without transport, it would become the favourite crag of some outstanding performers. Despite pioneering forays to more distant venues, they would repeatedly return to the sleeping shelter under a great boulder by the lake to plan new endeavours on the various facets of the range of crags above it.[5] In 1971 Christy Rice and Pat Redmond climbed

The Gannets on the Main Face using three aid points which would gradually be whittled down to yield a free route in the upper grades. Of equal importance to the majority of climbers were two climbs of middle grade which enabled them to experience the pleasures of the left flank of the Main Face – Claidheamh Solais by Tom Hand and Jim McKenzie, and the much more delectable Cling-on by Rice and Redmond – although there is uncertainty regarding which climb was done first.

Glendalough barely attracted pioneering interest, with McKenzie and Christy Rice being the principal leaders. Very little development occurred at Fair Head from 1971 to 1973, probably because of the revival of interest at Luggala and the effects of the Northern Irish Troubles, but McHugh and Billane managed routes there in 1971 as did Roger Greene with D. Chambers in support.

Harold Drasdo's fascination with Donegal's big faces was further demonstrated when an additional four pitches were added to The Direct on Bearnas Buttress in the Poisoned Glen by Maxfield, Drasdo and J. Williams. Andrew Maxfield, who had pioneered so much in Donegal and Glen Inagh, was to die climbing on sea cliffs near Aberdeen in the following year.[6]

In the Mournes, Crymble, R. Creighton and D. Bruce revived interest in the surprisingly neglected Slieve Beg (not forgetting Jenkin's and Moore's Poetic Justice and some easier climbs by Mick Curran) when they added a harder second pitch to Roy Johnston's splendid Devil's Rib, while John Forsythe and Marshall featured elsewhere. Lindsay Griffin, an Englishman who would become well known in international mountaineering circles, used one point of aid on Late Opening on Eagle Rocks with Robin Merrick as partner. Griffin demonstrated the English climbers' readiness to disregard local ethical tradition by repeatedly top-roping Asterisk on Hen Mountain before soloing it.[7] A few easier routes were done at Dalkey that year, unremarkable but for the appearance on the climbing scene of Jim Leonard and Joe Mulhall.

A tall, newly arrived English expatriate, Steve Young, put in the initial work on Dance of the Tumblers on Luggala's North Buttress, a fine piece of route finding with airy situations and an apt name given that it had taken several attempts and a number of falls to reach a conclusion. His companions were Joe Mulhall, Bob Richardson and Mike Harris.[8] Bob Richardson was a somewhat flamboyant American who led the crux on that successful day. Bob would open a climbing equipment store, The Mountain Hut, in Dublin's Stephen Street, a short-lived venture which was probably premature, as was a previous venture by Ernie Lawrence in Harcourt Street, given the small, if increasing, number of climbers. Richardson along with Young, Mulhall and others breathed new life into the IMC during the early 1970s and seemed not to hear the Spillikin Club's siren call. Mulhall and Young added Bearcats to the lengthening list of new climbs on the crag while Rice and Milnes continued their exploration, and their predilection for multiple points of aid, with a number of climbs, including the impressive Banshee, all eventually E-graded. Dónal Ó Murchú led the more moderately graded Taktix which runs beside, and overlaps, Pine Tree Buttress. In the Mournes, professional instructors Joe Rotherham, Teddy Hawkins and Telford put up the fine Cabin Cruise on Spellack.

The owners of the Luggala estate were tolerant and relaxed about all this activity taking place only a few hundred yards from the main house, albeit hidden both by the size of the crag and its easterly facing aspect. A conversation with the rod-wielding owner as a po-faced gillie kept their boat still by the lakeshore was more akin to a polite exchange with a curious visitor than with the proprietress of all that could be seen extending miles to the west and south. There was some confrontation with managers of the estate in the late 1970s and again in the early 1990s. They were concerned for the large herd of hybrid Sika/red deer and for the peregrine falcon nests on the expanse of crags, but these sensible men and the owners were amenable to various compromises and to a change of access route to the crag which led to a path being beaten from the Military Road to the top of the climbs.[9]

In August 1972, John O'Connor, Cathy Whyte, Young, Leonard and Mulhall, all IMC members who had been washed out of a meet in the Twelve Bens, drove to County Clare in response to the urging of Joe Whyte, a caver. Having been put off by the looseness of the

Cliffs of Moher they moved up the coast to the Burren to look at Ailladie, a crag of more modest height just south of Fanore.[10] Although taken aback by the smooth sheerness of Mirror Wall as viewed from above, they found their way down to the extensive, sea-washed terrace which became known as the Dancing Ledges and put up six climbs on weaknesses in the steep walls, the best of which were Genesis and Moonrill. One can imagine their exultation in finding this untouched spot with its unique ambience and beauty. In October and November of that year a further nine climbs were added, including some of very good quality led by McKenzie, especially Pis Fluich which the 2008 guidebook describes as having 'gained a ferocious reputation with stories of savage lay-backing on greasy rock above jagged boulders and a wild ocean'.[11] Richardson, and Alan Douglas with Ó Murchú, contributed to the growing list and Joe Mulhall led Box of Chocks, a classic which was to suffer a fate all too common on seacliffs when it was later washed away by winter storms.

Pioneers at Ailladie in 1972. *(L–r)*: Cathy Whyte, John O'Connor, Joe Whyte, Jim Leonard and Joe Mulhall. IMC ARCHIVE

Ken Higgs was intrigued by the nomenclature of climbs at Ailladie. These reflected the zeitgeist, along with the nationality and sometimes political leanings of mixed new and older generations. McKenzie's interest in Gaelic culture, of which one aspect was exemplified in the musical pubs of nearby Doolin, gave his routes Irish names (Amhrasach, An Fhuiseog). Young's English predilection for quirky names (Obscene Sardine) was obvious while Richardson was influenced, according to Higgs, by his American background.[12] Such manifestations of prevailing culture, including contemporary musical tastes, from Bob Dylan to Jimi Hendrix and Luke Kelly, would become even more evident at Luggala and Fair Head as the decade rolled out, especially when an even younger generation of climbers appeared.

No new climbs were done at Ailladie or elsewhere in the Burren in 1973 and there is no account of any activity there. However, other coastal crags were being developed: at Cork's Sherkin Island by English hard man Nat Allen; at Carrigan Head by McKenzie with Dave Mitchell, and at lovely Port Bay in Donegal by Young and Leonard. Torrans made a return sortie to Fair Head from his base in England's Lake District where, during a two-year stay as a 'postie' (or postman), he had ample free time to develop contacts and his own skills.

Young continued to make his presence felt in Dalkey, in Glendalough where Ó Murchú partnered him on Georgia, and at Luggala. In1973, on Benwee Head on the north-west Mayo coast, he and Ó Murchú ventured onto the western end of the broken line of crags looking out on Donegal Bay. The pair did a number of loose, easy climbs and later became involved in what was probably Ireland's first combined swim and Tyrolean traverse during a failed attempt and benightment on a cliff face in a fierce storm. (A Tyrolean traverse is a method of bridging a gap, as between the land and an island, by the use of ropes slung across the void.)

Further south and inland, UCD people Sheridan, Sheila Willis, Sean Darby and Mick O'Shea, along with Lynam, put up routes in the great corrie on Mweelrea facing out over Doo Lough.[13]

In the Mournes, the development of Slieve Beg continued with the aided ascent of Satanic Majesty by Crymble, Curran and D. Chambers; and with Sweetie Mice, a classic route by J. McGuinness and J. Bruce. The interest in Slieve Beg continued into 1974 and 1975, with Billane and newly returned Torrans raising the ante. A number of routes were put up on Beg, Ben Crom and Pigeon. The best of these were probably Slipstream on Beg by Roger Greene, along with his and Ricky Cowan's Penny Black, firstly done with aid, on Pigeon.[14] At a less exalted level some very good climbs were found, Surplomb Sundae on Eagle Mountain by Kerr and Mick Curran in 1976 being among the best. Dawson Stelfox's name appears for the first time, on a climb on Binnian Tors in 1976.

In the spring of 1974, Jimmy Leonard opened up the sea crag at Malinbeg in south-west Donegal. With Benny Kinsella he put up some climbs which would later fall into the sea. On that first visit, Dave Walsh and Joe Mulhall also climbed new routes. The crag would grow in popularity and by 1979 there would be sixty-eight routes of all grades to HVS, many of them associated with climbers named elsewhere in these pages and with individuals who would later become members of the Rapparees club. The IMC maintained its interest with Kevin Byrne, Peter Coakley, Sean Barrett, Brendan Proctor and others making a contribution.

Jim Leonard, pioneer on Ailladie and Malinbeg, *c.* 2013. LEONARD COLLECTION

Interest in the special challenge of Donegal's big mountain routes was maintained as, in 1974, Redmond and Walsh did Kongen with three points of aid on Ballagheegha Buttress in the Poisoned Glen. Shortly afterwards professional instructors made an appearance when Ray Finlay led H. Moore and Teddy Hawkins up Anaconda Corner on the Last Small Buttress. Sheridan and O'Halpin were active in Glenveagh, as were P. Brennan and J. Rafter. Also in Glenveagh, Torrans and Billane with Denis Rankin put up the crag's first modern hard route. More modest lines at Lough Belshade by Walsh and Richardson, followed in 1975 by Joe and Kathleen Bent with Paul Donnelly, kept IMC climbers in touch.

In 1974, at Bray Head in Wicklow, Gerry Moss and Ted Forde began their extensive development of the inland outcrops above the cliff path, and of the various sea crags and pinnacles below the railway line. By 1978 when the FMCI produced a guidebook, this pair had put up fifty new climbs here, assisted in the later stages by

Luke Brady, an amiable personality who would become familiar to an entire generation of climbers as he ambled around Dalkey Quarry, dispensing advice on technique and the location of hidden holds. That guidebook, edited by Lynam and Liam Convery who as a pair also did a number of routes at Bray, would include details of several minor crags in Dublin and Wicklow, including Ireland's Eye, Howth Head, Dunran, The Scalp and the Devil's Glen.

Gerry Moss would go on to be by far the most creative and successful developer of sea cliffs and noteworthy minor crags stretching down the east coast, along the south and up through Clare to Roundstone. Gerry – softly spoken, bearded, of compact, hard build – had the common experience of coming to climbing through the scouts and hillwalking. Throughout his mountaineering career he would be an inspiration to novices – usually hand-picked from IMC rock-climbing courses – and Alpine companions. He did much by his solid, understated but intense level of activity at

a respectable grade to deflect the disdainful dismissal of the IMC by those who felt themselves to be the climbing elite.

Gerry Moss on the Meije in France's Dauphiné Alps in 1989, perhaps cogitating on a new Irish coastal crag.
MOSS COLLECTION

Inland, Steve Young and Dave Walsh did the first two recorded ascents at Lough Dan. Also in 1974, Walsh, Donnelly and Ó Murchú climbed the first route on the North Crag in Glenmalure where, over the next few years a handful of climbs, mostly VS, would be done mainly by IMC climbers.

Steve Young was the dominant pioneer of harder new routes in the IMC for a number of years. Tall and bespectacled, he had whetted his skills in Cornwall where he put up a number of routes. He was involved in the first British ascent of the left pillar on the

North Face of the Pizzo del Ferro in Switzerland's Bregaglia and climbed the Cassin Route on the North-East Face of Piz Badile before he took up his engineering post in Avoca Mines in Wicklow.[15] His eagerness for new routes, and an attitude towards the use of aid derived from his Cornwall experience,[16] may have led him, in common with his compatriot Milnes, to use aid to solve difficult rock problems which others would be inclined to eschew until better protection – or more able climbers – appeared. But that very readiness to buck local tradition helped him to complete a remarkable list of new routes, including some outstanding ones without aid.

Steve Young at Glendalough in 1973. D. Ó MURCHÚ

More conventional or purist in his approach to aid – indeed he seemed to specialise in removing it – was Jim McKenzie who was brought up his first climbs by the author. No account of the late 1960s and of the 1970s can ignore Jim's contribution to Irish climbing. A coachbuilder by trade and later a prosthetic-limb fitter, with his strong physique he was steadiness itself on climbs and a sometimes difficult character off the crag. His climbs were marked by their bold lines and cleanness of ascent. Muskrat Ramble, which he did at Luggala in 1975, along with December and Hell's Kitchen at Fair Head were typical of his style. Almost invariably, one could be assured of a climb of character. He was gentle with newcomers but sensitive to perceived slights by his peers. Almost every climber of note had a falling-out with him, yet he remained well liked and respected, and there was usually a rueful reconciliation.

Besides Muskat Ramble with its magnificent second pitch, Luggala, in that year of 1975, saw the creation of new routes which marked the arrival of Ken Higgs, Tom Ryan, Anthony Latham and the three Windrim brothers. That group, as the guidebook has it, would produce routes thick and fast. Indeed, the sextet would be one of the major driving forces of Irish climbing in the second half of the decade, effectively lessening the dominance of working-class lads. Latham had already shown his mettle in putting up Frenzy in Dalkey in the cold of the previous February; Ryan had produced Blood Crack there in the following month while Sean Windrim had also built a reputation at the quarry. This group, except for expatriate Englishman Higgs, were TCD students, who were young, uninhibited and not overawed by their predecessors. Higgs' ownership of a van was an indispensible boon to the hard-pressed youngsters.[17] Their freshness of approach and exuberance and their struggle to manage on students' budgets brought a new and unexpected dimension to the Irish climbing scene. They could barely afford to contribute to petrol costs and Sean Windrim, who began climbing when he was sixteen, recalls the kindness of an older climber who brought pints to a thirsty and penniless threesome sitting forlornly outside the Royal Hotel in Glendalough. They regarded the IMC as 'a bunch of old fogies' whose jargon-filled talk about alpine arêtes and rimayes was pretentious coming from people whose climbing abilities, the youngsters considered, were no match for these newcomers.[18]

This talented bunch from TCD, whose subsequent careers would lead to a fair degree of prosperity and to several professorships, did much to enhance Luggala's popularity. Higgs's All Along The Watchtower, and Sean Windrim's Definitely Not The Beach,

Donal Windrim leading the first ascent of Curved Air at Luggala, with Ken Higgs, in 1976.
HIGGS COLLECTION

both climbed in 1976, were just two of the many worthwhile lines the group was responsible for in the latter part of the decade. Although most of these were in the harder grades they also put up many fine routes of medium standard, effectively scotching Luggala's somewhat fearsome reputation. During their three most active years from 1975 to 1977 the number of climbs at Luggala was doubled.[19] They learned lessons as their skills developed. An attempt by Sean Windrim to do the first free ascent of Soyuz Ten resulted in a huge fall which left himself and his second, his brother Donal, both hanging several metres out from the cliff face.[20] Competition with Young and Richardson became fierce, and Young describes a dawn start with Mulhall in order to beat 'Higgs and Co.' to a climb in which he knew they were interested. On completion of a wet and muddy ascent they were greeted by the TCD lads with 'How did you find it? We climbed it in the dark'.[21]

Higgs and Latham were also active in Glendalough. Higgs, who had graduated as a geologist at Sheffield, that forcing ground of English cragsmen, would settle in Ireland where he eventually became a Professor of Geology at University College Cork, and would enjoy a longer stint of Irish rock climbing than most of his slightly younger companions who, on graduation, got caught up in the initial stages of their careers and, for some, emigration.

At Dalkey Quarry, these youngsters vied with the rather older Richardson and Young in setting new standards. In 1975, Richardson spotted the possibility of climbing the wall below Tower Ridge past which an entire generation of climbers had walked unseeing, and put up the superb Graham Crackers at a surprisingly amenable grade. Higgs added Crash Landing and then the popular Street Fighter to the left of the Shield. Sean Windrim established an important milestone in the quarry when he padded delicately up the Ghost E2 5b, a friction line which owed little to modern gear or yet-to-come sticky-soled boots; the climber's ability and confidence were all. Tom Ryan was also busy, as was John Colton, in helping these mostly young climbers to dominate developments in Dalkey almost to the end of the decade, generally climbing and putting up routes in the lower E grades. Probably the most significant of these in regard to grading were Young's Creeping Paralysis, the quarry's first E2 6a grading, followed two months later by Sean Windrim's worthier Smouldering Stirrups at the same grade and later by a free ascent by Sean of The Shield, which, as Hebblethwaite and Browner say: 'is a superb popular test piece on which many people have had a chance to notch up their flying hours'.[22] Sean Windrim named Hoochie Coochie Couloir as a swipe at the IMC's supposed posturing in regard to alpine mountaineering terminology.[23]

Richardson returned to Ailladie in 1975 where he made a breakthrough with Marchanded Crack, an event much talked about back at The Mountain Hut,[24] and continued in the lower E grades in the following year with a clutch of routes, making good use of the continued improvement in gear which allowed better placement of protection. The Windrims and Ryan came to Clare in 1976 and availed of the second exceptionally fine summer in a row to add seven decent routes. The next year, 1977, was a fruitful one with twenty-three new routes coming on stream, no doubt partly the result of competition between several separate groups: the Ryan–Windrims–Higgs combination; Dermot Somers and John Colton with Joe O'Dwyer; and a party of IMC who would shortly break away to form the Raparees club. Tommy Irving was the outstanding talent in this last group which also included Brian Walker, Joe Hastings and the relative veteran Jim Leonard.

Somers, in his book *Rince ar na Ballaí*, evocatively captures the spirit of this period of expansion, of amicable rivalry between groups which sometimes coalesced or intermingled, and whose members constantly moved between climbing locations all over the country and abroad like bands of mythical Fianna warriors ('*Bhí grúpaí de shíor ar shiúl, mar a bheadh bandaí Fianna.*') The climbing culture of the time, he says, was vigorous and exuberant.[25] Sean Windrim recalls sunny sea-scented evenings at Ailladie eating camp-prepared spuds and freshly caught mackerel, followed by visits to still unspoiled pubs at Doolin for pure Clare music.[26] Climbers' goings-on added a new dimension to the experiences of those living in a county which, despite social problems and emigration,[27] was magical in its Tolkien associations, its geological and archaeological wonders, in the long lines of donkey carts and horse carts delivering milk to local creameries.

Not a great deal was done in the remaining years before the end of the decade. An Easter visit in 1979 by some English climbers resulted in five new lines. Sean Windrim remembers that the activities of some previous visiting British groups were regarded as somewhat avaricious, that they saw Ireland as a place where 'there was hay to be made' by banging in lines which had been disregarded by young enthusiasts keen on the deed rather than on making reputations.[28] More crags would be discovered inland, providing fun and fine views but none matched Ailladie.

At Fair Head, some of those who had been developing their skills in the Burren and Luggala joined Torrans, Sheridan and Billane in the new Dal Riada club which replaced the defunct Spillikin, and were well on the way to adding most of the forty climbs which would be put up at the Head between 1976 and 1980.[29] (The Spillikin had faded away, as one member put it, because of 'mots, mortgages and marriages'.)[30]

Dal Riada, Glendalough, 1980. (L–r): Emmett Goulding, Harry O'Brien, Ian Rea, Dermot Somers, Dawson Stelfox, Owen Jacob, Keefe Murphy, Stephen Gallwey and Calvin Torrans. HIGGS COLLECTION

Higgs, Ryan, Irving and Somers all contributed, as did Martin Smith and Robert Lawson, mainly climbing in the E1 range although Irving's White Lightning came in two grades higher. English climber Arni Strapcans' Wall of Prey at E4, 6a, put up in 1979, was harder to a considerable degree than anything previously climbed at Fair Head.

Sadly, Shay Billane fell to his death while abseiling on Fair Head in April 1977, ending a warm and productive group relationship made up of himself, his partner Val McCartney, Sheridan and Torrans. It is probably true to say that Billane was Ireland's most popular climber, as was evidenced by the numbers, from Belfast as well as Dublin, attending his funeral. He had little of the ego which motivates so many top climbers. Indeed, if it were not for his fine record at home and abroad it would be easy to think that he lacked the necessary drive, so relaxed did he seem in company and on the hill. He had twice decided to give up climbing, recognising its dangers and its effect on conventional social interaction (he was something of a romantic without being a 'ladies' man') but was unable to tear himself away from its friendships and excitements. A fairly typical episode in his company was an occasion in the 1960s when he and O'Leary found themselves in darkness when their candle blew out as they were midstream on stepping stones in a river in spate as they made their way to Luggala. Billane could not swim, but they almost fell in as his dry comments emanating from the darkness had them both helpless with laughter.

The Mournes were not neglected as the decade spun out but the creative energy and effort of Northern Irish climbers was concentrated to a large extent on Fair Head and on finding new routes and crags in Donegal. There was controversy in 1979 surrounding the tactics allegedly employed by some English climbers, including John Codling and expatriate Pete Douglas, in putting up some routes, including Mirror Mirror and Warhorse, both E4, 6a.[31] Ethical standards in Ireland, derived from the 1950s pioneers in Wicklow and the Mournes and inspired by British tradition, had not been compromised by the almost frenetic competition engendered since the late 1960s by climbing media and television in the UK and the resultant openings for mountaineering reputations and careers. Bolting, the use of chalk, secret red-pointing (not admitting to top-roping a climb before making a free ascent) and excessive use of aid were frowned upon, as were other practices which lessened the sport's inherent adventure, risk and demands on self-sufficiency. Peer pressure could be brought to bear on indigenous climbers but was less effective on visitors. But there was no doubting the difficulty or quality of these new routes which were among the hardest in Ireland at the time. There is usually some ambiguity in the approach to others' climbing misde-meanours, especially if these have not been directly observed. Some previously questionable practices sometimes come to be accepted, as would the use of chalk and roping down to clean a route as had occurred at Fair Head and which would become accepted usage in the Mournes. The Codling–Douglas controversy hinged partly on what is now known as 'openness and transparency'. In a later letter to *Irish Mountain Log* Codling disputed much of what had been said about his style.[32]

New crags were now being found all over the country and new routes were being done by the score each year. Tom Hand was to say of the 1979 *New Climbs Bulletin* that its total of 108 new climbs was at its disappointingly lowest since 1976.[33] Calvin Torrans has postulated that the rate at which new discoveries were being made may account for the failure, if that is the right word, to climb at higher grades.[34] Clubs were being formed all over the country, and, though these were mostly hillwalking clubs, several also included rock climbers.

In Cork, Pat Long, Con O'Leary and friends in the newly formed Cork Mountaineering Club put up routes at the sea crag at Oysterhaven in 1978 and helped Sean O'Riordan, Denis O'Connell and others to start the development at the Old Head of Kinsale. Around the southern and south-western coasts, and inland, routes were being put up by a variety of well-known names but little of importance emerged. In 1976, at Loop Head in County Clare, Young and Ó Murchú put up the first routes on the slabby shales of a coastal crag, Croan Rock.

The Rapparees, a club set up in 1977 mainly by Jim Leonard as a result of tensions in the IMC, visited Rocklands near Wexford town in 1978 and ticked off about thirty routes, the best probably being Irving's Ivy Direct. In the last two years of the decade, in nearby County Waterford, Stephen Gallwey, helped by Owen Jacob, Walter Lee and Randall Gossip, had begun his development of the high, extensive crags in the magnificent Coumshingaun, the best of several routes at this early stage being East Face Direct.

Leonard's parting from the IMC was, partly at least, a result of what he saw as social class differences, but activist Dave Walsh disputes this rationale, as does that formidable cragsman and alpinist Tommy Irving who left with Leonard. It should be noted when considering this touchy subject that Tommy's working-class credentials are as indisputable as his remarkable climbing abilities. His views are similar to those of the Rice brothers who came from a not dissimilar background. Again, the dispute seems largely to have arisen from rival views of what a mountaineering club should be, and who should run it.[35] It is also possible that a more effective use of language by those accustomed to debate may have led to the opposition's frustration and departure.

Ray Finlay, Kevin Quinn and D. R. Henshaw were foremost among those putting up routes on the many smaller crags in Fermanagh, some of which had been discovered by Bruce Rodgers in the 1960s. Ricky Cole was busy at the biggest of these, the Englishman's House Crag, where the names of M. Smith and J. Dixon were also prominent. In County Sligo, Torrans, Sheridan, Somers and Ryan found the fine limestone crag at Tormore in 1977. Sheridan narrowly beat others to the first route. All the previously named Dal Riada climbers would feature here over the next few years.[36]

Back in Donegal, Tom Ryan's Flying Enterprise at Malinbeg, climbed in 1975, was to become a classic as was McKenzie's Bold Princess Royal, although this latter line was to be washed away with several adjacent climbs eleven years later. Walsh kept IMC participation alive and was one of a party who made use of a Tyrolean traverse to gain access to The Island where a number of routes were done. Dal Riada was also active on the short beetling routes at newly discovered Muckross Head further up the coast. Further north at Crohy Head in 1976, members of QUBMC – Kerr, Alistair (Waldo) McQuoid, and A. McKinstry – did a few climbs, from Diff. to VS.

From 1976 onwards, Alan Tees, Ray Lee and other members of the NWMC, along with other Derry climbers from two new and rather short-lived clubs, Feargortha and Strand, developed crags on Muckish and Inishowen. Across the border, Strabane Glen was added in 1978. Most of these early climbs were in the easy range, with an occasional harder one, as the NWMC climbers developed their self-taught skills. The entry on to the north-west stage of the more experienced Joe Rotherham and his fellow Feargortha members, particularly Brian McDermott, ushered in a period of rising grades, competition and more intense development, notably at Culdaff and Kinnego Bay, which would help to further galvanise the earlier climbers and attract outside interest during the coming decade. Others involved in the earlier development were Martin Manson, Paddy Grant, Barney Patton and Jim Logan.[37]

Tragically, Joey Glover did not live to see all this development in his beloved Donegal. As a truly poignant reminder that Irish mountaineering can be caught up in politics he was shot dead by the IRA in November 1976 in an all too common case of mistaken identity.[38] Des Agnew too would not see the end of the decade. In June 1976 he died quite suddenly while traversing the Haute Route from Chamonix to Zermatt.[39] Groups and individuals from most of the active climbing clubs continued to travel to Scotland in the winter. A medical student and member of QUBMC, Martin Murray, died in an avalanche on Ben Nevis in March 1978.[40]

By the end of the 1970s there were at least thirty-two clubs in the whole of Ireland, most of which had some rock-climbing members. The IMC had become just another club, albeit a large one. Ten years before, consistent climbing at VS was a sufficiently high standard to allow one to be regarded as a hard man. The hardest climbs were graded Extreme, without any apparent distinction in degrees of difficulty at that grade. Now, HVS was high middle grade and top climbers climbed consistently at the lower E grades.[41] However, the highest grades still lagged behind international standards.

Hillwalking

Most of the clubs formed during the 1970s had more active hillwalkers, or what might be called general mountaineers, than rock climbers or serious alpinists. Some would respond to the challenges presented by the Atlas Mountains, the Pyrenees, easier Alpine peaks, or by Scottish winter traverses, where enterprise and some knowledge of basic roped techniques and snow and ice equipment were useful. But their normal weekend fare was the hills of home which only occasionally involved some scrambling. Bearing in mind that there were no unclimbed hills in the country, it is difficult to chart developments in this aspect of mountaineering, unlike the situation in rock-climbing where the discovery and scaling of new crags and routes can be fitted into a historical narrative. There were still some record times on 'challenge walks' to be noted. But the chronicling of these would become largely meaningless when hill-running, along with organised, monitored and sometimes logistically aided walks became common. Questions of access and environmental degeneration, hardly of import until this decade, would acquire more importance and will be briefly dealt with in chapter 11.

New clubs such as that at University College Galway (UCGMC) founded in 1970, and Sligo MC, were mainly focused on hillwalking but had some rock-climbing members. Cork MC and the much older NWMC would become quite active in the development of their local crags, with the latter group also ranging widely as it trod across the hills of almost every Irish county as well as the Scottish Highlands. Members of the IMC, in Belfast and Dublin, including some of its more able rock climbers, would continue the long-established practice of hillwalking and summit camping in the winter. Young, a rock-climbing specialist, describes what he regarded as miserable snow camps on Lugnaquilla and an occasion when his friends tramped up from Glen of Imaal, pitched tents on the summit and then descended to Fenton's pub for an evening's jollity before 'retiring' to their tents.[42]

What had been long, seldom-completed walks such as Art O'Neill's and the Lug Walk became almost commonplace. Some such walks became annual organised outings, usually arranged by a local club, which attracted scores and then hundreds of participants who were timed and monitored. By 1979 there would be seven of these 'challenge walks' and there would already be controversy about the environmental effects and the propriety of such ventures in what had previously been regarded as an individualistic or small-group activity. Nevertheless, some with good individual credentials took part in these, with Christy Rice smashing his brother Niall's record for the Lug walk on 18 June 1977 when he arrived at the summit of Lug in a time of 5 hours 38 minutes.[43] In the North, Denis Rankin of the Belfast section of the IMC took first place in the Mourne Wall Walk and, in 1978, Jim Patterson broke the 4-hour barrier for the same walk.[44] On 24 September 1976, Niall Rice and Eddie Gaffney did Hart's Walk in the remarkable time of 17 hours 39 minutes, beating their own previous best time of 19 hours 50 minutes.[45] Eddie had previously completed the Bohernabreena–Lug–Bohernabreena round trip some twenty years after it was first completed. Sensibly, he arranged to be accompanied by a relay of friends, thus ameliorating the perils of sleep deprivation.[46] Tommy Irving, a brilliant if transitory rock climber and alpinist, was another fast walker, completing the Lug walk 'many times' including one effort in 7 hours and 30 minutes.[47] In 1978, old hands Brown and Masterson did the third recorded Bohernabreena–Lug–Bohernabreena trip, experiencing some decidedly odd sleep-deprived hallucinations on the return journey.[48]

Uinseann Mac Eoin continued his ticking off of Scottish Munros on his odyssey aimed at being the first Irish-based person to do the lot. The first two of the Irish Walk Guide series edited by Joss Lynam appeared in 1978, an event which would not have been worth a publisher's effort ten years previously.[49]

Indications of the ageing of Irish mountaineering, and mountaineers, were the deaths of several early pioneers. Jack Coleman, who had been an early president of the IMC and was very active in the Kerry and Cork hills, died in a car accident in 1971.[50] Noel Lynch, one of the small group of working-class climbers introduced to rock climbing by Peter Kenny, died due to a fall while walking on Mullaghanattin.[51] In 1975 Tom Quinn, the Grand Old Man of An Óige hillwalkers, the first to do the Lug Walk (besides non-mountaineering tramps such as O'Sullivan Beara's trek and Sarsfield's Ride), died in 1975.[52] It is difficult to think of anyone who was such an inspiration to young hillwalkers who sought the less-trodden way.

And then there was the murder of Joey Glover, founder of one of the oldest clubs, explorer of all that Donegal had to offer and busy participant in a variety of mountaineering endeavours. His leadership of outings became legendary and deserves more space. There are accounts of summit bonfires, usually in winter, on Errigal and other peaks. The tone of obituaries and contemporary comments was one of loving regard for this wonderful pioneer, tinged with a little chastened exasperation at having to share the consequences of his more eventful endeavours.[53]

Joey Glover *(centre)*, with Ruth Burns and Denis Helliwell. ALAN TEES COLLECTION

7

The Walker Spur and Freney Pillar

Emmett Goulding's almost single-handed demonstration during the 1960s had shown that at least some of the Alps' major routes were not beyond the capabilities of the best of Irish climbers. But standards of Irish alpinism had fallen further behind those of the more successful international practitioners. In the early 1950s the top Irish alpinists were but a couple of years behind their British counterparts and perhaps a decade behind the outstanding performers from Alpine countries. But now, in the 1970s, as Irish climbers were set to follow Goulding's Alpine lead onto ED routes, British, continental European and Americans climbers had moved onto winter ascents of the very hardest Alpine routes; they had tested themselves on 8,000m giants and were pioneering the ascents of the more difficult facets of the world's highest peaks.

Fewer numbers, a later start in the mountaineering world and less ready access to the financial resources and professional opportunities which facilitate more ambitious endeavours account to some extent for this lesser Irish momentum; other possible reasons become evident as this narrative progresses. None of this detracts from the personal competence of those few Irish climbers who would, over the next few decades, overcome the handicaps of Ireland's isolation, climate and modest altitudes to tackle the best of the Alpine routes. Nor would it dilute the essential challenge of individual mountaineering experiences or lessen the enjoyment of those pushing their limits. The average club mountaineer would still delight in the encounter with granite face and alpine arête, and would sometimes display considerable skill and spirit in doing so.

In the Alpine valleys, as at home in Ireland, a certain innocence was lost. In Chamonix, English-speaking climbers were now viewed askance in equipment shops and supermarkets. The trust long established with people like M. Snell who had proffered advice and cheerful support at his sports shop, had diminished, as it had with Toni Gobbi in Courmayeur and Signor Grivel at his equipment workshop. Zermatt and Chamonix were no longer villages. Mountaineering had become worldly.

There was an odd start to the Irish Alpine experience of the 1970s. There seemed to have been a pause for breath in 1970 as a new generation girded itself while the more experienced rested or withdrew. Two newcomers to Chamonix attempted the South-West Pillar of the Petit Dru, the difficult Bonatti Route. Christy Rice and Doug Milnes, an English wool-buyer based in Dublin, followed the normal practice of using a 'back door' route to reach the pinnacled ridge known as Flammes de Pierre. From here they aimed to gain the base of the Bonatti Pillar by abseiling down the upper part of the big stone-strafed couloir described at the beginning of chapter 4, but they went astray and were obliged to climb with some difficulty back up to the ridge, suffering one bivouac below the crest.

Milnes left for home but Christy joined with John Fullalove, aka Daniel Boone, in an attempt on Mont Blanc's Central Pillar of Freney. This was the most remote ED climb in the Alps and the setting for tragic events when it was first attempted by some of Europe's top climbers in 1961, four of whom died during a storm-assailed retreat led by Bonatti. Rice and Fullalove also failed, having been caught by a storm somewhere short of the crux brilliantly forced by Bonington and Whillans during their successful ascent some weeks after the first sad attempt. Enduring forced bivouacs and a long retreat, Rice and his companion went without food for three days. Christy Rice had much to think about after this, his first Alpine visit. (The *IMC Journal* of 1971 reported that Christy and friend had bivouacked 150m from the summit, but it seems more likely that they were that distance from the end of the difficulties.[1]) Several Spillikin people were also in Chamonix including O'Brien and Nugent again, as well as Billane, Redmond and Hand. The weather must have been bad as there are no details of climbs done apart from a repeat ascent of North Ridge of the Peigne by O'Brien and Nugent before they escaped to the Calanques, an area of sunlit limestone sea cliffs and sandy coves between Marseilles and Cassis.

Chamonix, 1970. *(L–r)*: Pat Redmond, Frank Nugent, Harry O'Brien, Shay Billane, Doug Milne, Tom Hand, Christy Rice and Paul McHugh. HARRY O'BRIEN

In this same year, there was some activity by Northern Irish climbers in the Dolomites. The East Face of Catinnacio was done by Rankin and Ken Price. Above Chamonix, Nick Prescott and Michael Stitt did the Papillon Ridge of the Aiguille du Peigne, a peak and line already well accustomed to the echo of Irish accents, the clamour of which it would have to further endure in the years to come.

Two expeditions (see p. 150), one to Greenland, the other to Afghanistan, diverted many activists from the Alps in 1971 but the few from the Spillikin Club who did come to Chamonix made their mark. Pat Redmond and Sam Crymble repeated McDermott's ascent of the Frendo Spur. Sam and a friend had just completed the first Irish ascent of the North Face of the Triolet, one of the district's great ice routes. Paul McHugh did the second Irish ascent of the West Face of the Blaitière with Redmond and then, with Crymble, gained the much sought-after prize of one of the great north faces of the Alps, the Walker Spur of the Grandes Jorasses. McHugh's understated description makes the climb, completed with one bivouac, sound straightforward and fairly uneventful but this was an important milestone, one that breached a psychological barrier, even if recent rising standards had rendered its ascent predictable if not inevitable.[2] Goulding was no longer the sole Irish leader of the really hard routes. It was a loss to Irish mountaineering that McHugh did not return to the Alps. It had become apparent by this time that Irish climbers were testing themselves – consciously or not – on routes previously done by compatriots whose abilities they were familiar with from Irish crags, before advancing to harder Alpine routes. The more they could call on friends' previous experience, the quicker would be their personal Alpine development. This would explain the number of repeat ascents mentioned here. Thus, experience and achievements would advance during the next few decades.

Poor record keeping around this time makes it difficult to ascertain what was going on but it is clear that bad weather prevented much being done in the Alps in 1972. Torrans repeated what Crymble had done on the North Face of the Triolet.[3] Shay Nolan and Pat Redmond, along with O'Brien and Hand, did what was probably the first Irish ascent of the North Buttress of the Aiguille du Chardonnet, a fine climb at a reasonable standard. The former pair went on to repeat the Old Brenva on Mont Blanc, and the Grands Charmoz.[4] Ski mountaineers Noel and Ingrid Masterson completed a 220km trip in the Bernese Oberland, skiing from Les Diableret to Meiringen, taking in five summits, including the Monch and Wildstrubel on the way.[5]

Ingrid Masterson skiing the Haute Route Chamonix-Zermatt, 1973.
INGRID MASTERSON

During the following year the Mastersons, having completed the exciting and extremely beautiful ski run from the Aiguille du Midi through the Vallée Blanche to Montenvers and Chamonix, then followed the Haute Route to Zermatt, perhaps the first Irish ski traverse of the route. Ingrid went on with Sylvia Yates to climb a number of peaks in the Urner Alps (Eastern Oberland) including the Galenstock by the South Spur, and Bergseeschijen, South Ridge. IMC parties were in the Écrins and Arolla. In the Écrins, Dave Walsh and party did the first Irish unguided ascents of Mont Gioberney, Pointe de la Pilatte and Pic Nord des Cavales. In Chamonix, expatriate American Bob Richardson and a South African friend did the North Face of the Charmoz, but it may be stretching things a bit to claim this as a second *Irish* ascent.[6] Paddy O'Leary and Brian Walker, besides one of the usual training routes on the overgraded EDs on the flank of Aiguille de l'M/Point Albert, did the first Irish ascent of the South Ridge of the Petites Jorasses, and Willie Cunningham joined O'Leary on an easy route on Pointe Gamba as well as on the Bionnassay Ridge approached from the Italian Miage Glacier. Walker and Cunningham also did the only recorded Irish ascent of the easy normal Italian Route on the Aiguille de Leschaux. Later, Cunningham completed, solo, an ascent of the ordinary route to Grandes Jorasses and a traverse, Gouter-Midi, of Mont Blanc.[7]

Shay Billane celebrated – or at least observed – New Year's Day 1974 by completing what is almost certainly the first new Alpine route climbed by an unguided Irish person since those done by Kirkpatrick some eighty years earlier, when, with Lindsay Griffin, he did a winter ascent of what became known as Hidden Couloir (TD) on the North-East Face of Mont Blanc du Tacul. Its difficulty and the effect of winter storms can be gauged from the time – three days – they took on the 600m face, and the five subsequent days it required to get back down to Chamonix.[8] Having endured a very miserable bivouac (Griffin's second worst of his lifetime), beneath the cornice at the top of the route, they vainly attempted to find the way from the top (point A in photo) in thick cloud on fairly easy slopes to the Midi téléphérique station. They were forced to

North-West Face of Mont Blanc du Tacul with labels indicating some locations connected with the ordeal of Griffin and Billane in January 1974. LINDSAY GRIFFIN

shelter in some rocks (point C). In the afternoon there was a clearing and they set off. However, some distance down, at point B, a large section of the slope gave a loud crack and threatened to avalanche so they were forced to retrace their steps, losing much time climbing the vertical back wall of a crevasse which they had jumped on the way down. They managed to regain shelter in the rocks as darkness fell. They tried two other possible lines the next day and struggled against strong, bitter winds which caused Billane to fall over repeatedly and lie exhausted in the snow. They bivouacked again in the same rocks in temperatures of -20 ºC. In worsening weather the next day, they followed yet a different route (point D in photo) to the Grand Mulets glacier, bivouacked again, this time without food, before reaching the glacier with frostbitten toes and fingers. They spent another night on the glacier, sleeping under a clear sky. They luckily found animal tracks which brought them through a maze of crevasses the following day but not before Griffin, whose turn it now was to be exhausted, lost balance on a steep slope over a large drop and was fortunate to manage an ice-axe brake. They descended through woods to Chamonix in the dark and went straight to hospital in the middle of the night.[9]

Billane joined Torrans that summer to do the first Irish ascent of the West Face of the Petites Jorasses (unless Wathen's assertion that he was an honorary Irishman is accepted), and in a further portent of things to come, did repeat Irish ascents of the Frendo Spur and the West Face of the Blaitière, with Griffin joining them on the latter route.[10]

No one from the Belfast Section of the IMC is recorded as having been in the Alps that year of 1974 and most of the others with Irish connections stuck to well-tried favourites apart from Tom Quinn, Noel Masterson and Tom Wolfe who were in the Julian Alps.[11] Gerry Moss began his long association with the Alps, and his penchant for long traverses, in Arolla where he and Tony Clancy reached eight summits.[12] A Tiglin group was in Zermatt where, with Shelley's help, we reached seven summits including three 4,000m peaks.

In 1975, Belfast Section members John Forsythe, Mick Curran, John Kerr and Derek Howard, did the South-West Ridge of the

Aiguille des Pélerins, a climb which seemed to have escaped previous Irish attention except for a failed attempt by O'Brien and Nugent in 1968. In various combinations they completed some old favourites. Veteran Dublin Section members Brown, Masterson, Hannon and Alan Pope repeated the Forbes arête of the Aiguille de Chardonnet, which had its first Irish ascent by fellow-members twenty-two years previously. Hand with O'Brien did what they thought was the first Irish ascent of the South-West ridge of Petites Jorassess. In the Dauphiné, Lynam, Ingrid Masterson, Ó Murchú and Cecil O'Gorman between them did a number of routes including Aiguille de Dibona by the Voie Boeli and the North Ridge.[13]

The kind of people who had been in the Spillikin Club and would form the core of Dal Riada would continue to forge ahead and were regularly climbing at a more advanced level. Torrans, in particular, had a very good season. With Lindsay Griffin he succeeded on the South Face of the Fou, a most difficult rock climb rarely done since its first ascent by Americans twelve years previously, and the pair then went on to put up a new route which involved interesting mixed climbing on the South-East Face of Mont Maudit. Torrans also did the Swiss Route on the Courtes and, with Clare Sheridan, his life partner, climbed the North Face of the Tour Ronde as well as making a repeat ascent of the North Buttress of the Aiguille du Chardonnet. Moving to Arolla with Griffin, he helped put up a new route on the North Face of Blanche de Perroc, besides making the first Irish and British ascent of the North Face of Mont Brulé and the first Irish success on the North Face of Mont Blanc de Cheilon.[14] So now, largely due to Griffin's drive, there were three new Alpine routes in the modern era with Irish names attached.

In 1976 a large party from the IMC were again in the Écrins where Lynam and Ingrid Masterson traversed the Meije, probably the first Irish to do so since Kirkpatrick, seventy-four years previously. The rest of the party in various combinations did Mont Pelvoux in addition to four other peaks which had previous Irish ascents. In Chamonix, Richard Dean and Tony Latham (both, like Bruce Rodgers before them, from Portora and DUCC) did the second Irish ascent of the Walker Spur on a diet of nineteen Mars

Bars, soup, bread and cheese, while Curran, Kerr, Forsythe and Terry Mooney managed the Cosmique Arête on the Aiguille de Midi before bad weather forced a retreat to the cliffs and beaches of the Calanques.[15]

There were no fewer than five Irish expeditions to distant ranges during 1977, which removed a number of the more forceful personalities from the Alpine setting for that season. Belfast members of the IMC did a traverse of the Courtes, the Polish Route on the rarely climbed Aiguille L'Éboulement near Aiguille Talèfre, (probably the first Irish unguided ascent) besides completing ascents of the Ryan–Lochmatter on the Plan and the fine North Buttress of the Aiguille du Chardonnet. (By a curious coincidence L'Éboulement, Talèfre and the Ryan–Lochmatter all were climbs first done by guided Irishmen in the Victorian or Edwardian eras.[16]) O'Brien and Nolan succeeded on several routes which included what was probably the first Irish ascent of the North Face of the Col du Plan.[17]

The summer of 1978 brought a large contingent of Irish to the Alps, including thirty-one Dublin IMC members, most of whom were on an official meet. Those on the meet stuck mostly to old favourites. Moss and Clancy fitted a traverse of Les Courtes into a fairly full schedule. Some mountaineers showed that to experience real adventure it was best not to follow the crowd, and that it was not necessary to climb at the very highest levels to do so. Charlie McManus, Noel Maguire and Con Collins in the course of a typically imaginative and energetic outing began in the south of the Mont Blanc massif with ascents of Petit Mont Blanc by its north-west spur, east peak of Aiguille de Trélatéte by its east-north-east spur and its South Peak by the South-West Face. They then did the Aiguille des Glaciers and Aiguille Sans Nom before crossing to the Argentière area where they managed a traverse of L'Index, along with the south-west flank of Aiguille d'Argentière and the Forbes arête of the Chardonnet. Pat Redmond and Paddy O'Brien did the first Irish climb of the Pioda North Ridge and Sciora Innominata in the Bregaglia. Bad weather forced an exodus from Chamonix to the Verdon Gorge, a very new venue for people from this island. Donal Enright and Gerry Smith were very busy in Arolla before doing a traverse of the Matterhorn by the Italian and Hörnli Ridges in such poor conditions that they were out for four days.[18]

Old hand Goulding did the first Irish ascent of the North Ridge of Mont Dolent with Harry O'Brien and went on to Tour Ronde where unstable snow on the north face obliged them to divert to a variant on the right side before they tackled the tricky ice climb up Gervasutti Couloir on Mont Blanc du Tacul. They left the range to do the Grand Paradiso in the Graians.[19] Tommy Irving, on his first Alpine outing, demonstrated his talent by doing both the Bonatti Pillar and the first Irish ascent of the American Direct Route on the Petit Dru before tackling the North Face of the Plan, the Rebuffat line on the South Face of the Midi and the East Face of the Requin.[20]

The fun, the successes and the displays of prowess were yet again overshadowed by tragedy when Seamus O'Brien of UCDMC was killed in a crevasse fall on the Aletsch Glacier in July.[21]

The last Alpine season of the decade saw an unprecedented intensity of activity as various clubs from north and south of the border did many of the usual routes in Chamonix and Zermatt in a busy season which would hardly be matched again in the coming decade in the number of routes done. That year of 1979 saw Irish parties busy on various south-facing facets of the complicated and immense Italian side of Mont Blanc. Tommy Irving did the first Irish ascent of the Central Pillar of Freney, a remote climb difficult of approach, demanding in execution and fearsome of reputation. Tommy led all the way and shared the final bivouac with his English companion, Don Barr, just 150m from the summit of western Europe's highest mountain. Before this Irving had scaled, with several different partners, the North Face of the Petit Dru, the West Face of the Blaitière and the North Face of Les Droites, all outstanding climbs, the latter being a first Irish ascent.[22]

Irving and others, like Goulding before them, had turned on its head the situation which existed in Victorian times when the Alps were the playground of academics and the landed wealthy who had the time and resources to spend prolonged seasons, to acclimatise slowly, to wait out bad weather and climb numerous routes. Now, modern career demands on the one hand, along with a reduction in those of the leisured class interested in mountaineering, and, on the other hand, a growth in the number of those young climbers who were free to choose a lifestyle, led to a very changed situation. Cheaper travel and other conveniences resulted in young climbers – and not just those in the working class – taking long breaks, living simply and devoting entire seasons to indulge their climbing passions, somewhat like their surf- and ski-bum counterparts. Teachers like Collins, Maguire and McManus had both the time and resources to get a lot done; others would put their careers on hold and take up other jobs which they could casually leave for extended periods. Increasingly in the coming decade climbers would find employment as guides or similar posts which would enable them to earn a living while climbing full-time. Well-known figures such as Bonatti and Bonington were able to combine climbing with photojournalism or similar professions and this also would eventually occur to some Irish mountaineers.

Goulding, with less freedom to suit himself now that he was married, nonetheless maintained his high standards. With Harry O'Brien, and accompanied by fellow Dal Riadans Dermot Somers and Torrans, he did Route Major on the Brenva Face, Goulding's second ascent of this elegant rock and ice buttress. He and O'Brien had been heading for the Pear Buttress in order to complete the last element of an inspired triptych of stylish lines (Sentinelle, Major and Pear) first put together mainly by British climbers in the 1930s, but conditions dictated that they divert to Route Major.[23] Further to the right as one faces the mountain, and past the looming threat of the Great Couloir, Con Collins and Gerry Smyth made yet another Irish ascent of the Old Brenva Route. This pair had also completed what had become a favourite Irish traverse, that of the Bionnassay arête. Collins went on, with Maguire and an English friend, to do the Hörnli–Italian Ridge traverse of the Matterhorn, returning to the Hörnli Hut seventeen hours after departure – an admirable performance. They also did some of the old Irish Zermatt favourites and Collins went on to do what was probably the first Irish completion of the Nadelgrat, one of the Valais' finest traverses.[24]

Sarcophagus in Glendalough, County Wicklow, in the 1990s; Conor O'Connor leads. IMC ARCHIVE

The Matterhorn. The Z'mutt Ridge is on the right skyline with the snow-covered North Face to its left. The Hörnli Ridge is between the shadowed North Face and sunlit East Face. AUTHOR'S COLLECTION

Síle Daly on Dance of the Tumblers at Luggala, County Wicklow, in the early 2000s. JOE LYONS

Ken Higgs leading the first ascent of Jet at Ailladie in the Burren, County Clare, in 1978. HIGGS COLLECTION

Classical Revival at Lough Belshade in the Bluestacks, County Donegal. The climber is Geoff Thomas. 2014. ALAN TEES COLLECTION

Kev Power on Sharkbait on Ailladie in the Burren, County Clare, *c.* 2005.
PAT NOLAN COLLECTION

Calvin Torrans on the North-West Face of Half-Dome, Yosemite, in the US, 1981.
SHERIDAN COLLECTION

Gola Island, County Donegal, has climbs of all grades in beautiful surroundings. ALAN TEES COLLECTION

Gerry Moss and party on Monte Rosa in the Alps in 1994. MOSS COLLECTION

Ivan Counihan dealing with winter conditions on North Face of Les Droites in 1994.
MARTIN REDEKER

Dawson Stelfox on the Eiger's summit following his ascent in 1988 of the Nordwand. ANDY MCFARLANE

Orla Prendergast in the Alps, 2005. PRENDERGAST COLLECTION

Old men of the mountains: the Anglo-Irish Jaonli Expedition 1991. *Back row (l–r):* Richard Brooke, Mike Banks, Jim Milledge; *front row (l–r):* Paddy O'Leary, Mike Westmacott and Joss Lynam. AUTHOR'S COLLECTION

Dal Riada climbers in various combinations did Grépon's Mer de Glace Face, another route well-trodden by Irish climbers; the South-East Ridge of Le Minaret, a fine TD climb brought to the attention of alpinists by Gaston Rebuffat's writings; the East Face of the Requin; the North-East Face of the Courtes and the North Spur of Les Droites.

Some of the routes completed by the more than thirty climbers from Northern Ireland in the Mont Blanc area were Alan Currans' ascents of the now popular Frendo Spur and the Vaucher Route on the Peigne; Joe Rotherham and McQuoid's climbs on the Chevalier Route on Les Courtes and the East Face of the Requin; and Ian Rea's nine climbs including the North Buttress of the Chardonnet and what was probably the first Irish ascent of the North Face of the Argentière.[25]

(There may be some overlap in the lists of Dal Riada and Northern Irish climbers' routes but it is plain that the northerners were no longer satisfied to stick to run-of-the-mill outings.)

In Zermatt, Currans did what was probably the second unguided Irish ascent of the Z'Mutt ridge. The Dufourspitze was gained by Mac Eoin and John Murray. In the Bregaglia, Lynam, Convery and Donnelly did what was probably the first Irish ascent of the long North Ridge of Piz Badile. Sean Lyons and Paul McGrath of the IMC, having completed a first Irish traverse of the Barre des Écrins moved to Chamonix to do the Ryan–Lochmatter on the Plan and then went on to do the Matterhorn. Conor McGrath was successful on the Frendo Spur and the North Buttress of the Chardonnet. In Austria's Stubai, Tollymore Mountain Centre introduced thirteen novices to the Alpine experience.[26] Many of the listed climbs were already well-used to Irish boots but the sheer number of climbers and climbs done in this year is worthy of note.

Distant Ranges

The decade began quietly, just as it had in the Alps, for Irish mountaineers who ventured outside of Europe. In Washington State, in 1970, exiles Norah and Brian Moorehead did Mount Shuksan (2,781m) near Mount Baker.[27] The tempo quickened in

1971 with Lynam's second expedition to Greenland and Slader's Ulster Afghanistan Expedition to Mir Samir (6,059m).[28]

The Greenland party was a strong one whose leading lights included Billane, Christy Rice and Griffin, strongly supported by Milnes, Nolan, Tim Cashman, George Garrett (who had been on the 1964 Rakaposhi trip), Rankin and Jim Colgan. The team made eight first ascents of peaks including the Minster (ED) by its North Ridge by Rice and Milnes. The most notable climb was the first ascent of the North Ridge of Cathedral by Billane and Griffin, the summit of which was first reached on another route by the 1968 Irish expedition. This long ridge took seventeen hours of climbing, broken by one bivouac, and was graded ED. The descent was difficult in a snow-storm. As has happened to several Greenland expeditions (and to Gribbon on Baffin Island), the boat which was to pick up the group at the end of its month-long stay failed to arrive at their fjord-head base camp so three members – Billane (a non-swimmer), Rice and Rankin – volunteered to walk to a radio station where a boat could be summoned.[29] The trip, undertaken without tents, took three days in heavy rain and involved a series of six river crossings made more difficult by rain-fed spates. Most crossings were achieved by tricky boulder-hopping which sometimes needed roped protection until they reached the final and biggest river which emptied a large lake. They waited for some hours to allow the level drop some 4 feet (1.2m) before Rice undertook to swim across:

> Christy stripped and put on his long johns [underwear], a jumper and his balaclava. He tied a rope around his waist and . . . after hitting the water he was swept away downstream, the waves covered him and his head disappeared. We thought he was going to drown. He grabbed an underwater boulder. He was kneeling on the rocks, then standing and shouting to Denis and me. He made it.[30]

Rice found a rowing boat on the other bank, got it up to the lake and took the others across. They reached the radio station shortly afterwards.

In Afghanistan, the Ulster team led by Bert Slader climbed Mir Samir which was thought to be 6,059m in height but the Alpine Club had it at 5,809m. The mountain, which had been made famous by Eric Newby in his *A Short Walk in the Hindu Kush,* had been first climbed in 1959. The team, in common with so many organised from the province, was made up of a group of teenagers and experienced mountaineers, the idea being to give youngsters a taste of adventure besides learning something of local culture. Two new routes were done, the harder one by a couloir on the South-West Face which was climbed by Mick Curran, Trevor Mitten and Phil Blake; the other route on the South Face was climbed by John Anderson, Dick Jones and Mitten. The group also made first ascents of three 5,000m peaks in the Chamar valley.[31]

In 1972 Nick Lynam and Gwynn Stephenson did Peak Lenana on Mount Kenya.[32] In the following year O'Leary was baulked in an attempt on Nelion, one of Mount Kenya's twin summits, when he was obliged to recover the body of a fallen German climber and to accompany his widow down. In 1975 Dave Walsh renewed the Irish connection with Greenland and the Kap Farvel (Cape Farewell area) when he led a combined Belfast/Dublin party to Ilva Fjord. Encountering some of the usual difficulties associated with Greenland – impassable ice floes, engine breakdowns, rain and mist, long climbing days – the team made twelve first ascents of peaks, some of them quite hard. With Walsh were Joe Mulhall, Ray Finlay, Phil Holmes, Paddy O'Brien, Dave Mitchell, Alan Douglas and Roger Greene.[33]

In 1976, in Afghanistan, Maguire, McManus and Pat Blount trekked to the summit of a peak in the Panjir Valley area which they thought to be about 5,800m in height.

In the following year Calvin Torrans led Latham, Goulding, Lynam and Clare Sheridan to an area in Kishtwar in the Indian state of Jammu and Kashmir which had been reconnoitred the previous year by Billane, Torrans, Sheridan and McArtney. Attempts were made on the Eiger (6,000m), Cathedral (5,550m) and an unnamed peak, but all failed because of bad conditions, poor weather or unexpected difficulty. As a final effort Torrans, Latham and Lynam climbed a peak they called Khel Parbat, a 5,000m peak by a route considered to be TD. On the return trek Clare Sheridan had a frightening experience when a human chain broke as they made a river crossing and she was swept away, weighed down by a heavy pack. Her friends fished her out, shivering, onto a small island that was in danger of being inundated by rising water. Nomad horsemen then came to the rescue.[34]

In that year of 1977 another expedition to India was mounted by Ulstermen Curran, Kerr, Forsythe, Foster Kelley, Peter Lamont and Mooney. Their objective, Hanuman Tibba in Kulu was out of condition so they transferred to Karcha Parbat (6,269m), a peak in Lahul quite close to Lynam's field of exploration almost two decades earlier. The summit of Karcha Parbat was reached for the first time on 18 September by IMC members Forsythe, Kerr and Curran, along with their sirdar Tara Chand.[35]

The Ulster Alum Kuh Expedition to the Takhti-i-Suleiman in the Elbruz range of Iran was led by the dynamic Bert Slader and was again run in his inclusive style with twenty-one members, including mountaineers, trekkers and seven young climbers, one of whom was a young student, Dawson Stelfox. The most notable climb was the 610m Stenaur Route, TD, on the North Face of Alum Kuh (4,846m), which was completed with one bivouac by Joe Rotherham and Raymond Rowe.[36]

Another professional instructor, Ray Finlay, led the Ulster South Greenland expedition to Pamiagduluk Island where twenty-two peaks were climbed, mostly first ascents. Other members were Teresa Finlay, G. O'Neill and Roy Huddlestone.[37]

Alastair McQuoid led a QUBMC expedition to Kackar Dag in Turkey having been refused access to their original goal, the Cilo Dag area in the politically sensitive south-east. During the three weeks they spent in the area they climbed five peaks of almost 4,000m in height, three of them first ascents, and two rock spires. In tackling eleven different routes they encountered interesting mixed climbing with grade III/IV ice, and rock up to VS in difficulty.[38]

In 1978 there were no excursions to little-known ranges but there was a fair degree of interest in the United States where Dal

Riada climbers were active in the Yosemite area in what was almost certainly the first visit with serious intent by Irish climbers. A group from Ardnabannon Outdoor Education Centre visited the Tetons, and Dick Jones, with Willie Annett, was in the Wind River range which had previously been visited by Emlyn Jones. In Yosemite, Torrans and Sheridan moved up to Tuolomne Meadows where they did a number of medium-grade routes. Torrans then did the Nose on El Capitan with two other climbers in two and a half days. He ascended Snake Dike on Half Dome which had already been soloed by Dermot Somers. Somers and John Colton also climbed the Steck-Salethé Route on Sentinel Peak, a great classic enhanced by historical associations with some of the legendary characters of American climbing.[39]

There was an Ulster College Expedition to the Lyngen Peninsula in Norway. Corkman D. Wallace was on Kilimanjaro,[40] a harbinger of later ascents when every Tom, Dick and Enda would be rushed to the summit by guides already thinking of their next assigned group. In the last year of the decade, in Alaska, new ground was broken when Billy Ireland succeeded on the Cassin Ridge of Mount McKinley (Denali), enduring arduous experiences which would eventually become more familiar to Irish climbers. Flying in to a glacier landing some 17 miles (approx. 27km) from the mountain, he and companions hauled gear and food by sledge to the foot of the south face. Some hard climbing in deep snow and bad conditions got them to the top in poor weather where they camped for three days waiting for a clearance which would enable them to find their way down. The descent took another two days.[41]

O'Leary co-led a commercial group through the Rolwaling valley in Nepal and over the 5,755m-high Tashi Lapcha pass, a 'back door' route to the Khumbu region and Everest, climbing Ramdung (5,930m) on the way, but failing on an attempt on Parchamo (6,187m).

8

Coastal Tour

Home

Two English climbers, both of whom had upset the Irish rock-climbing establishment, got the 1980s off to a fruitful start at Dalkey Quarry while at the same time proving their undoubted abilities and wiping the eyes of their Irish detractors. Expatriate Steve Young, by far the lesser target of local strictures, put up a direct and harder finish to Gargoyle Groove in April 1980, and at about the same time John Codling with Pete Douglas and Ulsterman Martin Manson did the upper arête of Asterisk, a climb which had been vaguely attributed to, and named by, mythical supermen in the mid-1940s.[1] Codling diminished the route by avoiding the difficult crack at the beginning of the climb. This omission was remedied by Belfast's Eddie Cooper four years later when he led, on sight, the entire route. The loss of a crucial flake made the climb even more difficult and it would be 1990 before this new problem would be overcome.

Codling went on to do the first ascent of Lifeline on Camaderry's Upper Cliffs. Controversial tactics on this fine route prevented its getting a technical grade until it was done free by Howard Hebblethwaite, yet another expatriate Englishman, in

1985. In a year in which home achievements were largely over-shadowed by Irish doings abroad, Torrans was responsible for two other developments at Glendalough. In October 1980, with Sean Darby, he completed the long-awaited first free ascent of pinnacle-less Spillikin Ridge, restoring proper distinction to this fine classic and giving it a new grading more worthy of the line. In November, with Sheridan, he tackled the obvious arête to the right of Ifreann Direct to yield Ifreann Arête. Apart from these happenings it was a fairly uneventful year.

It may have been a relatively quiet year on the crags but, in print, blood flowed as two accomplished polemicists, Dermot Somers and Ian Rea, separately involved themselves in guidebook controversy in their respective bailiwicks, Dalkey and Mournes. Somers pitched into the newly published (1979) and second of Steve Young's guides to the quarry, claiming with much justifica-tion that there were anomalies and that it seriously under-graded many routes. In passing, he took a sideswipe at the new Mourne guide. Rea, also writing in *Mountain Log*, called the Mourne guide a 'dismal affair' and detected a lack of enthusiasm and passion on the part of the editor John Forsythe. He accused Forsythe of not climbing, indeed of not being capable of climbing, many of the hardest routes which he under-graded. He described the guide as being poor 'by mainland standards', by which, one assumes, he did not mean continental standards. There was another letter on climbing ethics signed by Rea, Dawson Stelfox, Gary Murray and Joe Rotherham. Forsythe's unsurprisingly ruffled replies further set the unfortunate tone for years of reciprocal bitterness which found its way into several editions of future Mourne guidebooks as well as the *Log*.[2]

Much of the fulminations of Somers and Rea, then and later, were directed at the Irish Mountaineering Club. Rea gave as his authority on the subject certain articles he had read and Torrans' verbal anecdotes.[3] Each excoriated the IMC and blamed it for everything from producing a poor journal – of which there were only three issues that decade – to being stuffy; Rea asserted that recent doings of the Belfast Section were insignificant in historical terms. Rea's critique of Phil Gribbons' account, in a *Peak Viewing* article, of early Mourne climbing – an assessment which he (Rea) may not have meant to be as begrudging as it reads – could be said to be ahistorical itself. (See chapter 10 for further comment.) Somers accused the club of being 'largely moribund' and of having driven out, stifled or antagonised any talent 'in its vicinity', but had the grace to lace his asperity with somewhat Swiftian humour.[4] He was answered by Dave Walsh who pointed out that the IMC had nurtured the various talents in the first place, that for many in Dublin at the time it was the only entry route to mountaineering. He went on to argue that clubs like Dal Riada did not foster talent so much as they acquired it, depending for their 'raw material' – high-grade rock climbers with proven record – on people who came as ready-made, able activists from clubs like the IMC.[5] This denigration of the IMC continued through the 1980s and into the following decade. Windrim's comments regarding the club have already been noted. Howard Hebblethwaite was to remark that he and his contemporaries regarded the IMC members as 'bumblies' who still wore climbing britches when he and his friends were bedecked in lycra.[6] An image is conjured up of booted, hooded and storm-lashed alpinists encountering lycra-clad and bare-chested figures on one of Windrim's derided arêtes or couloirs.

The level of rock-climbing competence evident in 1980 was a foretaste of a continuing rise in standards in most aspects of Irish mountaineering during this decade. There were a number of key issues which dominated development and discourse. Domestically, the opening of climbing walls – fairly basic ones at first – and an associated increased emphasis on fitness and training, would help to raise general standards to a level which would hardly have been imagined in previous decades. At the walls and places like Dalkey the exhibitionism which was always part of climbing in public places, albeit somewhat muted to avoid suggestions of showing off, now became open, as the colourful lycra mentioned above was matched in Californian boardwalk style by bare upper bodies and flexed muscles. The days had gone of heavy drinking and off-season idleness – feigned or otherwise – to be replaced by intensive training in the style of UK climbers like Pete Livesey and his US counterparts. Northern Irish climbers would jostle, if not entirely dislodge, their southern counterparts from their accustomed dominance of the sport. More women would tackle hard routes and appear prominently and independently in the Alps and other high places. There would be far more Irish alpinists with a particular focus being directed by a few towards the great north faces. There also, Northern Irish climbers would feature far more than hitherto, as they would in seeking out harder challenges in the greater ranges. The Irish would again venture onto 7,000m peaks. There would be much agitation in regard to threats to the mountain environment and some incipient concern about access to the hills.

Climbers from outside the larger cities, North and South, would make their presence felt, most predictively in Munster. This was the first decade in which it could be said that rock-climbing activity and, to a certain extent, interest in higher ranges extended almost nationwide. An interesting phenomenon would be the emergence of professional climbers, mountain guides and others, whose dedication to the activity had much the same effects as professionalism would have in sports such as rugby – greater longevity at a high level, more attention to fitness, a spread in the awareness of technical finesse. Whatever social distinctions that may have continued to matter into the 1970s would become utterly irrelevant. Continued reference in this history to climbers' occupations will mainly be to account for the sometimes sudden departure from the scene of talented climbers due to career demands, or to explain how others found the time to continue climbing. Antipathies, clashes of very strong climbing egos and elitism bordering on the overweening replaced class-determined differences.

The following paragraphs attempt to describe the range of new developments and to present the growing cast of characters involved. In the decade's first year, Douglas and Manson, using two rest points, put up Mad Dogs, a fine route on Spellack in the Mournes which would remain the hardest in the area until near the end of the decade, when Cooper's removal of aid made it harder.

In the next few years, two Northern Irish climbers – Rea and Stelfox – would make their presence felt on what should have been the territory of southern climbers as they took turns in producing new lines at Lough Belshade high up in Donegal's Bluestacks. Climbers from south of the border were entirely absent from developments in the Bluestacks during this decade except in minor if essential roles at the blunt end of the rope. Perhaps the finest achievements on these remote, long granite crags with their real highland feel were two climbs by Stelfox which bracketed the decade: Classical Revival in 1981 on which Stelfox led Rea and Ursula MacPherson, and Act of Destruction, 'for which superlatives don't suffice' with Martin McNiff in 1989. (Two points of aid were removed on this latter line, no doubt with a little respectful envy, by Donie O'Sullivan and Fenlon in 1991.) Willie Brown-Kerr, Paula Turley, Derryman Brian McDermott, Paddy Mallon, McNiff and Alan Currans all notched up routes here.

Rea and Stelfox would also blazon their mark on many of the Mourne's crags, Stelfox mainly at the beginning of the decade with Rea coming into his own near the end, as they and others assailed almost all the area's crags in a very productive period of good quality routes which reflected a more widespread dissemination of the dynamism shown at the end of the 1970s. Now, some of those who were active in the Bluestacks and, of course, Douglas, were joined in the Mournes by Alistair McQuoid and Martin Smith and, a little later and at a lesser intensity but similar quality, by Paul Clerkin, Steve Reid and the pairing of John Harrup and E. Johnson. The latter half of the decade was much influenced by Gary Murray who had a particular penchant for hilltop tors, and shared with the similarly prolific Simon McIlwaine a liking for the Mournes that ran so deep that their names can scarcely be found in the guidebooks of other areas. Torrans made an occasional foray from other haunts, almost always to good effect. Others, too numerous to mention, also contributed, including Kevin Quinn and, at a more modest level, John Forsythe. Southern input was limited to one route by Peter Coakley. Quite late in the decade, the remarkable talents of Eddie Cooper were displayed on a series of outstanding routes when he interrupted his doings at Fair Head and Ailladie to produce some fine routes which presaged his outstanding contributions in the 1990s and his transformation from being the first among equals to his being a virtually undisputed rock-climbing master.

The Northern Irish Troubles which affected so much of Irish life during this period also had their effect on mountaineers. Stelfox has said that at least some of his motivation and a great deal of his enjoyment of the hills came from a desire to get out of turbulent Belfast at weekends.[7] Southern climbers did venture north, albeit in lesser numbers during this period, to Fair Head as well as the Mournes. Their much-reduced numbers were to an extent due to their involvement in Ailladie and the Wicklow crags, but ferment in Northern Ireland played its part. It is difficult to describe to a later generation the feeling of relief when one recrossed the border going south, relief from a tension one was not consciously aware of while in the hills or engaging with Northern Irish friends. Perhaps some Northerners felt a similar emotion when climbing in the south, which would explain the absence of all but a few of them from crags in the Republic – excepting Donegal – and their absolute non-presence, save for Wicklow resident Torrans, from guidebooks to places like Luggala.

Torrans and his wife Clare Sheridan would continue to play important roles in the development of Fair Head. Their dedication to the exploration, for such a lengthy period, of this steep and extensive crag, exposed and northerly, is remarkable; an exploration and development which is of undisputed importance on the international climbing stage – perhaps the only domestic climbing achievement of which this may be said. Torrans came from Belfast's Shankill Road and took to youth hostelling where he was tentatively introduced to rock climbing. Following a stint in the British army, where he had some experience as a mountaineering instructor, he teamed up in the mid-1960s with Calvert Moore and others in Glenfoffany club where class, religion and political leanings had little meaning and had no bearing on climbing partnerships or the intense enthusiasm which so impressed visitors to their hut a few miles outside Newcastle.

He brought with him an intense dislike of what he saw as the climbing establishment in Northern Ireland and especially of the IMC. He had implacable views on climbing ethics, on climbing politics and those he labelled as bureaucrats, views which were stubbornly and obdurately aired.[8] This stance was at variance with his more genial, huge-grinned and helpful approach to beginners and those seeking his advice on

Calvin Torrans at Ailladie, County Clare.
SIMON MCEVOY

mountaineering matters. He influenced Irish climbing to a remarkable degree and it is considerably due to his proselytising zeal that the advent of chalk and bolts were so long delayed. He earned his living as a mountaineering instructor and then as a guide. It would be tendentious to argue that at any given time Torrans was the best, but his consistency at a high level, the long duration of his career, his pioneering work at Fair Head and other places, his extensive experience in high ranges on several continents, together place him in the very front rank of Irish mountaineers – and a place in their history.

Sheridan, quite separately, had a profound effect on Irish climbing in the way she became a role model, an exemplar of the lofty positions to which women climbers could aspire, all the more so as she had not set out to inspire emulation, nor did she herself have a need for such a model; she simply climbed almost exclusively and on equal terms with men, adjusting her techniques where necessary to make up for the lack of brute strength. It has been said that Clare was even more rigorous than Calvin in her approach to climbing and climbers, but her views were moderately expressed in a manner appropriate to her middle-class, convent-educated background. Following a family transfer to Dublin she became a member of UCDMC and began to climb. She met Torrans in Chamonix on her first climbing season and they began a partnership in which they put up more than a hundred new routes together, in addition to those done with other climbing partners. Before children came along they managed together to fit in a year's climbing in North America, busy Alpine seasons and trips to the Himalaya and the Andes.[9]

Clare Sheridan in the Vanoise, France, in 2004. SHEILA WILLIS

Sheridan, a teacher, has explained how, as parents, they seldom climbed together and how on one occasion on a new route at Fair Head she looked after a baby while Calvin climbed the first pitch and then abseiled down to allow her to lead the top pitch while he played his part as dad.[10]

The Torrans–Sheridan partnership and its friends were still finding new climbable areas on the line of cliffs even into the late 1980s. Climbers from the south of the border were still active at the Head, albeit in fewer numbers. Ken Higgs and old hand McKenzie contributed, as did others who were increasingly applying lessons learned on the steep walls of the Burren and Tormore. Keefe Murphy's Baptism of Fire E5, 6a, 6b (1983), the Head's hardest climb to date, in addition to a number of his later ascents, showed how well these lessons were applied. His partner on Baptism, Tom Ryan, also led several good routes. Donie O'Sullivan was there in mid-decade and his friend Robbie Fenlon put in appearances at the end of the period. There were a number of British visitors, including Pat Littlejohn, whose Above and Beyond (1984) trumped Murphy's efforts.

Dubliners' dominance of the Fair Head was beginning to wane, that of Northerners to grow. Robert Lawson at the beginning of the decade was very busy at the crag with token contributions from Stelfox and a 'last hurrah' from Ricky Cole. Rea started off slowly enough but his route count over the decade was impressive, even if the impression is left that Fair Head was not quite his cup of tea. Eddie Cooper also began gently, albeit at a higher grade, but soon vied with Keefe Murphy in the quality and technical level of his routes. Their competitiveness showed in the several routes on which they each eliminated aid placed by the other. Cooper's prowess and eye for good lines were well demonstrated and augured even greater deeds in the 1990s.

Elsewhere in Ulster, Derry-based climbers were busy demonstrating a considerable rise in technical expertise on crags of various rock types across the border on Inishowen and other Donegal locations. Rotherham, Paula Turley who worked at nearby Altnagelvin Hospital, Paul Dunlop and Al Millar all contributed, as did Tees with Gareth Colhoun, Richard Smith, Alan Ward, Davy Hyndman and others. Several Belfast climbers joined those based in Derry, including New Zealander Andy McFarlane. Tees ventured tentatively on to Gola Island where he and friends put up the first climbs. Niall Grimes appears as a leader for the first time at Crockanaffrin in 1989. Development continued at Cruit Island, mainly by IMC members, on Horn Head where UCD climbers contributed,[11] and at Crohy Head.[12] The making of new routes at Muckross Head went out of fashion for almost the entire decade.

Throughout the country, climbers were making the assessments of Hart and Dickinson in the early days of Irish climbing seem ridiculous. Climbable crags, major and minor, were being ferreted out on all sorts of rock, to an extent that developments have to be dealt with in general terms without giving due mention to all those involved. In Sligo, on Tormore's limestone, Dal Riada added routes throughout the decade. Climbers associated with Fermanagh's Gortatole Outdoor Centre helped to develop a sandstone crag on the Sligo coast and also renewed interest in the gritstone of the Playground on the Cavan/Leitrim border by adding a number of lines to those pioneered by the Spillikin Club in the 1960s.

Continuing on an anticlockwise tour of coastal counties, Mayo yielded new crags and routes at a number of places, and would gradually become Tom Ryan's climbing kingdom. With Joe Lyons, Ryan did various harder routes on Mweelrea above Doo Lough. Gallwey joined Ryan and Owen Jacobs who had begun the development of a quartzite crag at Erris Head. In Achill the most important routes were on quartzite sea crags which were developed firstly by Terry McQueen and Alison Lyttle, both from Northern Ireland, in 1985 and later by Stelfox and McFarlane. In the wild but accessible cooms of the sandstone Maumtrasnas, long easy routes were put up in Srahnalong, and an E1 route in Coom Gowlaun. Further south, in Galway, numerous easy routes were found by the IMC on the gabbro crags of Errisbeg near Roundstone which were originally found by Winder and J. Brown in 1970.

Still further south, the Burren's smaller crags were yielding routes, mainly to IMC climbers David Walsh and Gerry Moss. At Murroughkilly, Torrans and Sheridan did some harder routes in the mid-1980s, as did Rea. Andy McFarlane and Paula Turley (now a married couple) added several routes of varying standards later in the decade. Limerick man Mike Keyes, a founder member of the quirkily named Limerick Climbing and Crochet Club, was seconded by Somers on a HVS, Wounded Knee, in 1989. Ailladie remained at or near the forefront of Irish climbing, serving as a forcing house of new talent and as a sociable place where techniques were honed for use on the bigger walls of Fair Head. Keefe Murphy and Tom Ryan did the lion's share of the work here in the first few years of this, the most fruitful decade at the crag (almost seventy routes were recorded). Murphy raised standards in 1982, as he would later do at Fair Head, by climbing Virtual Image which was graded at E4, 6a, making it the hardest in the country at that time.[13] It was later downgraded but retained its technical grading. Classics like Wall of Fossils fell to Murphy and Ryan as did the first two E5s on the crag, Blockhead and The Rack. Cooper made his presence felt with three good routes in 1984 and Point Blank in 1985, the hardest route to date with one rest point. Murphy's emigration in mid-decade left the field open to Cooper who swooped down from his northern eyries in 1988 to pounce on some notable routes of considerable difficulty, including Joker Man E6, 6b.

As one would expect, Torrans had been busy, adding routes as well as producing a new guidebook in 1986. In 1985, visiting English climbers Gary Gibson and Codling, accompanied by Manson, bearded the Irish lion by completing seven routes in the higher range, including the Fall of Wossils. However, Codling, in the local view, dirtied his bib again by making what the 2008 guidebook calls a tainted ascent of what is an otherwise outstanding pitch on Refraction. According to the 2008 climbing guide to the Burren and Aran Islands, Gibson's ethical approach to the making of new routes aroused criticism in each of the two following years.[14] Back in 1985, newcomer Donie O'Sullivan showed the abilities he was to apply in several Irish climbing areas and overseas by soloing Dead Ringer and leading the strenuous Eliminator, albeit with some yo-yos, the first two of a number of good routes he was to add in the 1980s and 1990s. Howard Hebblethwaite who had been making waves at Dalkey also stirred the water here with his 'vicious' Sharkbait with one rest point, besides 'brilliant and intense' Grey Dawn. In 1986 Paul Daly found a crag just north of Doolin Pier which yielded a few routes.

Sheridan was so dominant throughout this time that, but for the mention of the likes of Paula Turley, it might be thought that women were not contributing. Perhaps they were not prominently involved in new routes but they were making their presence felt. The Quadrockers and friends were a group of enterprising young women in the IMC who, besides Joan Flanagan's lead of Dalkey's Ghost, asserted themselves at various venues. Here at Ailladie, Flanagan led the existing The Ramp and Black Widow climbs which were by no means easy.[15] Vera Kelly belonged to that group as did several others whose names appear in Alpine and Himalayan accounts. Other women from colleges and some outdoor centres were independently active.

The intensity and spread of all this activity was reflected in the various guidebooks produced during the decade. These included Donegal (Stelfox, 1985), Wicklow (Higgs, 1982), Fair Head (Torrans and Sheridan, 1989), Mournes (Forsythe, 1980), Mournes (group of nine climbers, 1988) and Burren (Torrans, 1986). All were published by the FMCI as were annual New Climbs bulletins.

Further south in Munster the most significant happening of the decade was the contribution made by local climbers in Kerry.

Kerry

Kerry, the Kingdom, warrants a section to itself, not only because it contains the highest and most serious peaks and mountain traverses in Ireland. It is also because its development as a climbing centre, virtually all of which is on sandstones of various types, is simultaneously an example of how clubs came into being outside the two largest cities and an exception to that model because it happened, almost spontaneously and with little outside help, in an entirely rural sub-montane area. Early hillwalking and rock-climbing endeavours by outsiders have already been noted, but the idea of venturing into the hills for pleasure was long regarded as a dangerous folly by the tough sheepmen who lived on the lower slopes.[16]

The Tralee Mountaineering Club had been in existence since 1954 but largely confined itself to local hillwalks and hardly affected the outlook of hill people. The relatively rare but growing interest in ascents of Corrán Tuathail led to several accidents in the 1960s and the setting up of the Killorglin-based rescue team and its associated Laune Mountaineering Club (see chapter 4). However, skills and experience remained at a modest level.

The few individuals who were involved in the development of Kerry mountaineering in the 1980s were interesting and dynamic characters and deserve more space than is available here. Mike Barry as a youngster was excited by the sight of snow on the hills rising above his home town, Tralee. 'The light was lit,' he said, so that in his mid-twenties it was natural for him to seek out those involved in Kerry Mountain Rescue and then, in an effort to develop skills, to partake with Tiglin in two winter trips to Scotland in the late 1970s. He was back in Scotland in 1980 with John Riordan of Milltown when they introduced seventeen-year-old Con Moriarty to the peculiar joys of the winter environment. Barry, while remaining active at home, went on various enterprising foreign trips as described in this and following chapters. In 1980, he and P. J. Quirke tested their still-developing skills in opening up a seaside crag at Dunmore Head near Coumeenole on the Dingle Peninsula. His inclination to bigger things took him to Mount Brandon's East Buttress in 1983 where, with, Pat Quinn, he put up Place of Penance, a 165m VS route. He also climbed a route which he called Mystic Ridge, in partly icy conditions. At a section on which they were climbing unroped one of the party fell and disappeared into the cloud below, from which a succession of crashing sounds echoed upwards. Barry, fearing the worst, made his way back down and found that his friend had repeatedly landed on his rucksack as he bounced from ledge to ledge and was lucky to suffer only a broken ankle. It was easier to effect a rescue upwards than down, and a long and difficult evacuation ensued which tested Barry's skill and resolution. In 1984 Mike Barry, Tony Macken and an experienced and able northern climber, Adrian Devlin who now lived in Kerry, produced a cluster of climbs varying from V. Diff to easier E grades at Dunshean Head, one of Kerry's best coastal crags. An accessible sea stack added to the fun.[17]

Devlin would go on to climb with Aidan Forde in the Gap of Dunloe. Forde, who grew up in nearby Fossa, had started climbing at the age of sixteen when he put up a Hard Severe in the Gap. He went to TCD, climbed with DUCC and on his visits home, within easy walking distance of the crags in the Gap, he did a number of routes with Con Moriarty who lived just at the Gap's mouth. Con had been messing around among the crags since he was a schoolboy and taught himself ropework from books such as Bill March's *Modern Rope Techniques in Mountaineering*. He put up a few climbs in 1983 and would be responsible for a considerable number of routes in the Gap of Dunloe over the next few years. But it is to Aidan Forde that we must turn to see the remarkable progress made in this area so neglected by climbers from the cities. Over the next twelve years or so Forde would put up over eighty climbs on various crags in the Gap of Dunloe, including some in the lower to middle E grades. According to several who knew him, Forde was a very forceful and innovative climber. (He was in Scotland when he was eighteen and, without previous experience on ice, soloed grade

III/IV winter routes on Ben Nevis, including Comb Gully.) Other local lads were recruited, including Mike Shea from the nearest village, Beaufort, as well as some enterprising young women.[18]

These locals, and some climbers from Cork, were well positioned to exploit the obvious potential for winter climbing on the peaks encircling Coom Caillí (the Hag's Glen) but which always seemed to be out of condition when outsiders made the long journey south. In 1984 Kevin Croft and Jim Crowley, two students from Cork, found a 245m runnel of ice on the north-east face of Corrán Tuathail, climbed it and gave it the unfortunate name of The Lick and a grading of Scottish IV. A shorter Grade IV nearby called Looking Glass Falls which had been first climbed by Devlin and Barry was then done by Forde and Croft. The winter of 1985–86, which also brought out ice climbers in Wicklow, the Mournes and Comeraghs, provided ideal conditions on this impressive face of

Howling Ridge, Corrán Tuathail in winter. Climbers circled. VALERIE O'SULLIVAN

Ireland's highest mountain where climbs start at over 600m and some finish almost at the summit at well over 900m. Forde and John Armstrong from Dublin went on that year to do two grade V routes – the Ramp, along with Death and Destruction – which would not be repeated until well into the twenty-first century.[19] Croft and Crowley did The Ultimate Sin, grade V, to the right of the latter climb in what has been described as a tour de force on thin ice.[20] Three Cork climbers were caught in an avalanche in Curved Gully (grade II) in February and the resultant rescue and evacuation led, according to Con Moriarty, to much soul-searching and to the drafting of new standards for the rescue team. Other climbs, such as Primroses (Moriarty and Garland, 1981) and Howling Ridge, which was first climbed by Moriarty in February 1987, would become classic long, easy summer routes.[21]

Moriarty was easily the most colourful of the Kerry climbers. His love and knowledge of the hills under which he was reared was undisguised and an article he wrote for *Irish Mountain Log* is the most authentic and authoritative essay written by an Irish mountaineer about his local hills and the people who inhabit their fringes.[22] A big man, larger in temperament, vivid in expression and given to embellishment, he would be responsible, like the understated Barry, for notable achievements abroad.

Con Moriarty on home ground in the MacGillycuddy's Reeks. MORIARTY COLLECTION

For reasons which are hard to probe there was a considerable degree of antagonism between the majority of climbers from the major cities and their counterparts in Munster and, in particular, in Kerry. This could give rise to humorous comment about outsiders having to pay the ferryman to venture into the region across the Styx, and less friendly remarks about Cork and Kerry climbs being encompassed by a sinister xenophobic silence.[23] To those who have experienced rural Kerry hospitality such tensions are strange, but it is true that for a long time information on new routes in the area was not forthcoming.

On Kerry's extensive sea coast, Northerners Terry McQueen and Alison Lyttle had opened up a small crag with easy climbs at Carrigard far out on the Dingle Peninsula in 1983 and 1984. In 1985 Cooper and Torrans sniffed out harder lines on newly opened Dunshean Head. Wide-ranging Stephen Gallwey made two sorties from Waterford to put up good routes near where Winder and McCall had climbed thirty years before on Sybil Head. He was with Edward Hernstadt in 1986, and in 1989 with Owen Jacobs. On Great Blasket Island, during two week-long visits by Tiglin groups in 1981 and 1984, over thirty new routes of various grades were climbed near the harbour, the best of these being led by Richard Dean. Cork MC added a few routes in 1981.

In neighbouring Cork, Con O'Leary, Pat Long, Denis O'Connell and Sean O'Riordan continued their exploration of local crags as they opened up routes, including some at HVS, on a cliff at Seven Heads in the early 1980s. Keefe Murphy added two E-graded lines a few years later.

A little further north-east, in Waterford, Stephen Gallwey started the decade by getting into his pioneering stride in the Comeraghs with two 60m climbs, Emperor's Nose and Dark Angel, both on the north-facing conglomerate crags of Coumshingaun. As the decade progressed Gallwey continued to work on the south-facing crag in Coumshingaun as well as the back wall of the coom. On both facets, because of the steep slopes beneath and the fact that some of the climbs begin on upper tiers of this vast amphitheatre, the exposure and big mountain feel is even greater than the lengths of the routes would suggest. With Hernstadt and Jacobs, a number of steep, worthwhile climbs were done from 1982 until 1988, when Jack Bergin then did his bit. Of particular note in the earlier period was Jabberwock, a 95m HVS in the upper tier of the east-facing back wall, on which Gallwey and Jacobs shared leads on a climb which begins 100m above the lake. When Bergin came along

he worked on crags outside the coom, in the Mahon valley and on
Foil na Priosun (or Foilanprisoon as the Ordnance Survey has it),
as well as on previously undeveloped areas in Coumshingaun itself.
Few outsiders ventured into the great corrie and none of the other
top performers pioneered routes here. On the nearby coast at
Bunmahon, Martin Daly and Frank Nugent opened a small crag.

Stephen Gallwey *(left)* and Jack Bergin in the 1990s in Coumshingaun, County
Waterford. JACK BERGIN

Having made a circuit of those coastal counties in which
almost all Irish climbs exist, the climber finds himself back on the
granites of Wicklow and Dalkey. Ken Higgs was still active at
Luggala and in Glendalough, as was Richard Dean, a very tall,
sensitive, likeable man, who put up Silent Movie on Glendalough's
Upper Cliffs with his Tiglin colleague Paccy Stronach. Standards
were rising as Keefe Murphy and Hebblethwaite kept upping the
ante, the latter making the first free ascent of Lifeline, Wicklow's
first E4, followed in 1986 by Bathsheba, Wicklow's first E5.
Contraband was climbed at Glendalough by Donie O'Sullivan
who was one of a group of young climbers who would contribute
much during the coming years. Another of this group, Robbie

Fenlon, managed to find the big, bare-looking slab left of Cuchulainn's Groove sufficiently dry to put up Blue Moon in 1986.

At Luggala, O'Sullivan put up some hard climbs from 1986 to 1988. Joe Lyons had begun his comprehensive development of the hitherto neglected buttresses left of the Main Face at Luggala, besides making his own imprint at Lough Dan and Glenmalure north crag. In doing so, Joe exemplified that breed of very competent climber – Gerry Moss, Alan Tees, Dave Walsh were others – who did not climb at the very highest contemporary grade but who avidly sought out new crags and routes. These climbers, and some who operate at a more modest level, are there in every generation and often exhibit an imaginative approach in the Alps and further afield. In 1983, a small, worthwhile crag of unusual andesitic rock was found at Hollywood in west Wicklow by Jack Bergin (early IMC climbers had also explored here),[24] and was developed in the next few years, mainly by Jack, Joe Hastings and Dan O'Connor.

Dalkey, the fountainhead of so much talent and progress, and which several times had been thought to be worked out, yielded almost forty routes, some of them excellent. At the outset of the decade, Paul O'Sullivan was busy. Later, American Joel Grube, Tony Burke, Hebblethwaite, Donie O'Sullivan, Dean, Colm Ó Cofaigh and Fenlon all tagged on new lines, with the first three named being the most prolific. Hebblethwite's Haunted on the left arête of the Ghost slab was one of the most breathtaking and aesthetically pleasing contributions. Of course, most of the activity at the quarry did not consist of pushing up new routes. With increasing numbers, more climbers were succeeding on harder middle-grade routes as evidenced by Walsh's ascent of the Ghost and the doings of climbers in the various other clubs. Dalkey was unique among Irish crags in its serving almost as an outdoor climbing wall with the consequent social interchange between novice, the casual climber at easy grades, and the elite rock experts, an interchange continued in nearby McDonagh's pub where weekends, Alpine trips and expeditions to higher ranges were planned or talked up.

Increased competence could also be seen in Irish performances on snow and ice. On the rare occasions when decent Irish winter conditions allowed, more people than before could be seen on places like Lugnaquilla's North Prison, MacGillycuddy's Reeks or Eagle Mountain,[25] but such widely spaced outings could not fully be relied upon to develop the sort of techniques which new methods and equipment now demanded from ice climbers and alpinists. For this, Scotland was preferred. Modern equipment and the methods it facilitated made more difference in this branch of mountaineering and in the scaling of great Alpine and Himalayan faces than new gear had in rock climbing. Shorter metal or composite ice-axe shafts that were ergonomically designed, drooped picks, better ice screws, better designed 'step-in' crampons, 'dead man' belay plates, made the long wooden shafts, barely curved picks and the single 9-inch-long blade piton used by Goulding and O'Leary only twenty years before seem ridiculously antiquated.

Placed somewhere between home climbs and those further abroad, climbs in Britain do not form part of this narrative but Scotland in the winter is a special case. Many Irish climbers developed their ice skills there on high-grade mixed ice, snow and rock routes, often in harsh weather, which provided mountaineering experiences of the very best kind. Indeed, winter trips to Scotland, had become almost a prerequisite for good Alpine performances on hard mixed routes, as they had with Irving and others in the 1970s. There are accounts of Scottish winter trips which included fairly frequent ascents, including solo ascents in 1983 by Rea, of Zero and Point Five gullies on Ben Nevis, and of climbs on the Orion Face. Rea also climbed Astronomy with an American partner, an undertaking rightly described as significant at the time.[26] By 1986, Gary Murray was able to report much activity by northern climbers including the ascent of both Point Five and Zero in one day by Paula Turley and Phil Holmes. Murray himself soloed Zero, having already climbed several other routes on the same day. He went on to do Point Five with McNaught and then soloed the Curtain. Rea, Stelfox and Somers also climbed on the Ben in that year as did numerous others from north and south of the Irish border. Climbs were also done in the Cairngorms and Creag Meagaigh. Hastings and Mick Scanlon of the IMC, Burke and

Donie O'Sullivan, Walsh and Ó Murchú were also active at fairly advanced levels, while Gerry Moss led an IMC party on Crowberry Gully on Buachaill Etive Mor.[27] Throughout the decade, groups from Tiglin and Tollymore Centres experienced traverses such as Aonach Eagach ridge and Carn Dearg arête, along with grade III gullies, as they learned their winter skills during several weeks each winter.

There were also the all-too-common incidents – benightments, minor avalanches, falls, even rescues – which occurred to inexperienced parties from Ireland or from south of the Scottish border. Scotland being Scotland, incidents also occurred, if less often, to more-experienced Irish parties.

Hillwalking

The era of exploration of the Irish hills, as referred to in the *IMC Journal* of 1955–56 was long ago ended.[28] While there were still some ridge lines without paths on their crests in the ranges along the western seaboard, there were some signs of the increased usage that was to come, and there were established networks of well-trodden ways already forming on the oft-frequented ridges of Wicklow and Mourne. The initial part of the Wicklow Way, the first of a nationwide network of signposted walking trails was opened in 1980 thanks to the work of J. B. Malone; a section of the Kerry Way would follow in 1985. Similar waymarked paths would follow in places such as the Slieve Blooms. The Ulster Way had opened in 1974 but, unlike its counterparts south of the border, avoided intrusion into the upper reaches of the hills. *Mountain Log* was already, in 1980, publishing advance notices of so-called 'Challenge Walks' which had monitors and checkpoints, such as the Comeragh Bog Trot and the Glover Marathon, just two of a number of such walks which brought large groups into the heart of the hills.[29]

A few of the forty or so clubs affiliated to FMCI by the end of the decade commonly brought groups of over fifty members deep into the hills; one such group on an occasion in 1987 had about ninety tramping over Billy Byrne's Gap.[30] In the Mournes, the annual Mourne Wall Walk organised by YHANI was attracting over 3,000 starters. Objections to the numbers of participants and spectators, along with associated problems of traffic, path erosion, safety and noise from attendant helicopters aroused much controversy, so YHANI decided in1984 to stop organising the event.[31] Under these circumstances, fresh hillwalking experiences of historical mountaineering significance were hard to come by. Those seeking such experiences would attempt to beat records on various well-known 'challenge' walks or to try their skill and stamina on new versions of these. But real comparisons with past efforts were hardly valid now that hill-running had become a competitive activity and challenge walks were so comprehensively serviced. Individual adventures in more rugged hills in bad conditions were still possible, of course, but this is the very stuff of common mountain experience and usually goes unremarked.

One of the few recorded feats worth mentioning was the traverse of all of Ireland's 3,000-foot peaks in less than 24 hours, the first time this was done in a day. This was completed in 1985 by two members of NWMC, Paul Marshall and the redoubtable Alan Tees, who took 23 hours 10 minutes, including driving time. This time was beaten the following year by Mike Berry, Niall Carroll and Justin McCarthy of Peaks Climbing Club who completed the round in 20 hours 36 minutes.[32]

Another example of the way in which politics affect mountaineering was the loss of NWMC's club records in a fire caused by a car bomb in Coleraine.[33] Another fire, an accidental one, marked the end of a thirty-year-old institution which had served mountaineering well for much of its life. The IMC hut, the Bloat House at Dunnywater, burnt down accidentally in November 1989 and two members were lucky to escape with only broken limbs after they jumped from an upstairs window. Its loss undoubtedly led to the demise of the Northern Section two years later.[34]

A number of deaths occurred to hillwalkers during the 1980s. Two of these are mentioned because of their special circumstances. On 13 December 1981, UCDMC student Peter McDonnell died in high winds and heavily falling snow, as a result of a fall down

Lugnaquilla's North Prison in an unfortunate mirroring of part of the tragedy which befell a UCD party twenty years before (see chapter 4). Other members of McDonnell's group spent the night on the open hillside.[35] In December 1987, Angela Kenny of the Limerick Climbing Club drowned while attempting a roped crossing of the swollen Gaddagh River in the Hag's Glen in County Kerry.[36]

Various problems pertaining to access and to conservation were causes of dispute, to an extent not previously encountered, between the mountaineering community on one hand and, on the other, local authorities, landowners and government. These will be covered in chapter 11.

9

On Five Continents

No new routes were created in the Alps by Irish mountaineers during the 1980s. Irish creativity during the decade became increasingly directed away from Europe towards more exotically located and unclimbed distant peaks and faces. These early ventures to distant places also brought deaths which are too often the price exacted from the venturesome.

There would be ample proof of an advanced level of individual skills as some of the Alps' most difficult grand courses were tackled by Irish climbers for the first time, but all these had been done before by other countries' climbers, some of them many times. Robbie Fenlon, who came to know the western Alps really well, has commented that most new Alpine routes were done by locally based climbers steeped in local lore, whose families and friends had become familiar over a long period with the mountains on their doorsteps, and who were well aware of unclimbed lines.[1] Bigger countries, even non-Alpine ones, with larger climbing populations would naturally have extensive knowledge of such things and would not be overanxious to share. It was not surprising, then, that the few new climbs on which the Irish were involved during the 1970s were instigated by Englishman Lindsay Griffin, who could draw on such a resource. It became increasingly rare for any Irish party to have a route to itself, even a quite difficult one, as hundreds of high-grade climbers from all over the world tackled climbs which once were the preserve of the few, while thousands – tens of thousands – could be found on peaks all over the Alps. The Irish, in their own way, had developed a store of knowledge which would be availed of by up-and-coming activists to emulate and then build on, but there was too much repetition to allow for a breakthrough to greater things.

Three expeditions to faraway ranges left Ireland in 1980 and there were several individual ventures. Calvin Torrans led the Irish Andean Expedition to the Cordillera Blanca of Peru, the list of whose members makes for intriguing reading in view of later antipathies. The peaks climbed were 5,500–6,000m in height. None was a first ascent but for a new route of about TD Sup standard climbed by Torrans and Tommy Irving on the North Face of Caraz II (6,020m). Other peaks included Artesonraju (6,025m), which was climbed by Torrans, Sheridan, Hand, Irving, Harry O'Brien and Goulding. Somers and Lynam, as well as some of the others, were foiled by bad rock or ice on other peaks. Things had changed considerably in Peru since 1968 when we had met no other mountaineers or trekkers except for a small British expedition. Goulding was surprised at the number of climbers in the Cordillera Blanca and the fact that trekkers passed by the Irish campsite every day, numbers which prompted Tom Hand to remark, 'Jaysus, it's like being camped beside the Naas Road!'[2] Tom, a much-liked individual who was a keen reader of Flann O'Brien and astute parodist of some of his characters, fell to his death on descent from Artesonraju and his body was never recovered.[3]

Alistair McQuoid led a Northern Ireland Andean Expedition to the same region. A team of thirteen climbers, including Rea, Stelfox and others who would go on to become major figures in Irish mountaineering, spent seven weeks in the area. Artesonraju was traversed via its East and North Ridges. Several other courses were completed including a new TD route on the East Ridge of Nevada Ulta 5,880m.[4]

A QUBMC team led by Alistair Acheson visited Prins Christian IV Island in the Cape Farewell area of Greenland. During a six-week stay the seven-person team (a mixed-gender one like the two Andean expeditions) made forty ascents of twenty-six mountains of 1,300–1,500m height, twenty-one of these claimed as first ascents. There was little technical difficulty, the main effort being one of long slogs and endurance.[5]

Undoubtedly the best individual effort, and the most notable Irish achievement in higher ranges in 1980, was Billy Ireland's success with his Swedish companion Ulf Bjornberg, on the seven-day first ascent of a route on the north face of Alaska's Mount Hunter in July.[6] Although reported at the time as being an ascent of the much-attempted but unclimbed North Buttress, their line was an objectively dangerous one on the right of the face which is unlikely to have had a second ascent.[7] Nevertheless, this achievement on a difficult route in a region that makes great demands physically and on self-sufficiency is further evidence that mountaineers who make little impact on home crags can sometimes find strengths in cold, high places.

In Kenya, Alan and Jimmy Tees with other NWMC members climbed Point Lenana and minor peaks in the Mount Kenya massif.[8] In Nepal, O'Leary again led a group which crossed the Tasi Lapcha from Rolwaling to Khumbu, climbing Ramdung and Parchamo on the way (although O'Leary himself, suffering from frostbite, did not manage the latter).

In 1981, Choc Quinn, Sean Maguire and Jack Bergin completed the first known Irish ascent of the 'ordinary' route, the West Buttress, on Mount McKinley. The three, who had met on a Tiglin course, encountered the usual hardships which feature so much in stories of attempts at that peak. The successful summit bid by Maguire and Quinn was made from a snow cave, Bergin having had to turn back with cold feet and defective crampons. They were not very experienced at the time. Bergin became quite well known in Irish climbing circles while Quinn, who had just emigrated to Canada continued to climb in North America and was on K2 in 1986 (see p. 191).[9]

Denali (Mount McKinley). West Buttress Route follows left skyline. WIKIPEDIA

The following year, in September 1982, Ian Rea led a three-man first ascent of the North Face of Bhagirathi II (6,512m), in India's Garhwal, probably the most difficult Himalayan climb to that date by Irish mountaineers. Rea, Stelfox and Tommy Maguire spent four days on the 2,100m snow and ice face above the Gangotri Glacier before summiting on 10 September. Whilst nearing the end of a descent of the east flank, 23-year-old Maguire fell some 250m, sustaining injuries which led to his death a few days later.[10] He was buried on the mountain. This new route was a very significant advance in Irish Himalayan climbing but Tommy's death had a traumatic and lasting effect on his companions and must have raised doubts about the rationale behind undertaking alpine-style ascents on such a formidable face. Indeed, Stelfox has since said that they did not have enough experience and there is an obvious element of truth in this.[11] He himself had served an apprenticeship on a series of outings to high peaks in Turkey, Afghanistan and Peru. Once the experience of big Alpine faces has been acquired a climber has to adjust to vaster scales and the necessary acclimatisation to greater heights. And that kind of adjustment can only be achieved on the spot.

That Alpine expertise had shown itself in 1980 when Rea and

Maguire followed other Irish ascents of the North Face of the Plan, Maguire having already, with D. Byrne, emulated Irish successes on several good routes including the North Face of Les Courtes. In 1981, Rea and Maguire, Stelfox and Somers did the first Irish ascents of the Cassin Route on the Piz Badile, and the latter pair went on to complete the North Face of Cima Grande de Lavaredo and the scarier North Face of the Matterhorn. (Rea and Maguire were obliged to escape to the Matterhorn's Hörnli Ridge near the Solvay hut when Maguire was injured by falling stones.) These three faces were done as part of that knight-like quest entailed in the climbing of six great north faces of the Alps, a set of classic problems not all of which retained their original reputation. Their successful completion admitted one, if not to the pantheon of greats, then to a meritorious brotherhood of possible candidates. Stelfox had set his sights on this Holy Grail and, though Somers did not then consciously see it as a goal,[12] their successes so far were seen as the first laps of a friendly race to be the first Irish climber to grasp it.

Somers had already established himself as a proficient climber of hard Alpine routes and in 1980 had done, amongst other climbs, the Petit Dru's Bonatti Pillar, Swiss Route on Les Courtes North Face, and the first Irish ascent of the Gervasutti Pillar on Mont Blanc du Tacul with Sean Darby.[13] Then, in 1981, when the others left on their Indian expedition, he did the third Irish ascent of the Walker Spur, another of the sought-after six faces, with English climber Tommy Curtis. As a grand finale to a splendid season he repeated Irving's climb of the Central Pillar of Freney, again with Curtis with whom he had established a close bond. His description of the climb in *Mountain Log,* and of its demanding night-time approach, is vivid. In the best tradition of clear mountaineering description, it can be read almost as a route-guide while capturing the essential challenge and magnificence of the route. Avoiding lyricism, going into details of equipment and food (ice axes, ropes, 'Friends', cheese, sleeping bags, gas stove and so on), his spareness includes passages which are illustrative to layman and climber alike – 'Like all good rock the Pillar looked blankly unassailable from a distance and then yielded at close quarters to a reassuring maze of cracks, corners, slabs and ledges.' And, 'I hung on a crucifying belay, scarecrow in a gale, shivering and blaspheming, freezing tears congealing on my cheeks.' The crux of the climb gave them a measure of Irving's achievement two years previously:

> The crack flares at the top into a vicious slot leaning out over the Lombardy Plain (well, overhanging at any rate!). A weathered tangle of grey slings trails down from pegs in the roof like spaghetti stuck to a ceiling. You trapeze on these, squeeze-chimneying towards the mouth of the slot. It was a serious mistake not to have left my rucksack on the belay with Tommy. I felt like an acrobat trying to perform with a gorilla on his back. Hanging horizontally in mid-air I clipped at f-u-l-l s-t-r-e-t-c-h into a perlon loop and swung out into flared space. Panic zipped wildly up and down my nerves – the perlon sheath was severed all the way through and I was suspended from a single spidery thread of its core. A light lunge with strenuous delicacy, if you know what I mean, and I pulled out retching for breath onto a providential belay ledge.[14]

The Slot on the crux pitch of the Central Pillar of Freney. This photograph, taken by Bruce Normand in 1998, depicts John Hawkins whose experience of the pitch was similar to that of Somers. OLIVE HAWKINS

The tricky night-time approach via the Brenva glacier had taken them ten hours and they were two days on the face before they exultantly summited.

Elsewhere, the South Face direct of La Meije, a good TD route in the Écrins group, had its first Irish ascent by Richard Dean and Martin Smith.[15]

The 1981 season had instilled confidence in Somers to the extent that he felt ready for the Nordwand of the Eiger, the most serious of the faces. In 1982 he did this *con brio* with Curtis and then finished his quest with an ascent of the North Face of the Dru in a prolonged and frightening thunderstorm which tested ex-Catholic Somers' atheism. Two naive, ill-equipped Belgians probably owed their lives to Somers and Curtis who looked after them, not entirely for altruistic motives as the Irishmen had lost their own guidebook. On reaching the summit Somers had completed his six north faces, the first Irishman to do so. Throughout the storm they had worried about Stelfox and Rea who were on the Walker Spur which, being considerably higher than the Dru, was more exposed to the dangers of the tempest. However, that pair had continued climbing through the turmoil and, having descended into Italy, made their way back to their campsite in Chamonix and what should have been a mutually relieved and jubilant reunion with their friends. But, before the other pair returned from the Dru, Stelfox was dealt a crushing blow by the news that his girlfriend Angela Taylor, when descending from the Aiguille de Peigne, had been struck by a falling climber causing both to plunge to their deaths.[16] Angela was a second-year medical student at QUB.

Dermot Somers had a somewhat enigmatic, butterfly-like flair, so full of multi-hued contradictions that it is difficult to pin him down for analysis. Of middle-class Roscommon stock, a graduate of UCD, a proficient *Gaeilgeoir* (Irish speaker), an already promising writer and for a time a teacher, he transferred his adventurous interest from scuba-diving to mountaineering at the age of twenty-seven, quite late for someone to take up climbing. Lean-featured, short of gaunt, he turned to working as a builder's labourer and then a freelance builder which, besides keeping him fit, allowed him the freedom to climb and write. Above average height (which would make him taller than most of his predecessors), he was not one of the very best rock climbers but had considerable ability and a passion for the sport which extended to Alpine and Scottish winter climbing. Crucially, he had the intelligence, drive, imagination and a feeling for the history of the sport which led to his Alpine successes. Moreover, he had a knack of striking up apt friendships which intensified his experiences and enabled resultant partnerships to tackle a selection of routes as described above. His Alpine successes – we haven't finished with them yet – were of an order quite exceptional among Irish alpinists and, like Goulding before him, he sought out big routes away from the trendy bustle of the Aiguilles. Still, he raised hackles, especially when his writer's fondness for the apt phrase seemed to make him oblivious to the likely reaction. He could exhibit disdain for those of lesser deeds (or those with overblown reputations, he would argue) but was modest about his own achievements and abilities. Unusually among top climbers, he had the insight and self-awareness to modify his views of people and of certain mountaineering ethics, thus making him an influential figure when the Irish ventured onto 8,000m peaks.[17] His influence on Irish Alpine climbing is not so easy to assess but his writings and climbing initiatives must surely have convinced the up-and-coming that mountaineering is not just about climbing.

Dermot Somers in Bregaglia, Switzerland, 2012. DAWSON STELFOX

In that same season of 1982, veteran Goulding did the North Face of the Triolet with Harry O'Brien and Higgs, enduring a difficult bivouac on descent which resulted in hospitalisation, with frostbite, of O'Brien and Higgs.[18] Torrans, in 1980, with Sheridan had made what was probably the first Irish ascent of a TD route on the East Face of the Moine and then climbed the American Direct and West Face on the Dru with Curtis. Sheridan and Torrans were now, in 1982, on an extended working/climbing tour of the western United States and Canada. In the Bugaboos they made a one-day ascent of the Becky-Chouinard Route on South Howser Tower and climbed the East Ridge and Face of Bugaboo Spire. They also visited Joshua Tree and in Yosemite climbed the North-West Face of Half Dome. Torrans climbed the Salethé Wall on El Capitan with a Canadian friend. In Yosemite as well were McKenzie and Paul McGrath who climbed the classic Royal Arches, the North-West Face of Half Dome and the East Buttress of Middle Cathedral.[19] Further afield in 1982, Trevor Mitten led the Kashmir Himalayan Expedition which had thirteen members from Northern Ireland, including the inspirational Poor Clares Sister Mark Hollywood. Four unnamed 5,000m peaks were climbed and also Kang Yisay (6,400m) which was climbed by Mitten, Brian McBurney, Damien Murray and Terry McClatchey. This peak, which was, according to the *Himalayan Journal*, 6,090m high, had previously been climbed by a Japanese team.[20] Con Collins and Sean Maguire were thwarted on an attempt on Menthosa (6,443m) in Lahul, when they were stopped by a huge crescent-shaped crevasse at about 6,000m.[21] At this time, when there was scarcely an awareness in Ireland of Nepal or of trekking, an Irish party climbed a trekking peak, Naya Kanga (5,846m) in Nepal's Langtang Himal.[22]

According to Clare Sheridan the weather in Chamonix in 1983 was the hottest and driest since 1947.[23] The amount of activity reflected this, as did a shift of interest to other areas. Sheridan herself, with Torrans, made a first Irish ascent of the Cordier Pillar of the Aiguille de Roc. Torrans followed this with the Voie des Dalles, TD-, on the Aiguille Pouce in the Tour Rouge area, with Lipp as his companion. Another first Irish ascent was completed by Sheridan and rising star Donie O'Sullivan on the Cordier Pillar of the Grands Charmoz before they did the West Face of the Petites Jorasses. O'Sullivan and Keefe Murphy were active on several other routes, including the Dru's American Direct, as were 'Waldo' McQuoid and John Anderson. Goulding and O'Brien did the North Face of the Dru – a repeat for Goulding – the Walker Spur on the Grandes Jorasses which was a long wished-for project of Goulding's, and then the Gervasutti Pillar on Mont Blanc du

Tacul.[24] On the descent from the Tacul they were caught in an avalanche on a much-used slope overlooked by threatening seracs. O'Brien, a trade union official unafraid of confrontation and an experienced climber in the middle grades, suffered a broken arm but insisted in the face of further looming danger on staying with the trapped Goulding. However, with his arm broken in two places he could not be of assistance and was persuaded to stand clear, leaving his axe to allow Goulding to begin cutting himself free. Other climbers came to the rescue.[25] O'Brien was ubiquitous and had qualities which led to his being a trusted partner by a number of the very best practitioners on some notable routes.

Ian Rea was determined to press the case for Irish efforts on bigger ranges, and to make these efforts in alpine style. He led a small group – Torrans, Cooper and Alan Currans – in attempts on two different routes on Shivling (6,543m), a dramatic peak which faces across the Gangotri Glacier to Bhagirathi II. They retreated from the unclimbed North-West Face having spent five days coping with heavy snowfall and then attempted the West Ridge on which they turned back when confronted with a difficult section where the ice 'had the consistency of bullet-proof glass'.[26] (True alpine style entails climbing a mountain from base camp without porter support and without a build-up of prepared camps. Climbers start at the bottom and keep going until they reach the top, bivouacking or camping en route if necessary. Compromises with this idea of a 'pure' ascent are not uncommon and ambiguities abound.)

This was followed in 1984 by an attempt led by Dawson Stelfox on a big peak, Churen Himal (7,371m), in Nepal. Following an unusually long walk-in of two weeks and a spell of bad weather at Base Camp the climbers – Stelfox, Holmes, Manson and Malcolm McNaught – spent a week making their way up the previously unclimbed South-West Face to a point at about 6,600m where they encountered unreliable snow conditions and some near misses from constantly falling stones. They were forced to retreat, passing the grisly remains of two Germans lying there since the previous year among the remnants of their avalanche-wrecked tent.[27]

Churen Himal in 1984. DAWSON STELFOX

Another Irishman, Terry Mooney, who was on an expedition led by the impressive Doug Scott, reached the summit of Nepal's Baruntse (7,162m) in 1984, the first Irish climber to reach the summit of a 7,000m peak, showing once again that one's doings in one's home mountains is not necessarily an augury of quality of performance at high altitudes. Hundreds of kilometres to the west, Dónal ÓMurchú and Gordon Simpson of the Irish Zanskar Expedition reached the top of Z8 (6,050m) on 23 July, to be followed nine days later by Lynam, Hastings and Ravi (C. P. Ravichandra, the Indian liaison officer). These were the first official ascents but it is thought that there may have been a previous ascent unauthorised by the Indian government.[28]

Also in 1984, in Africa, that enterprising Kerryman Mike Barry and Northern Irishman Adrian Devlin made what was probably the first Irish ascent of Nelion, one of Mount Kenya's peaks, and later climbed Kilimanjaro by the tourist track.[29] O'Leary was in Zaire (later the Democratic Republic of Congo) where he walked through fumarole-peppered jungle to the top of volcanic Nyiragongo (3,468m) in the Virunga range and then, from the wreck of an abandoned hut, climbed the worthwhile North-West Ridge of Point Albert (5,087m) in the Ruwenzori. Because of

Zaire's febrile political situation, by far the safest part of the trip was on the mountains.

Throughout this busy time for those at the forefront of Irish alpine mountaineering, and of innovation at different levels in distant ranges, the ordinary club climber – that term covers a wide range of competence and commitment – still followed in Leslie Stephens' giant strides across their Alpine playground, spending the limited time of their annual holidays in this wonderful arena of exalted rock, fluid ice, idyllic valley. (Leslie Stephens was an early member of the Alpine Club, author of *Playground of Europe* and father of Virginia Woolf.) No doubt ego played some part in their tussle with verticality and the elements – in what human endeavour does it not? – but it was subdued in comparison to that of some pushing at the boundaries. They reacted in a way largely unaffected by testosterone to the challenges, the beauty, the thrill of the exposed arête, as mountaineers everywhere have done since the Golden Age of alpinism in which Stephens had played a prominent role. Some of the top men had by now become almost full-time mountaineers or had so arranged their lives that long Alpine seasons, sometimes preceded or followed by trips to distant ranges, did not disrupt their careers. This further distinguished them from

Snow on the equator. Ruwenzori from the Zaire side. Brendan Moss and Sean Rothery had made separate ascents from Uganda side in the 1950s. AUTHOR'S COLLECTION

those whose careers or family obligations resulted in shorter Alpine sojourns. The doings of these less single-minded climbers, the majority of alpinists, were becoming more ambitious, more widespread, and more difficult to record in detail. Nevertheless, the geographical extent and the variety of what they were doing can be gathered from the following selection.

In 1980, Lynam with a Dutch companion did an old Irish favourite, the classic South-West Ridge of the Moine, which was also climbed by the MacPherson sisters, Maeve and Ursula. IMC member Sean Lyons completed what was probably the first Irish traverse of Barre des Écrins,[30] before repeating good routes in Chamonix. In 1981, Gerry and Lily Moss blitzed eleven peaks in the Zermatt/Saas-Fee area, a coup which included a traverse of the Dom, the highest peak wholly in Switzerland. Other IMC climbers were in Chamonix and Zermatt, as they were in most years. Groups from Tiglin were in the Mont Blanc area almost every year during this time, led by several of those who were making a name for themselves on the great north faces. Paccy Stronach of Tiglin was on the Old Brenva with Rea in 1981. Somers and Maeve MacPherson were on the North Ridge of the Badile. Also in 1981, Owen Jacobs brought news from Calpe of the wonderful opportunities to climb, both sports climbing and traditional, in Costa Blanca's winter sunshine. The vertical virtues of Buoux, the Verdon Gorge and other rock-climbing destinations had been realised in the late 1970s. All were magnificent and usually sun-warmed limestone crags to which tired or storm-chastened Irish alpinists would decamp throughout the next generation.[31]

IMC parties were scattered throughout the Alps in 1982, from Grossglockner to the Dauphiné. In the latter area Ann Spencer, Oonagh McElligott, Sue Dempsey and Joan Flanagan, all Quadrockers, were busy reaching the top of seven peaks. Gerry and Lily Moss with Gerry Forde were in the Vanoise where they completed their usual whirlwind itinerary including several traverses and an ascent of Gran Paradiso. Joe Hastings soloed a route on Pic des Agneaux in the Écrins in July of 1983, leaving the Mosses and Bill Hannon to indulge themselves – needless to say making several long traverses, as Gerry would continue to do in several areas throughout the decade. In the Bregaglia, Paula Turley and Norah McElroy were breaking new ground for Irish climbers by completing ascents of the North-West Ridge of Scioretta, North Ridge of Piz Ginelli, West Ridge of Punta Pioda, besides climbing the North Ridge of Piz Badile and other routes which had been climbed by Lynam, Convery, Ingrid Masterson and Paul Donnelly in the previous year.[32] Throughout this time, family-tied climbers, such as Nugent, would drive to various Alpine venues and tick off some of the old classics, soloing when they had to.

It would be more than tiresome to go into all that was being done in the Alps throughout the 1980s but each year brought increasing numbers at all grades. In any event, neither *Mountain Log* (later *Irish Mountain Log*) nor the *IMC Journal* was at its best during the late 1970s and early 1980s so the activities of those from both parts of Ireland who repeated many of the Alpine classics, from easy slogs to Chamonix EDs, were not always recorded. There were a few well-written articles on Alpine and higher ranges outings in the much-praised annual *Irish Climber* from 1983 to 1985. Edited by Clare Sheridan it was brought out as another FMCI publication and good writers like Rea, Somers and Sheridan herself contributed. In the 1984 issue, there is a fine account by Rea of the climbing of Couloir du Diable in winter and the subsequent descent from Mont Blanc du Tacul (shades of Griffin and Billane, but easier, quicker, in clear moonlight) in which he manages to convey something of the hardship and risk. Previously, as they leave for the climb he is beset by doubt:

I, not having landed a job, am living on handouts from my wife who has . . . In truth it is sometimes hard to understand the impulses that drive us. Watching my wife wave goodbye to the ever-ascending téléphérique gnawed at my heart like an unbearably sad metaphor. My throat clutching I waved in unison until she became invisible.[33]

But, as climbers do, he went ahead.

In 1985, Tralee native Mike Barry was in Patagonia with an ascent of Fitzroy in mind; 'the innocent abroad' he says of a rather naive approach to this difficult peak. He and Adrian Devlin then travelled north to try Aconcagua, the highest peak in the Americas at 6,962m. Devlin's acclimatisation problems led to Barry making a successful solo ascent, a feat which would lead to considerable changes in his mountaineering career.[34] Yet another Irish attempt on Mount Kenya, this time, enterprisingly, on Batian's North Face, resulted again in an Irish failure for Des Doyle, Sue Dempsey and Liam Campbell.[35] Mount Kenya is notorious for acclimatisation difficulties which add to the problems of occasional unseasonal weather. Con Moriarty and Aidan Forde climbed Wyoming's Devil's Tower.[36]

In July 1986, during an attempt on the Biancograt of Piz Bernina, David Walsh was knocked to the ground by lightning and, along with Paul Donnelly, endured a frightening few hours in a bivvy bag before emerging only to be caught again in a strike. They retreated safely but a German pair who insisted on going on were never seen again.[37] In the same area, Gerry Moss with Vera Kelly and Emily Hackett did traverses of Piz Palu, Piz Bernina, Piz Badile and several other peaks.[38]

That year of 1986 was an excellent Alpine season with Irish climbers in various venues. Rea had a particularly successful summer with Andy Cunningham, doing the Croz spur, a fine TD route to the right of the Walker Spur on the Grandes Jorasses, and the Bonatti–Zapelli line on the Eckpfeiler buttress of Mont Blanc which Bonatti, possibly the greatest alpinist of his era, had considered the hardest of his mixed rock and ice routes. The pair went on to do the Cretier Route on Mont Maudit and the South-East Spur of Bec d'Oiseau, a notable TD route. That list shows Rea at his imaginative best, ploughing new furrows in ground previously undisturbed by the Irish. Other Irish included Phil Holmes, Gary Murray and Donie O'Sullivan who, along with Rea, repeated some of the harder but by now well-worn Chamonix climbs, O'Sullivan's venture on the Walker Spur being the most notable.[39]

In the higher ranges, Margaret Magennis, Paula Turley and Jenny Clarke joined Stelfox, Brown-Kerr and John Armstrong in the Shimshal area of the Hunza Karakoram where the bad weather and deep snow which comes with the monsoon season prevented attempts at an unclimbed 6,400m peak but they managed some easy 5,000m summits.[40] A Cork group, led by Thorley Sweetman, with Dave Coulter, Pat Mulcahy, Paul Tassie, Marian Sweetman, Niall O'Sullivan (camp manager) and Dave Hayden (doctor), failed on an ambitious attempt on Pinnacle Peak, a 6,970m summit in the Nun Kun group in the Zanskar area of Kashmir. Their Indian liaison officer, Sanjay Shukla, was drowned during a river crossing.[41]

Choc Quinn set an Irish altitude record when he reached Camp III at a height given variously as 7,950m[42] and 7,800m[43] on the 1986 American K2 Expedition which attempted that giant's very difficult North Ridge, approached from the Chinese side. The summit assault trio reached 8,000m before the entire team retreated safely to base. Given Choc's experiences in Ireland and his success on Mount McKinley it was unfortunate that his efforts were overlooked back at home.

In 1987, there was a second Irish success, at last, on Mount Kenya, by Ruth Lynam and Don Short who climbed Nelion, bivouacking some distance above De Graf's variation.[44]

In the Cordillera Blanca of Peru a Northern Irish group (Ian and Moira Rea, Robert Moncrieff and Gary Murray) climbed six 5,000m peaks as well as Nevada Huandoy (6,395m) and Huascaran Sur, Peru's highest summit at 6,768m. Moira probably set an Irishwoman's altitude record on reaching the top of the latter peak.[45]

Zhangzi/Changtse

In 1984, the Chinese authorities opened Tibet, in a limited and tightly regulated way, to foreign mountaineers. Joss Lynam, who had become quite influential in the UIAA (the coordinating body for the world's alpine associations), used his contacts to obtain permission to attempt Zhangzi (7,553m), a peak in Tibet just to the north of Everest and referred to in the West as Changste, meaning North Peak. When Frank Nugent, who became deputy leader, wrote about it in early 1987 he said that a success on Changtse would not only be an Irish altitude record but would be 'a necessary stepping stone for a future 8,000m climb'.[46] According to Nugent, the team was originally meant to consist of IMC members but he and Shay Nolan were also included as were Dermot Somers and Welshman Phil Thomas who had worked at Tiglin. In September 1987 the Irish team arrived at Base Camp near Rongbuk monastery, a place famous in mountaineering annals and now being visited again by mountaineers who had for decades been prevented from doing so by the Chinese authorities. Changtse had been climbed once, by Germans in 1982, and the Irish team planned to attempt a new route via the South-West Spur. Conditions ruled out that option and attention shifted to the North Ridge. A reconnaissance by Nugent and Phil Thomas from Advanced Base Camp at 5,001m brought them to the Chang Changtse La, a col to the north of their objective from where it was judged that this route also was not feasible.

Another attempt by the same pair, this time supported by Somers, Nolan, Barry, Ó Murchú and Richard Fry, was made on the South Ridge via the North Col (7,030m), that famous scene of so much drama when pre-war British expeditions had camped there during repeated attempts on Everest's North Ridge. Heavy snows made the position of the Irish/Welsh pair in a tent on the col a very precarious one. A retreat back down the notorious avalanche-prone west flank would be extremely perilous, so Nugent and Thomas had to climb down the east slopes to the East Rongbuk Glacier on the opposite flank of the ridge from their route of ascent. A two-day trek brought them back around the mountain to anxiously waiting friends. When the weather cleared, a second foray from the North Col by Nugent and Thomas floundered to a halt in unstable snow resulting in retreat but not before all those named above had topped 7,000m. Dónal Ó Murchú was lucky to survive a bout of cerebral oedema at the outset of the trip and owed his life to prompt evacuation to lower altitudes and to the care of the expedition doctor, Geraldine Osborne, who, with her husband Danny, Sarah Gillen and Leslie Lawrence made up the rest of the team.[47] Lessons had been learned, not least the one that demonstrated, yet again, that a sound climber who has not reached the stellar heights of the technically brilliant – in this case Nugent – could adapt better than most to the travails of high altitude.

Perhaps it was this revelation that he performed well at great heights that strengthened Nugent's intention to move on to 8,000m peaks and especially to the greatest of them, Mount Everest. It was agreed by Stelfox and himself that they would mount attempts on Manaslu (8,156m), in 1991 and Everest (8,848m) in 1993.[48]

Frank Nugent in 1987. His performance on Zhangzi (Changtse) led to leadership roles on Manaslu and Everest.

NUGENT COLLECTION

In 1988, the great Alpine north faces again attracted competent parties. Gary Murray did the Eigerwand in addition to the north faces of the Courtes and Matterhorn. Stelfox also did the Eigerwand with Andy McFarlane. The latter climbed the Mittellegi ridge on the same mountain with his wife, Paula Turley, while other Northerners and Ursula MacPherson between them reached a number of Oberland summits which had tended to be neglected by Irish climbers. Northern Irish climbers, including QUBMC, were also active in Chamonix where old favourites, varying a great deal in grades, were repeated. Somers and Fenlon did the Blaitière West Face; Ian Rea and party did a route on the south flank of the Grandes Jorasses. Nugent and O'Brien had what mountaineers all too often call an 'epic' retreat in a storm from the South Ridge of Aiguille Noire de Peuterey.[49] Moss and Vera Kelly could not resist doing several of their hallmark long traverses during their stay in the Mont Blanc area.[50] Eddie Gaffney, long absent from the Alps during the early years of his marriage, was back to climb in the Bregaglia,[51] where a UCDMC team, including Paul Harrington on his first Alpine trip, did a number of rock routes and also managed Piz Bernina and the first Irish ascent of a route on Disgrazia's North Face.[52]

Further afield, in the USA, Ruth Lynam and Don Short climbed

Mount Rainier and Forbidden Peak while in Pakistan a mixed team of five women and three men, all but one of whom were IMC members, were in the Naltar valley near Gilgit. There, in mainly poor post-monsoon weather, Brian Searson reached the summit of Snow Dome (5,029m), and the party as a whole managed Sentinel (5,242m). By doing so, they demonstrated that an enterprising group with modest resources, moderate ambition, a restricted timetable and limited experience can enjoy all the thrill of exploring a little-known and exotic location combined with the excitement of reaching easier Himalayan summits.[53]

Neither *Irish Mountain Log* nor the IMC newsletters for 1989 and 1990 give any oversight of what was happening to Irish

Joan Flanagan on Snow Dome in the Karakoram, 1988.
PETER NEVIN

mountaineers in the Alps or higher ranges. There is an account in *IML* 13 by Harry Connolly of a 1989 failed attempt on the normal West Buttress Route on Mount McKinley which conveys the hardships inherent in an assault on a big Alaskan peak, involving landing on a glacier in a light plane, the hauling of heavy sledges, and encountering the huge snowfalls and devastating winds of the region. In *IML* 12, Tony Farrell describes suffering similar bad weather on an unsuccessful attempt in 1989 on Peru's Alpamayo in which he mentions a later successful climb on the same peak.[54] He also managed to fit in an unsuccessful effort on Mount Kenya's Diamond Couloir with Con Moriarty.[55] Moss and Hackett were traversing merrily in the Écrins.[56] Lynam and O'Leary, along with well-known English skier and mountaineering author Alan Blackshaw, were members of the first of a series of Anglo-Irish trips organised by old expedition campaigner Mike Banks and sponsored by *Saga Magazine*. The first of these was a pre-monsoon attempt in 1989 on the unclimbed South Ridge of Jaonli (6,632m) in Garhwal. Poor weather, the avalanche-prone south-east flank and a long approach over glaciers covered with melting winter snow stymied the attempt. Banks, Blackshaw and O'Leary reached about 5,800m. Lynam and liaison officer C. P. Ravichandra, who were assisted by base-camp manager Don Roberts, reached an outlier summit of 5,450m.[57]

Torrans was a member of a British expedition which attempted a traverse of Makalu, the fifth highest mountain in the world and only a short distance from Everest but failed, mainly because of bad weather and consequent avalanche risk.[58] Dawson and Margaret Stelfox with Somers and Maeve MacPherson spent the last two months of the decade – spilling over into 1990 – doing trekking-peaks in Nepal and between them managed Thorung Peak and Chulu Far East in the Annapurna massif and Island peak in Khumbu.[59]

An unusual undertaking in 1989 was Kieran Furey's month-long race around Europe with his English friend Peter Eagan, during which they reached the highest summit in each of the twelve countries which then made up the EC.[60]

10

A Shift Sideways

When I returned to Ireland in 1994 following nearly two years spent in India I was surprised to see the number of mid-range cars crowded into the car park at Baravore Ford in Wicklow. At first I assumed that a hunt was in progress, beagling perhaps, but then realised that these were vehicles driven by hillwalkers, and were a reflection both of how Ireland's economy was changing and of the increasing popularity of various aspects of mountaineering. These linked phenomena had undoubtedly sprung shoots before I had gone away but I had been too engrossed in work and study to notice. The extent of changes in the mountaineering world which would continue throughout the 1990s was unprecedented, and astonishing to someone who had once hitchhiked to the hills alone or with a very few like-minded companions.

There are all sorts of reasons for this growth in participation, and at least some of these can be linked to the normal developments of recreational activities in expanding economies. I was still coming to terms with what was happening as I walked and climbed during the next few years. Once, I met some local young men wearing their parish football colours atop Mweelrea, some of whom were returned emigrants who had picked up the 'hiking' habit when working in New England. I cannot remember having previously met such local recreationists on Irish hilltops. One could not help but be aware of more foreign accents on crags and even quite remote hills, of more people from mountaineering or walking clubs based in Irish towns and villages.

Every facet of mountaineering seemed to be involved in these changes, from attendance at indoor climbing walls – which would grow exponentially as the decade progressed and which would result in considerable financial investment in the new millennium – to outdoor bouldering; to remarkably large numbers camping at newly discovered rock-climbing venues such as Gola; to Alpine venues which would attract up to a hundred Irish climbers in places where once we had struggled to find partners. There were so many ventures into higher ranges that one cannot do justice in describing them.

It is difficult to decide which of these various developments was the most significant but several were of considerable, even dramatic, importance to Irish mountaineering. The huge and in some ways gratifying increase in the numbers of people taking to the hills led to a diminution in the enjoyment of those who sought solitude and adventure; and increased usage had inevitable environmental impacts. Nearing the end of the decade a tendency could be detected by which, as one well-known climber noted, Irish mountaineering began to move sideways,[1] towards increased use of climbing walls, towards bouldering, towards a more socially interactive form of climbing, towards acquisition of ever-higher technical skills, and away from increased participation in the arcane pleasures of unguided and self-reliant greater mountaineering. These changes in emphasis would have unpredictable consequences in the new century. A few mountaineers became celebrities, again with unpredictable consequences for an activity which at its heart is one which is indulged in far from the public eye.

Along with new developments in climbing, some of which were considerable personal triumphs for the talented few, there came significant changes in the financing and administration of the national governing body, in training, in environmental pressures on the hills, in relations with hill farmers. Exchange of information, the very lifeblood of modern mountaineering, was made a great deal easier with the advent of the Internet. MCI, *Irish Mountain Log*, and their various officers first published their email addresses in 1996 and the organisation acquired a website in 1998. *Rock Climber* magazine had one in the previous year. The *Log*, in autumn 1997, gave instructions to its readers on how to send and receive emails.

Although winding down, the Troubles in Northern Ireland were still of immediate concern to climbers. In Belfast two outdoor shops which served the mountaineering community were destroyed in 1992. Jackson's Sports was blown up in January,[2] and Beaten Track was burned out shortly afterwards.[3] An unrelated happening was the dissolution of the Belfast Section of the IMC in 1991, just short of forty years since its formation.[4]

Hillwalking
The growth in participation was only loosely correlated to the number of new clubs, mostly hillwalking clubs, affiliated to the national body, which had changed its name to the Mountaineering Council of Ireland (MCI) in January 1990. In 1990 there were roughly forty clubs; by late 1999 there were 102.[5] Accurate figures are not available but most commentators agree that the number of people independently participating in hillwalking far outnumbered those in clubs. These numbers exacerbated problems which had become apparent during the 1980s. In order to cater for the increasing interest in outdoor leisure, and to provide for the needs of tourists, the number of way-marked trails, not all of them in the hills, increased to twenty by 1995.[6] The number of organised walks also increased. *Irish Mountain Log* saw nothing wrong with giving details of twelve of these organised walks,[7] nor in devoting space to accounts of well-attended annual Art O'Neill walks, none of which were recorded as having completed the original escape to the site of Hugh O'Byrne's fortress at Ballinacor.[8] In 1991 there were 350 people on the Maamturks walk.[9] In 1997 the annual Lug Walk run

by the Ramblers had 249 starters but weather conditions led to 192 of these dropping out, leaving only 57 to finish,[10] an indication of the potential dangers of less well organised long walks in similar conditions. A new departure was the holding on behalf of charities of organised walks such as Hart's Walk.[11] In the Mournes, 130 walkers and runners were attracted to the second holding of the Seven Sevens walking event. In an effort to lessen environmental damage, organisers invited participants to visit, in any order they liked, the tops of each of the Mournes' seven peaks over 700m in height.[12] The *Irish Mountain Log* also gave details of mountain running events.[13]

A related happening, which can be looked at as both cause and effect of the above phenomena, was the very welcome publication by the Irish Ordnance Survey of a series of 1:50,000 maps to replace the totally inadequate half inch (1:126,000) and one inch (1:63,000) series on which hill-users had to rely previously. Depiction of crags in both of these old series varied in precision from sheet to sheet, as did the interpretation of what a crag was. The larger scale map was somewhat better but the contour interval above 1,000 feet (*c.* 305m) was 250 feet (*c.* 76 m) which, inter alia, resulted in many prominent subsidiary tops – and useful navigational waypoints – being omitted. Tiglin had tried to deal with its own training problem in the mid-1980s by producing a map of the Glenmacnass area at a scale of 1:25,000. This may have been the first map of that scale south of the border and was surveyed and drawn by staff member Barry Dalby who would later found the excellent East-West Mapping firm. In 1988, that cartographic genius Tim Robinson brought out a 1:50,000 map of the mountains of Connemara drawn by orienteer Justin May which, although printed on less than good quality paper and with a number of errors, was a boon to mountain recreationists in the region. The great cliffs of Glen Inagh could now be seen graphically for the first time at a scale that was useful to hillwalkers. In 1989 the Ordnance Survey (OS) brought out a Preliminary Edition of Sheet 78 (Kenmare) at a scale of 1:50,000 and a contour interval of 10m which was followed rapidly by similar maps of Wicklow and the Slieve Blooms.

These were an enormous improvement and allowed accurate dead reckoning across entire sheets for the first time. With the co-operation and assistance of the Dermot Bouchier-Hayes Trust the OS published a 1:25,000 map, the *MacGillycuddy Reeks*, in 1990–91 which allowed, for the first time, the accurate depiction of many features in the range, a representation which may have saved lives had its equivalent been available earlier. Like the Robinson map, which had an attached guide by Joss Lynam to some walking routes, this Reeks map had a route guide by John Murray. The OS went on during the 1990s to produce the well-known and gratefully received *Discovery* series covering the entire country at 1:50,000.

Long before this, the Ordnance Survey of Northern Ireland (which had been hived off in 1922) had developed a 1:50,000 series with 10m contour interval in the period 1978–1985, garishly coloured at first but moving to the *Discoverer* series which was fully compatible with the *Discovery* series south of the border. As early as 1981 the OSNI had produced a 1:25,000 Mourne Country Outdoor Pusuits map, again with a 10m contour interval.

As in the 1980s there was little done in regard to hillwalking that merits the interest of historians but there were plenty of indications that Irish hills provided challenge along with physical and transcendental joy to many. Among the many articles submitted to *Irish Mountain Log*, pieces by Helen Lawless,[14] Liam Reinhardt[15] and Con Moriarty[16] catch the imagination; all three articles deal with memorable experiences on the Iveragh peninsula, with Liam describing a five-day camping trip across the peninsula. A description by Philip Gormley of the walk from Teelin to Maghery with its combination of mountain and coastal magnifi-cence must have tempted many to south Donegal.[17] An article on Cavan–Leitrim's Playbank by Gerry Moss in the *IMC Newsletter*, whilst contained in a rock-climbing context, spoke eloquently and sensitively of a problem familiar to any discerning traveller in the Irish hills – that of a vanishing, distinctive culture, of depopulation and abandoned cottages on marginal hillside land.[18] Some achieve-ments were still being recorded, including Hugh Sharkey's completion in 1992 of the double Maamturks walk in 15 hours 45 minutes.[19] In 1994 Mike Begley and Brian McCabe reached the tops of all 14 Irish Munros in 15 hours.[20] Late in the decade Paul Cullen was one of a party which completed the round of the Five Peaks, the highest hills in Ireland north and south, and in Scotland, England and Wales, taking a total of 41 hours 19 minutes. Much time was saved, according to Paul, by good driving on the roads.[21] In 1995 two orienteers, Paul Nolan and Mark Caslin, in less than one year, got to the tops of what they reckoned were all the hills over 600m in Ireland, 282 all told. Running or walking, carrying heavy gear or not, it was quite an undertaking.[22]

Howard Hebblethwaite on Spillikin Ridge
c. 2008. JOE LYONS

All this interest in mountain walking inevitably led to much increased interest in trekking in distant places and to outings by non-mountaineers to peaks such as Kilimanjaro on behalf of some charitable organisations. The various problems arising from the increase in numbers, such as those relating to rescue, the environment, training and access are dealt with in chapter 11.

Rock climbing

In an interview in 1993, Howard Hebblethwaite asserted that 'Irish development is very slow,' and that those involved in rock climbing were more or less the same people as twenty years before.[23] Twenty years later he was saying much the same thing in regard to climbing development which he saw as lagging behind that of the UK. At this later time, he commented on the 'incredibly small scene' and its tendency to be dogged by personality clashes.[24] At about the same time, Paul Harrington reminisced about the Irish climbing scene in the 1990s and saw its small size as being a good thing, where activists knew almost everyone else and were consequently aware of what was going on. Foreign climbers, he said, were favourably impressed by the connectedness of Irish climbers and the casual interchange of information and banter.[25] Dermot Somers, on being reminded of his earlier remarks about the amicable intermingling of Irish climbers in the 1970s, was quick to point out that this amiability had not lasted.[26]

All these statements are true to some extent and would not merit comment were it not for the effects which small size had on mountaineering development. Hebblethwaite's view that the dramatis personae were virtually unchanged was modified by a further comment that there were 'those who came for a short period and were forced to leave the country for jobs or whatever'.[27] Young guns such as Tony Burke and Donie O'Sullivan, Joan Flanagan, Robbie Fenlon, Paul Dunlop and Paul Harrington were making their presence felt at home and abroad at the time of Hebblethwaite's 1993 interview but emigration would remove three of the above named as it had done with Keefe Murphy, and expose the small core of activists on which high-grade rock climbing and alpinism depended. The Irish climbing world would continue to be small despite the growth of interest in the outdoors. The death or injury of just one talented individual, or their absence due to career or marriage, had significant effects. It would seem self-evident that from such a small base it would be difficult to have an impact on the international scene. Whether this is necessarily a bad thing, given the individualistic nature of moun-taineering, is open to debate, but note should be taken of Harrington's views on the benign nature of littleness.

The major problem associated with lesser size and geographical isolation is the effect that interpersonal tensions and clashes can have on wider developments. It does not do to exaggerate such matters. Given the growing sociability fostered by climbing walls, the majority of easy-going Irish mountaineers were uninterested in what they would probably regard as unworthy animosities. The general public were both unaware and uninterested. These inter-personal and inter-group tensions stemmed mainly from disputes between a few of the older top rock climbers. Others arose from less fathomable unwillingness to recognise the doings of some Munster-based mountaineers on the part of those 'affables' who, with success, had acquired some 'typical' traits (see chapter 2). Whatever the source of these personal differences they were to have profound impacts on happenings in the greater ranges and on the mountaineering careers of some major figures in the Irish climbing world. It is not intended to explore the reasons behind such tensions nor to identify the antagonists, most of whom are alive, but readers need to be aware of such matters when happenings in great ranges are covered in chapter 13.

Unquestionably, the consistently top performer on rock through-out the decade was Eddie Cooper. Described by friends and contemporaries as elitist, driven, uncompromising and difficult,[28] Cooper was ubiquitous and very productive throughout the decade. At Fair Head, he 'dominated the development with a steady stream of high quality hard routes'.[29] Beginning with Back to the Future in 1990, he produced routes like Paralyzed Power E6, 6b/c in 1996, a climb which had still not had a second ascent when the guide was produced in 2002. Such a long delay in recording a second ascent 'must be a peculiarly Irish phenomenon'.[30] As might be expected, Donie O'Sullivan matched Cooper's performance in regard to severity if not to quantity with routes like Closing Time E6, 6c which he did in 1994. But interest in Fair Head was fading as the century neared its end despite the efforts of a few like Rea and Paul McArthur and, of course, Sheridan and Torrans. Sheridan has described the architecture of the cliff as Gothic.[31] One wonders if the oppressive atmosphere conjured up by one interpretation of such a term, and perhaps the first sight of this sheer precipice on a gloomy day, rather than the technical difficulties, accounted for the *fin de siècle* lack of enthusiasm.

Belfast-born Eddie Cooper, master rock-climber and creator of many outstanding climbs at Fair Head, in the Mournes and the Burren. SHERIDAN COLLECTION

Hardest Climb in the World?

In the Mournes, Cooper returned to Buzzard's Roost where he had put up Twist of Fate in 1989 and then, in 1994, The Spirit Level, E5, 6b, 6a with McArthur, and eliminated the rest point he had used on War Music, thus creating a trio of three-star high-grade climbs which, as a set, were probably unmatched in the country. Combined with Divided Years on the same crag which, at E9, 6c, was for a short time thought to be the hardest traditional climb in the world,[32] these routes made the Main Face of Buzzard's Roost a challenging arena for Irish and other climbers. Divided Years was put up by an English expatriate, Yorkshire man John Dunne, who was committed to a very rigorous training regime, building himself what he described as an elite personal climbing space in an outbuilding in Rathfriland, the design of which applied lessons he had learned from similar projects in the UK.[33] Divided Years, an extremely strenuous and 'necky' route up an outrageously overhanging nose, would not have been completed without transgressing – if that is the right word – the traditional Mourne and Irish ethical stance on the practising of moves prior to a first ascent.

It was generally accepted that such practice, together with the taking of huge falls on traditional gear, was understandable if not condoned, in view of the pioneering nature of the route. The same tolerance was not extended to his pre-practised route, No Rest For The Wicked, which he had put up on Upper Cove, especially when Cooper led it on sight and downgraded it. One recalls Sean Windrim's stricture pertaining to putting reputation before the deed. Cooper put up other routes in the Mournes, as did Rea, while Gary Murray continued his development of tors on Binnian, which were done in his typical style, 'bold, protection-less slabs conjoined with bursts of concentrated athleticism'.[34]

Mallon and Stelfox eliminated an aid point on a route on Slieve Beg which they had done in the 1980s, resulting in a climb called JP. While there were these welcome developments, Rea was to write in 1998 that little had changed in the local scene. Certainly there were few new names and the expansion in hillwalking to which Rea refers – and which may have something to do with the winding down of the Troubles – was not matched by a similar growth in rock climbing. Rea's remarks were contained in the historical notes to the *Mourne Guide* where he made some very good points in relation to climbing ethics, saying:

> Ethics remain a thorny issue in climbing because of the tension between necessary rules which give it a coherence and a context for assessing achievement and progression, and the desire to flaunt these rules in order to take [climbing] . . . into avenues of individual expression not previously explored.

In that same guide he also reiterated his criticism of something which he claimed Phil Gribbon wrote in a *Peak Viewing* article (see chapter 8) about Gribbon's era being a Golden Age of Mourne and of Irish climbing.[35] Rea, competent writer and polemicist as he was, must have been amused by the self-created fanciful world he had entered of a 'straw man' and Humpty Dumpty. It can be understood that Rea 'tells it as he sees it' but Phil Gribbon did not write of a

Ian Rea, rock-climber, alpinist, expedition mountaineer, pictured here at Fair Head in 1982. SHERIDAN COLLECTION

Golden Age in Mourne climbing. Having set up a straw man, Ian proceeded to demolish it by insisting, like Humpty Dumpty in *Through the Looking Glass*, that a word (or the term Golden Age) meant what he chose it to mean.[36] The Golden Age of alpinism, for instance, is universally accepted as referring to a defined period in the mid-nineteenth century.[37] It does not refer, as Ian would have preferred it, to the most productive era or to one of technical excellence.[38]

Cooper naturally gravitated to Muckross Head, which in the early part of the decade attracted most of the top climbers. In 1990 he put up four routes in the lower E grades, anticipating the visit there in the following year of O'Sullivan who blitzed the crag with about ten new routes, some of them of high quality. Muckross Head received sporadic attention during the rest of the decade from those able to deal with its outrageous overhangs. Of note was an amazing, almost ungradeable traverse by the very young Michael Duffy across the lip of an overhang, with a frightening finish to the top.[39]

One wonders what might have transpired if Donie O'Sullivan had not left the country, as his rivalry with Cooper on Fair Head and Muckross was also evident on Ailladie. At Ailladie in 1991, Donie managed to find Zebedee and Aileadoir to be followed by Cooper in 1992 with Damn the Torpedoes. Another one-time rival of Cooper's, Keefe Murphy, during a visit home from the UK in 1990, red-pointed Sunbane with Johnny Adams besides tacking on a bottom half to Cooper's Ship of Fools. One cannot help but surmise that if emigration had not removed so many top climbers, then the resultant rivalry would have yielded routes of really high international standards.

Just south of Ailladie, and about 1km distant, Ian Rea and Ian Dillon opened up a new crag at Ceann Capaill in 1991. About twenty-three routes of roughly 10m each, with gradings from easy to E1 were climbed. Ailladie's first E7 route, Very Big Springs, was done on sight by UK visitor George Smith in 1994 and the first free 6c pitch was put up by Peak District climber Dominic Lee in 1996 when, according to the guidebook, he made a reality out of the contested line claimed by Gibson in 1986. These were by no means the only instances in which visitors outclassed locals. As in other crags there were few new names other than those of visiting English climbers, some of them attracted by plentiful new opportunities on the Aran Islands which dominate the view from Ailladie. A well-known habitué of Dalkey Quarry, Ronan Browner, starting in 1995, added a number of fine routes to Ailladie over the next few years culminating in 1997 with his Earthling which had a grading of E6/7, 6c. This route and another he did with Hebblethwaite in the same year were subject to top-rope practice but were then done in good style. Another new name which appeared, all too briefly, in 1995, was that of John Hawkins, a

Corkman studying at University of Limerick who had pioneered some climbs on Inishmore. He took advantage of severe winter storms which had torn away considerable portions of the crag to put up, with John Beard, a route named Chocks Away, which replaced the vanished classic Box of Chocks, and then having practised moves on a top rope, climbed Crepuscular Ray with Finbar Desmond and Eoin Fitzgerald. For reasons which are not obvious, new routing virtually ceased from 1997 onwards although the crag remained popular. The slow build-up of new talent may be one factor, another the engagement in Himalayan ventures of some of the top men.

Climbing Walls

Climbers generally agree that the coming of climbing walls led to improved standards of fitness and technique which, for experienced outdoor climbers, transferred easily to crags. The opening of the first wall in the UK built by climbers (rather than architects and the like) was in Leeds in 1960 and was credited with a rise in standards in Yorkshire crags.[40] Ireland's first wall was built by climbers at Newpark School in a Dublin suburb in 1985 and was followed by Clondalkin in 1989 and by a rash of building in 1990 to 1993, mainly by Somers and Fenlon, at Tiglin, Cabra, Cork, Waterford, UCD, and DCU.[41] In Cork, in 1990 or thereabouts, Willie Cunningham supervised the building of a wall in the Midleton school of which he was principal. The first climbing competition, an inter-colleges affair, was held in UCD in 1992 and a bouldering league was in place the following year.[42] Derry's St Columb's climbing wall was opened in 1992, with a demonstration by Catherine Destivelle.[43] By now there was also a wall in Queen's which was due for expansion. More walls in Northern Ireland would follow. As yet, most walls were modest in size compared to some which were to be built in the new millennium but they were already attracting large numbers. While information is lacking, and there is need for Irish research in the area, it is apparent that if trends in the UK and USA were to be followed then the expanding economy, especially in the later 1990s, would lead to greater usage of such walls.[44] Research elsewhere had also shown that 22 per cent of climbers did their first climb indoors, that 15 per cent would never climb outdoors and 53 per cent would climb more indoors than they would on crags.[45]

Although climbing walls and bouldering competitions are indoor phenomena quite distant from mountains and crags, and do not form part of the main thrust of this history, their importance as training facilities and skills developers cannot be ignored; rock climbing and the rest of mountaineering underwent remarkable technical improvements because of them. Perhaps of equal import-ance in the close-knit Irish scene was the social aspect. Youngsters with little knowledge of greater mountaineering could meet with top performers and sometimes outdo them. For those mountaineering and rock-climbing demi-gods there was the opportunity to mix with those of lesser standing, to share enthusiasms and knowledge in a relaxed setting where class, gender and education were irrelevant. Many perceptions changed for good. It was always the case that, in the summer, Dalkey Quarry and such local crags served a similar purpose, if not on the same scale.

If there was a real threat to Cooper's dominance on so many crags it was presented by the usual denizens of Dalkey, either in the quarry itself or when they tested their abilities elsewhere. O'Sullivan, Browner and Hebblethwaite showed what could be done at Ailladie and elsewhere but were constantly reverting to the quarry to sharpen that cutting edge. Five routes by Tony Burke in 1990 included the frightening Phantom Raspberry Blower on the Ghost Slab, and Gulf Crisis on which he took a huge fall when a ledge he was swinging on gave way. Colm Ó Cofaigh put up a route near Crime in the City and Joe Lyons put up several routes of about VS standard at either side of Jacob's Ladder.

The next couple of years were fairly quiet except for the work of a visiting climber, Fernando Lomba; indeed, at the time Hebblethwaite thought there was stagnation. But 1993 was a year of drama and controversy. It is apparent from the descriptions of first ascents in this and previous chapters that not all climbers had Cooper's ethical approach. There was increasing resort to top-roping, practising of moves, pre-placement of protection, red-pointing and other means of ascent which departed from the traditionally accepted free lead done more or less on sight from the ground up. There had been some champing at the bit by young climbers – Tony Burke was one – at what they saw as conservative restrictions on their freedom to climb as they chose. It was such climbers who advocated the use of chalk, for instance.[46] So far it had been largely possible by means of peer pressure to avoid or modify what was seen by some as harmful innovation. The inevitable clash came when Ronan Browner bolted the wall right of Ripsnorter and climbed it at an initial F6c (a sports climbing grade). This was Indecent Assault and repulsed several attempted repeats. He bolted a second line on the overhanging sidewall of Tower Ridge to yield The Great Escape, F7a. The ensuing row led to a well-attended special meeting in January 1994 hosted by the MCI Technical Committee in Dun Laoghaire, County Dublin, at which it was agreed that bolting was unacceptable on traditional Irish crags.[47] Common gossip had it that Browner was unofficially told that if he did not remove the bolts then it would be done for him. He duly did as asked, placed a peg in The Great Escape, re-climbed the route and, giving some indication of how he felt, renamed it Bitter Aftertaste, a fine E6, 6a route.

Also in 1994, Tony Burke made a flying visit to complete Chomolungma, a route slightly harder than Bitter Aftertaste, which he had cleaned and pegged some time before. Browner also added routes, as did Terry O'Connor and Kevin Cooper, each putting up lines on the Ghost slab. Browner continued his almost single-handed ticking off of new routes in 1995, the most remarkable one being a free ascent of Indecent Assault, albeit after top-roping it, using two home-made pegs for protection. His partner was Jonathan Gillmor. The climb was now graded E7, 6c, the quarry's first climb at this grade. He almost equalled the grade in 1999 with Slapstick. Otherwise the latter part of the decade yielded little new, one exception being two climbs by thirteen-year-old Michael Duffy who did an E3 (top-roped) near Joas in 1996 and followed it in the next year with Body Fluid E5, 6c having previously top-roped and placed a wire. Terry O'Connor with two others, Conor O'Connor and Nick Keegan who made up a well-known IMC trio, did a route at a reasonable standard called Need a Drink, and Alan Sarhan displayed his ability with a new route in 1999.

The imminent publication of the new *Wicklow Guide* by Fenlon and Lyons saw a spate of routes by Donie O'Sullivan before he emigrated to the UK. He climbed three routes of E4/E5 on steep walls near Sarcophagus in Glendalough, and in Luggala he did two fine three-starred routes, Juniper Junction on the Main Face and Dreamtime on North Buttress. Joe Lyons added many more lines at Luggala and, at Hobnail Buttress in Glendalough, he and John Breen separately added some easy routes. Joe was also busy in Baravore Valley on the rocks near Great Gully where he did routes with Sé O Hanlon and others. Further down the valley Gerry Moss put up some routes with Hugh Sharkey and Terry O'Neill. Earlier, Gerry had found and climbed on small but productive crags in woodland settings at Carrick and Barnbawn. On both of these he was helped mainly by Liam Convery, Emily Hackett and Bob Norton, with some input also by Bill Hannon. Little was done in Wicklow in the latter half of the decade apart from some of these climbs, a hard route by Hebblethwaite at Glendalough called Deadlines and a medium grade line by Peter Keane and Peter Owens on the lower main face at Luggala.

For many climbers, the rediscovery of Donegal's Gola Island was the most warmly welcomed development of the decade. Easily accessible with lovely beaches, no permanent population, wild camping and an abundance of clean granite sea crags, the island was a climbers' paradise. Even the weather was thought to be better than on the mountainous mainland. Although lacking the broad terraces at the feet of some other seaside crags there were enough sizable platforms to allow relatively easy access to many routes. This was not a hard man's exclusive place of daunting lines, although it yielded a fair number of middle E grades, but a pleasant out-of-the-way venue with new route opportunities for climbers at every level. Discovered as a climbing destination by Alan Tees in 1981, it remained almost unknown to the climbing world until a 1994 article by Tees in *Irish Mountain Log*.[48] Tees and other Derry climbers got away some salvos of decent medium calibre before bigger guns in the persons of Paddy Mallon and Terry McQueen arrived in the summer of 1995, quickly followed by even heavier artillery in the form of Seamus MacGearailt, Traoloch O'Brien, Paul Harrington and Padraic Breen who, between them, put up ten routes in one day.

Gola Island, Donegal, a very popular climbing venue. Many small ledges allow easy access to climbs. ALAN TEES COLLECTION

Towards the end of the decade, large groups of climbers from clubs all over the country converged on Gola, especially at long weekends. If it were not for its distance from most major towns, the island was just what Ireland needed to encourage more participation at all levels. A number of other Donegal crags, coastal and inland, were found or re-found during this time, including Owey Island by Dave Walsh and Biddies Buttress above Barnesmore Gap by Tees (possibly one of the areas explored by Glover in the 1950s?). Skelpoonagh Bay, just north of the beach at Glencolumbcille, was opened up by Currans, Nolan, Allsop and Walls, and the Eglish Valley in the Bluestacks was discovered by Brian Johnston. The number and variety of crags which had now been found in Donegal, from long and committing mountain routes to short and strenuous coastal tests, combined with the choice of rock types, made the county a place of singular interest to climbers.

Developments elsewhere were so intense that a full chronicling is not possible here. An account of the more notable happenings is necessary although it lends emphasis to Hebblethwaite's remarks on the continued dominance of a few veterans. Those two somewhat isolated pioneers, Gallwey in Waterford and Ryan in Mayo, continued to make their mark locally early in the 1990s, after which other commitments removed them from the list of leaders. Tom Ryan was nearing the end of sixteen or more years of spearheading activity in various locations. Following a span of ten years' pioneering in Mayo, he was still, in the early 1990s, putting up routes of quality at Doo Lough, mainly with Simon McEvoy, and along the north Mayo coast at Glenloss Point and Erris Head/Danish Cellar with his regular partner Kevin McDonald. Paul Harrington, Gallwey and Willie Rock also partnered him. These coastal crags required nerve and an ability to find routes from above. One of these, typical in some ways but outstanding in quality, was Bohemian Rhapsody, described as a stunning route. Access was by means of a long abseil and a 7m swing to gain a belay ledge which was sometimes wave-washed. Tom, an extremely popular climber, was killed in 1997 in a work-related accident on a boat off the Mayo coast.[49]

The outstanding English climber Mick Fowler was also active on the north Mayo coast. Fowler's exploits as an 'adventure climber' tackling friable rock and using ice-climbing techniques on chalk cliffs may have seemed outrageous, but he was a brilliant climber of long standing and already well on his way to being one of the world's most successful climbers of breathtakingly difficult routes in greater ranges. On a trip to Ireland in 1990 he climbed the cliffs of Moher and the obvious sea stack, Branaunmore opposite O'Brien's Tower, before coming to Mayo to climb Dunbristy, a sea stack off Downpatrick Head which had remained inviolate since AD 1393 when it became detached from the land.

Tom Ryan, Mayo activist and popular climber, climbing in Wales in the 1980s.
HIGGS COLLECTION

Jack Bergin of Waterford Institute of Technology (WIT) and Stephen Gallwey continued their development of Coumshingaun, mainly on the north-facing buttress. The best route here was probably Talking God, a 30m route in the upper range of difficulty which was climbed by the pair in 1991. Stephen was involved, mainly as leader, in more than forty routes in Coumshingaun over a period of about fourteen years before easing off in 1992. He was to appear briefly again in the early part of the new millennium.

In Kerry, Aidan Forde became the undoubted master of the Gap of Dunloe putting up some forty-four climbs in the decade, mainly with Ivan Counihan. Most of his climbs were in the upper middle grades with one coming in at a higher grade. Moriarty and

Counihan also led climbs, the latter often with Forde. Richard Stack and Mike Shea shared leads on a number of climbs scattered among the Gap's various crags, most being in the mid-range of difficulty. A long-awaited guidebook to the climbs in the Gap was brought out as a limited edition (about 150 copies) in 1994–95. It was unfortunate that details were slow in emerging from Kerry, especially those pertaining to other inland crags in Iveragh where some worthwhile climbs were done. Con Moriarty, in explaining local attitudes, has said that details of routes were shared with those whom Kerry climbers had reason to trust. Moriarty has also said that there was a sense that climbing was a private affair involving a tight circle of friends and their relationship with landowners:

> The sensitivity of the unlimited access enjoyed was some-
> thing we were very deeply aware of along with the warmth
> and openness with which it was given and this was
> something we didn't want to see abused by others . . .
> While it was inevitable that people would one day discover
> these places, we weren't going to shout about them.[50]

But, from something else said by Moriarty, it is plain that resentment of what was seen as interference by the Dublin-based climbing establishment played no small part in his outlook.[51] Mike Barry, having established an early rapport with those mainly responsible for fostering the Irish rock-climbing ethos, was unstintingly open about his routes. Conflicting views make it difficult to identify specific reasons for the friction which marked urban/Kerry relationships but one object of contention was a small emergency shelter built by Moriarty and friends near the foot of Corrán Tuathail's north-west face where several accidents had occurred.

Discovery was still a leitmotif of Irish climbing with finds being made not only of the new crags already mentioned but also of sea crags on Cape Clear and on Sligo's Aughris Head. By 1997 there were 120 crags listed on a website maintained by Dave Hunt,[52] an enormous increase in the figures pertaining when the

IMC was founded, or even compared with those times in the 1960s when climbers struggled to locate anything new. However, Ireland still lacked sufficient numbers of good-quality, long and not-too-difficult routes of the sort which provide such enjoyment in several British mountain areas and which play an important part in attracting climbers high into the hills.

Throughout this time, when winters were kind – or harsh? – ice climbing was practised in almost every mountainous county. The infrequent and transient nature of opportunities for such climbing in Ireland still obliged climbers to resort to Scotland or to the increasingly popular frozen cascades around the Briançon region of the French Alps. Scotland, besides being a marvellous place for mountaineering, remained the place to develop skills on hard mixed routes, to learn those techniques so essential on the best of Alpine routes. It was at the beginning of a planned extended trip to the highlands that Bill Murphy was killed in an avalanche at the base of Buachaille Etive Mòr. Bill, a young Corkman who had helped re-galvanise UCDMC, had displayed much promise during his short alpine career.[53] His club had, over the years, become an important pillar of Irish mountaineering with very able walkers, climbers and big-range mountaineers such as Mick O'Shea, Keefe Murphy, Paul Harrington and Clare Sheridan.

11

FMCI/MI, Rescue Training

The purpose of this chapter is to describe what was going on in the background in those areas which are closely linked to mountaineering, form an important framework of its organisation, but are not intrinsic to the activity. The elements covered here had reached a fairly advanced level of development at this stage (1990s) in the narrative. The reader whose interest is confined to the sport itself can safely skip this chapter.

RESCUE

The little helicopter with the two-man bubble cockpit buzzed up the Slaney valley to where the IMC group clustered around the pathetic body of a young girl lying at the foot of Lugnaquilla's craggy North Prison. The tiny British aircraft had been sent from Ballykelly Aerodrome in Northern Ireland because then, in 1963, there were no such craft south of the border. It had fluttered back and forth over the club's search groups scattered across the mountain, and now, in response to a message relayed down to the roadside by word of mouth, it tried unsuccessfully to land near the group waiting for a stretcher which was to be brought up from the road. Standing off a few hundred yards from the crags it hovered over an inviting, flat green area. The group of mountaineers watched with gallows humour and knowing anticipation as an Irish Army liaison officer in brown shoes, smart uniform and glistening Sam Browne belt stood in the aircraft's doorway. He jumped with a little splash knee-deep into the morass.

The embarrassed young soldier had the presence of mind to heed the shouts of the mountaineers which informed him and, through him, the waiting police and public that the casualty would be carried down on the Thomas mountain-rescue stretcher, the only one in the country. The helicopter was obviously not designed or able to carry out such a task.[1]

This, in March 1963, was the somewhat ignominious circumstance which led within months to the commissioning of two French Alouette III helicopters,[2] later to be expanded to a Squadron, then a Wing, and a new rescue role for the Irish Air Corps. The unfortunate young woman victim, unsuitably clad and booted, was one of a group of UCD students on an outing of the L&H (Literary and Historical Society) to snow-covered Lug ,who had become disoriented in mist. She and a young man, together or separately, had slipped on the icy rim of the Prisons and fallen a considerable height. He had somehow managed to travel quite a distance down the valley before he too succumbed but she had died, probably instantly, at the foot of the crag.

The Dublin IMC had acquired the Thomas stretcher in 1962 and had it housed in Glendalough's Royal Hotel along with a comprehensive first-aid pack.[3] A makeshift stretcher made by a Dublin workshop had sufficed until then, and occasional cliff rescue practices were held at Dalkey Quarry or the Rocky Valley.[4]

The appearance on the Irish climbing scene of Aubrey Flegg, who had spent his National Service years with the RAF Mountain Rescue Team at Kinloss, led to the imparting of better skills, more practice and the acquisition of the Thomas stretcher. An arrangement was made with the Garda Síochána to initiate a call-out system, a rather woolly one at first, run from their Dublin

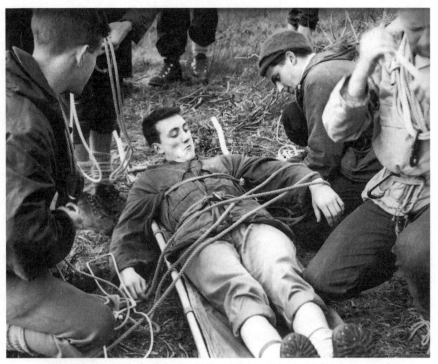

IMC rescue practice at Dalkey. *(L–r)*: Gerry Cairns, Dennis Moloney in stretcher, Niall Rice and Barry O'Flynn. The stretcher was made up in a Dublin workshop.
IMC ARCHIVE

Castle base. Aubrey coordinated the efforts of the thirty-seven club members who turned up for the Lugnaquilla search. The responsible Garda superintendant was glad to hand over the quartering of more difficult terrain to the mountaineers while the army and police stayed on the lower slopes.[5]

In the Mournes, Phil Wood of IMC Belfast initiated the Mourne Mountain Rescue Team in 1962 and there was also a Belfast team composed mainly of IMC members. The Mourne team members were almost entirely local residents. The team was supplied by the Northern Ireland Hospital Authority with a Thomas stretcher and some equipment which was supplemented with the aid of IMC funds. With the help of the Forest Service, a cottage near Newcastle Forest was acquired as a team base.[6]

Brendan Walsh took over from Flegg as IMC Mountain

Rescue Officer in 1964 and developed relations with a number of organisations, including some in Northern Ireland. Arising from this, and with the discreet and always effective influence of Bert Slader of the CCPR, a meeting was held in early 1965 at Lord Roden's home at Bryansford, with Roden himself as chairman. Attendees included Brian Gibson of the Mourne Team, Walsh and Slader representing IMC Dublin and Belfast, Joey Glover from NWMC, Brendan O'Connor from the Ramblers, some other interested bodies along with representatives of various youth and educational organisations. The Irish Mountain Rescue Association (IMRA) was formed here, a considerable achievement which would have been difficult to envisage later in that decade as the Troubles began. Walsh was elected secretary/organiser, Brian Gibson of Mourne Rescue was chairman with Bert Slader for IMC Belfast as deputy chair. Calvert Moore of Glenfoffany would become

IMC cliff-rescue practice in Dalkey Quarry c. 1961. (L–r): Niall Rice, Dennis Moloney on stretcher, Tony Kavanagh and Kevin Shelley. Note the primitive early mountain-rescue stretcher. IMC ARCHIVE

treasurer.[7] Slader was also a founder member of the Mourne MR Team. At the first AGM the following November, Mick Kellett and Phil Wood were elected to the committee with the core executive positions remaining in the same original hands. During the following year John Bourke of An Óige was co-opted.[8]

Two tragedies in the Corrán Tuathail area in April 1966 showed that the formation of IMRA had been indeed timely, and led to the formation of two additional teams. Late in the evening of 21 April 1966, a call-out led to sixteen IMC members leaving for Kerry, with one car diverting to Glendalough to pick up the stretcher. Arriving at the mouth of the Hag's Glen about dawn, the team later that morning found the body of an English student whose fall had been reported the previous day. The body was on Corrán Tuathail's north face in a spot accessible only to climbers. Walsh, Sean Rothery and Pat Colleran, supported by Peter Shortt, managed to attach a rope and lower the body to other team members waiting with the Thomas stretcher.[9] (Walsh recalls carrying the body strapped to his back for at least some of the lowering.) The body was then carried down to waiting locals and Gardaí.

Even before this, a well-known An Óige member, Myles Kinsella, had gone missing in the area but this was reported only on 22 April. An Óige members under Mick Kellett mounted a series of searches but it was not until the following November that the body of Myles was found by IMC members Colleran and Colgan.[10]

Natural concern and dented local pride arising from these incidents led to the formation of the Kerry Mountain Rescue Team (KMRT) and to a similar organisation in An Óige. A MacInnes stretcher, a more portable improvement on the Thomas, was placed in each of four An Óige hostels. A once-off, disposable Bofors stretcher was situated by the IMC at Lough Barra, where also, sometime in that busy year of 1966, a joint cliff lower was carried out by IMC Dublin and Glenfoffany. There would be a number of such practice sessions run jointly by various teams.[11]

The Kerry team, at the urging of Frank Lewis of the regional tourism body, was set up by Paddy O'Callaghan, Dermot Foley and Gearoid O'Sullivan of Killorglin, John Maguire of Muckross House and Jack Walsh of the Climbers Inn at Glencar. The team, which for many years was organised from Killorglin by the O'Sullivans and other families, would become a very effective unit, well equipped and drawing for its personnel mainly on members of the Laune Mountaineering Club which was set up for that purpose.[12] They were to become by far the busiest team in the country until the sudden growth of outdoor activities in the 1990s put a similar burden on Wicklow teams. For some time the IMC and Mourne teams were the only groups equipped, trained and capable of cliff rescue, while An Óige had a looser arrangement whereby large numbers could be called upon to carry out searches.

Having initiated much that had happened, Walsh retired as secretary/organiser in November 1966 but remained as chairman for a few years. He was replaced as secretary by Mick Kellett who now acted for An Óige and became a prominent activist for many years.

An inspired initiative of KMRT in 1973 was to affect mountain rescue in Ireland profoundly for a generation. The Laune club invited Bill March to run a week's course based in Glencar. Bill was chief instructor at Glenmore Lodge in Scotland and one of the foremost mountain rescue experts in a country which included the likes of Hamish MacInnes and John Cunningham. Quite apart from any improvements which subsequently took place in Kerry and the initial moves towards the setting up of the Galway MRT by a course participant, the week's thorough grounding led to regular and very amicable contacts between Bill and myself and as a result to later connections between Tiglin Centre and Glenmore Lodge. It also resulted in the acquisition of expertise and equipment and to further visits to Tiglin by Glenmore staff. Tiglin, in turn, imparted a range of skills to members of different clubs who went on to set up their own teams. Frequent liaison by Tiglin with the Air Corps helicopter unit resulted in a steep and risky learning curve on the part of both entities (see section on Training).

As mountaineering and walking clubs came into being around the country, so also did Mountain Rescue Teams. As these often sprang up following a particular mountaineering accident and operated independently for some time before being accepted into IMRA, it is not possible to be precise about dates of formation. In 1975, a team was formed in Galway,[13] and another in Sligo–Leitrim.[14] In the following year, a loosely knit group was formed to cover the South Tipperary, Kilkenny, Waterford area and by 1977 had become the South-East Mountain Rescue Association.[15] In Tramore in 1978 a Cliff Rescue Team, which had some previous connection with an inshore lifeboat team, came into being.[16] A resignation en masse by most activists in An Óige's team in 1984 led to the formation of the Dublin–Wicklow team and the cessation of An Óige's rescue role.[17] Before that, in 1982, a team was established by people who were mostly residents of the Glen of Imaal. The Glen of Imaal team and the Dublin–Wicklow group shared responsibility for mountain rescue in Wicklow.[18] A Mayo team came into being in 1989.[19] Together with Sligo and Galway they amalgamated in 1991 to form the Western Mountain Rescue Association but later reverted to their original form with WMRT acting to maintain liaison.[20] A Donegal team was established in 1984.[21]

Teams acquired skill, equipment and experience over the years which led to sometimes very sophisticated operations. Less busy teams sometimes faltered and seemed on the verge of extinction while those in Kerry and Dublin–Wicklow were called upon so frequently that they had little choice but to maintain a fully functioning service. All teams had tales to tell. One of the better known is the rescue of three Cork climbers who were caught in a snow avalanche in a gully on Corrán Tuathail and, on the same weekend in February 1986 the recovery of the body of a young doctor who slipped to her death in icy conditions in the nearby Cnoc na Tuinne area. KMRT needed all its resources to deal with the complicated evacuations and body recovery.[22] In Wicklow, the tragic 1981 reprise of the unfortunate incident which occurred to UCD students in 1963 has been mentioned in chapter 8, again a winter occurrence.

All this time-consuming and often dangerous work by the various teams was done on a voluntary basis with funds being

raised for equipment and transport through church-gate collec-
tions, raffles and all the usual multifaceted and ingenious ways so
familiar to rural Ireland. There were some instances of help being
received from local Health Boards. Then, in 1983, the right man,
Dick Spring, in the right place as a junior minister in the
Department of the Environment, announced, at the opening of a
new KMRA base in his constituency, the establishment of a
National Coordinating Committee for Mountain and Cave Rescue.
Funding became much easier to access on a regular basis from then
on. Troubles with radio frequencies were eventually sorted out
through the good offices of the coordinating committee, as were
firmer arrangements with various official bodies including the
Garda Síochána who remained the responsible body for mounting
and coordinating mountain and cave search and rescue. In 1986
Mountain Rescue was included in the emergency 999 call system
which brought it into line with the long-held practice in Northern
Ireland. The nifty Alouettes were supplemented by Dauphin
helicopters in that same year.

The funding issue and government involvement had been
sorted out much earlier in Northern Ireland. There, various health
and educational bodies as well as the police had helped with funds
or equipment from time to time. In late 1980 two new teams,
North-West and North-East, came into being at the same time as
the Northern Ireland Mountain, Cave and Cliff Rescue Coordinating Committee. That committee somehow got past its difficult
title to become an effective body with access to funds, initially
through the Department of Education. The North-East team later
stood down but the North-West continued to be responsible for
counties Derry, Tyrone and Fermanagh from its then base in Derry
city. The Mourne Team also had a secondary responsibility for the
Cooley peninsula in County Louth. There was a part-time Royal
Ulster Constabulary mountain-rescue team which had stores of
equipment in police stations in four locations in the province. Due
largely to Bert Slader's diplomatic skills, mountain-rescue teams
were later allowed access to these caches for training purposes, but
fears for their own security inhibited use by some team members.

Sergeant John Manning
demonstrating Air Corps
Alouette and use of hoist.
AUTHOR'S COLLECTION

Another result of the Troubles was that helicopter rescues by the RAF entailed having two machines, one of which carried a squad of soldiers who secured the rescue site. Irish Air Corps pilots on rescue practice with Tiglin took to carrying sidearms following the hijacking of a private helicopter which was used in the escape of republican prisoners from Mountjoy prison in 1973.

A Search and Rescue Dog Association came into being in Northern Ireland in 1979 and had spread to the Republic in 1983. It joined IMRA in 1993. The story of that very effective organisation and its constituent parts must await expert recounting in another publication.

In both parts of the island the Coastguard (Coast Guard when the term was revived in the Republic in 2000) had a role to play in cliff rescue. It was a Coastguard helicopter which lifted the dying Shay Billane from the bottom of Fair Head. The ins and outs of such government-run agencies and the shifting responsibilities of government departments is too complicated to follow but a brief outline is as follows. The Air Corps continued to provide search-and-rescue cover throughout the 1980s and acquired Dauphins in 1986. In 1989, a Dauphin was stationed at Shannon to supple-ment the Baldonnel craft. A decision to place responsibility for Search and Rescue in the hands of the Irish Marine Emergency

Service (later the Irish Coast Guard) led to a contracted company operating two Sikorsky S61N helicopters based at Shannon, beginning in July 1991. The Air Corps moved its Dauphin to Finner Camp in Donegal. Another company took over in 1996 and extended its service to bases in Dublin and Sligo airports.[23] The Air Corps provided a Dauphin at Waterford Airport in 1999 but suffered an immediate tragedy when a crew was killed in a crash at Tramore.[24] The Air Corps' proud involvement in Search and Rescue did not long survive this and its various new craft were used for military operations.

TRAINING

The year 1969 was an exhilarating time to be involved in adventure sports in Ireland. Many initiatives were happening simultaneously north and south of the border. These initiatives would result in the introduction of outdoor sports new to this country, to new bodies being formed, including the national body for mountaineering, to the setting-up of training structures in mountaineering. The term 'adventure sports' itself was introduced to Ireland.

In Northern Ireland, besides courses run by a climbing school which would evolve into the Glenfoffany club, formal government-aided training courses in outdoor activities had been run for a few years by the CCPR. Bert Slader of the CCPR was centrally involved in such training, as he was in organising that body's expedition to Turkey in 1964. He was helped by some club mountaineers on courses which were run from Lord Roden's Cottage in Bryansford in County Down.[25] By 1969, construction was under way of a purpose-built outdoor centre, Ireland's first, in Tollymore Forest near Bryansford. The centre, which became Tollymore National Outdoor Centre, was opened in 1970. Slader acted for some time as the centre's Warden before being transferred, as Head of Sports Development, to the Belfast headquarters of the new Sports Council for Northern Ireland which took over the running of the Centre in 1974 (or 1973 according to one source).[26] He continued to influence Tollymore and – as recorded in previous chapters – the practice of sending young people on supervised expeditions to distant ranges. Even when Slader retired, Tollymore was fortunate in having advocates at the very centre of policy making and the source of funding, as several former instructors occupied senior positions at head-quarters; one of them was to become the executive head of the Sports Council.

Bert Slader.
SLADER COLLECTION

In the Republic, a series of newspaper articles on adventure sports by O'Leary in early 1969 led to a meeting at his home in May of that year which was attended by very able personalities in a variety of adventurous activities.[27] Most of them were pioneers in their sports and founder members of their associations or clubs. The scuba-divers present had carried out their first dives at Greystones, County Wicklow, in winter dressed in their flannel long-johns; the canoeists had built their own boats. It was obvious to all that a shared approach to such matters as training, the environment, access and rescue would be an advantage. It was agreed to form a new umbrella body, the Association for Adventure Sports (AFAS), to which the still tiny national organisations of each adventure activity would affiliate. The mountaineers at the meeting, O'Leary and Lynam, were embarrassed by the non-existence of a national representative organisation for their sport at a time when newer pursuits had thriving, if small, national governing bodies. As a result, and at the invitation of the Spillikin Club, a number of mountaineering clubs came together as noted later in this chapter, and the FMCI was formed.

(Contrary to some reports which did a grave disservice to altruistic volunteers, those enthusiasts from a number of sports who set up AFAS were not motivated by the availability of government funding. A new government scheme which allocated funds for sports came into being more than a year after AFAS's founding.)

As in Northern Ireland, but unaware of what was happening there, training was identified as a priority. Activities such as scuba-diving and skiing had well-structured approaches to training and it was felt that much could be learned by running joint training courses. A number of these were run by AFAS on a voluntary basis using personal and borrowed equipment.[28] The mountaineers who acted as instructors on these courses set about applying what they had learned from other sports' training regimes.

Learning through 'apprenticeship' was the accepted and traditional way in which mountaineering knowledge, judgement and skill were imparted when numbers were small. With growth, clubs in Ireland tried to cope by organising courses for prospective members in places like Dalkey Quarry. This was first done in a structured fashion for its prospective members by the Dublin IMC in the 1960s and by several voluntary groups in the Mournes. Something more needed to be done to spread the net wider and to construct a suitable framework along the lines followed by sister organisations in AFAS and by the CCPR.

Much concern had been expressed in the UK about the growing number of mountaineering accidents, especially to those involving school and youth groups. It was feared that a similar pattern would develop in Ireland as participation grew. In both jurisdictions of the island, and scarcely aware of each other's existence, schemes for the training of group leaders were instituted.

In the North, Bert Slader became the first secretary to the Northern Ireland Mountain Leadership Training Board.[29] In the Republic, Mountain Leadership courses were run at first by AFAS.[30] The instigators of both Irish schemes designed their own syllabi which, when bedded down, transpired to be quite similar to what was in being across the Irish Sea. The first Irish Mountain Leadership course – soon to be followed by leader courses in other activities such as canoeing/kayaking – was run on an entirely voluntary basis by the author, Joss Lynam and Niall Rice. The first year or two entailed a fairly steep and sometimes painful learning curve for instructors and trainees alike.

Some governmental financial assistance became available through the new grant system for sports announced in October 1970. (That scheme had originally been intended by the Minister for Finance Charles Haughey as an initial contribution towards what he saw as a land-based version of the *Asgard* training vessel, but his fall from grace resulted in the fund being used for much wider sporting purposes.[31]) Equipment and a vehicle were acquired by AFAS. With the assistance of a priming grant from the Carnegie Trust and the kindness of An Óige, a residential training base was set up in the youth hostel at Tiglin in County Wicklow. Poorly resourced, not ideally sited and probably premature, this base became the National Adventure Centre and was the only such centre in the Republic. A VEC-run Outdoor Education Centre, which was also the first of its kind, was housed in a redundant vocational school on Achill Island. Under AFAS control and gradually moving into nearby premises, the Tiglin establishment would eventually be brought up to a fairly acceptable but spare standard through a Dublin Vocational Education Committee (VEC) grant.

Tiglin ran the Mountain Leadership and other mountaineering courses until Joss Lynam persuaded the FMCI to establish the Mountain Leadership Training Board (Bord Oiliúint Sléibhe or BOS) in late 1974.[32] Thereafter, Tiglin's mountaineering courses were run under BOS's auspices and its leadership courses were certified by that body.

Tiglin was run on a voluntary basis for the first year or two. It was AFAS's misfortune that its monies came mainly through the Department of Education, an organisation which was then utterly unsuited to dealing with adventure sports. Tiglin found itself increasingly involved in instruction for school and youth groups which, almost imperceptibly, led to an eventual involvement in Outdoor Education for schools and in specially designed courses and qualifications for teachers and others. This led to a certain diminution of its mountain training role.

A full-time director, the author, was appointed in 1972. A small number of suitably qualified staff trained in the UK were taken on, and more advanced qualifications were acquired through courses in Wales and Scotland. Voluntary instructors were still used, partly out of financial necessity but mainly to maintain links with the main body of active mountaineers in clubs. AFAS was ineffective at raising government and other funds, partly because its constituent bodies were vying for slices from the same small financial cake. Tiglin was funded from the small annual national body sports grant allocated to AFAS rather than being separately financed in a similar fashion to Tollymore. It struggled to sustain itself as a budding national centre of excellence. (AFAS received a total grant from the government of £2,000 in 1973, rising to £9,000 by 1975. Tiglin fought for its share of this.)

From its beginning, Tollymore was run professionally with funds allocated directly by the Northern Ireland Sports Council, although it too used voluntary instructors for much the same reasons as did Tiglin. Tollymore was affected by the Troubles when it was burned down in 1972, but funds were readily available to rebuild and expand. Teddy Hawkins, Willie Annett, Judith Annett, Dick Jones and Nick Harkness served the centre well, as did younger activists such as Alan Currans.

Local Education Authorities in Northern Ireland ran outdoor courses in a number of Outdoor Education Centres which were much more lavishly appointed and staffed than any similar centres south of the border. Again, the Troubles played their part. Northern Ireland, more than other parts of the UK, was felt to be in special need of funding for youth and sports projects, as was made plain by Lords Windlesham and Shackleton in a House of Lords debate in 1973.[33]

Tiglin could never adequately compensate or retain outstanding talent. Nor, until the 1990s, could it draw on a sufficiently large reservoir of professionally qualified people. Nevertheless, over the years, it would employ some of the very best Irish mountaineers including Richard Dean, Calvin Torrans, Shay Billane, Tom Hand and Robbie Fenlon, as well as equally competent multiskilled instructors, most of whose names appear as mountaineers elsewhere in this history. For more advanced Alpine and Scottish courses Tiglin instructors were sometimes supported by experts such as Stelfox and Somers.

New courses, including the Mountain Skills and Single Pitch rock-climbing trainer were initiated along with a more advanced rock-climbing qualification and early entry to the European Mountain Leadership scheme. These were not without their teething problems and were regarded with scepticism by UK Mountain Leadership Training Boards. A similar progression of courses occurred at Tollymore, perhaps a little more cautiously given the need to move in tandem with other UK national centres and Mountain Leadership Training Boards.

The variety of courses at Tiglin ranged from the first adventure courses in Ireland for physically disabled people to several mountaineering courses attended by supposedly incognito members of the Army Ranger wing. There were lighter moments. On an army mountaineering course run by Tiglin the author remembers an inspecting brass-hat looking at him handling ropes at a cliff top. An order was issued: 'tell that officer to get a haircut.'

Following on from an eye-opening course in Mountain Rescue run by Bill March in Kerry, and with further help from Glenmore Lodge in the Cairngorms, and recognition by IMRA, training courses in Mountain Rescue were run at Tiglin. Similarly, with the aid of the exacting Dr Ieuan Jones who had designed a Mountain First Aid course in Snowdonia, training courses were established in that discipline. Course participants included founder members of Mountain Rescue teams such as Tramore, SEMRA, Sligo, Mayo and Dublin–Wicklow, as well as staff from other centres.

On two or three consecutive years, full helicopter crews attended Tiglin's week-long mountain rescue courses, as did instructors from the Garda training centre in Tullamore, County Offaly. Arising from hard lessons learned, not without some risk, from frequent helicopter practices on Wicklow crags and bogs, changes in operating procedures were implemented by both the Air Corps and Tiglin. (One example was the modification to the rescue cables on Alouette helicopters following the emergency jettisoning of two of these expensive wires during a practice on Kippure's Eagle's Crag.) The Air Corps and mountaineers owe much to pioneer crews such as then Captain Hugh O'Donnell, winchman John Manning, winch operator Willie Byrne, and to their innovative Commanding Officer Fergus O'Connor.

Tiglin participated with Tollymore in a short-lived but worthwhile Diploma in Mountaineering Instruction which emanated from fertile brains in the Northern Ireland Sports Council. The six-month course had some academic input from colleges in Limerick and Jordanstown. There was also a comprehensive part-time course in Outdoor Education which was conceived by the Curriculum Development Unit attached to TCD and was run jointly by the CDU, Tiglin and a college of Dublin Institute of Technology. Technical and 'soft' skills acquired on this course can be seen in use throughout the country as this is written.

In 1991, EC funding became available to BOS for a pilot scheme to run courses which led to the *Accompagnateur en Montagne* qualification which authorised its holders to lead people in non-glaciated mountainous terrain in EU countries. Tiglin drew up a syllabus which was required to stick as closely as possible to that of the original French design, with some adaptation to Irish conditions. The course was run by BOS with mixed success at several locations during the following year and was operated by Tiglin for its second year of operation. Also in 1991 Tiglin secured some EC funding for the first time.

At a different level from the Accompagnateur scheme, a six-month FÁS (then AnCo) course in Outdoor Pursuits was initiated in 1985. It was designed and run for young people aspiring to make careers in outdoor centres and related establishments. A number of well-known climbers began or developed their careers on these courses. The Tiglin syllabus was accepted nationwide and was adopted by other training establishments.

Mountain Guides

In the late 1980s and continuing into the 1990s a number of Irishmen, across the thirty-two counties, qualified as Mountain Guides recognised by IFMGA (International Federation of Mountain Guides Associations). They fulfilled an important role in imparting advanced rock-climbing and alpine skills as well as guiding ski-touring ventures. They were also very effective in helping clubs, outdoor centres and the FMCI/MCI to run their mountaineering courses.

Centre Standards Board

As other outdoor centres came into being, both commercial and those run by such bodies as VECs, their senior staff became qualified (almost all through Tiglin). Some of these centres were approved by BOS to run mountaineering and leadership training courses at different levels. Arising from such developments, AFAS, in 1993, was charged by its constituent bodies to run an outdoor centre inspection scheme designed to ensure compliance with the safety standards of the various adventure sports bodies. AFAS did this through its Centre Standards Board on which various interested parties were represented. Inspectors provided their services on a voluntary basis. Although the scheme was approved by Bord Fáilte (the Irish Tourist Board) it was self-funding, with the centres and AFAS both contributing to costs. Later in the decade, through the work of a dedicated civil servant, the Minister for Marine and Natural Resources approved a once-off grant which, for a short time, enabled the Board to provide a professional service.

Takeover

Tiglin had achieved all it had been required to do by AFAS. Its mountaineering future depended on what role the FMCI/MCI felt it should fulfil. The MCI with the Irish Canoe Union took over the practical running of the National Adventure Centre in 1999 and at the same time assumed dominant roles in the governance of AFAS. The Centre Standards Board ceased operation a little over a year after that and Tiglin ceased to operate as an outdoor centre a few years later.

Tollymore was extended and improved in 1979 with the aid of a £70,000 grant from the Department of Education and underwent a major modernisation of facilities over three years in the early 1990s. In 1999, an area of the Tollymore's grounds was leased to MCI which erected Hotrock Climbing Wall, a project opened the following year.

Millennium Youth Initiative

MCI organised a few youth climbing meets early in the 1990s. It became actively involved in alpine training late in the decade when it held the first and well-attended MCI alpine meet at Ailefroide which had a strong instructional and mentoring element, provided mainly by Mountain Guides. This was followed closely by a three-year programme of training for young climbers under the umbrella of The Millennium Youth Initiative. This involved its young charges in a series of courses in Ireland, Scotland, the Alps and then, in the new century, in the Caucasus Mountains and Nepal. One can identify the hand of Stelfox in all this, given his background and what he had seen of Slader's initiatives. The FMCI, now MCI, had almost from its beginnings sent promising young climbers to Chamonix's ENSA (École Nationale de Ski et d'Alpinisme) on alpine courses at various levels.

FMCI/MI, ENVIRONMENT AND ACCESS

In 1970, a prominent member of the IMC wrote: 'We were under pressure from AFAS to form a Federation of mountaineering clubs'.[34]

In 1969 and 1970, that same 'pressure' or persuasion was being brought to bear on all the other mountaineering clubs, as it was on those other adventure sports represented in AFAS but which, as yet, did not have a national organisation. Mountaineering, Caving and Orienteering were the more obvious unfederated bodies. The idea of having a federation of mountaineering clubs was not a new one. The Belfast Section of the IMC had been advocating for some years that such a body be established,[35] and in early 1969 had given some thought to the setting up of an Ulster federation.[36] Both Glenfoffany and Tralee MC had made similar suggestions, so most doors were already open and some clubs did not need to be persuaded.[37] Sean O'Sullivan of the Laune club and first chairman of the Federation, writing about that exciting period of many initiatives remarked, 'very often the same personalities were involved'.[38] So it was that the Spillikin Club, relying on its positive experience of AFAS and of inter-club cooperation, invited other mountaineering clubs to the inaugural meeting in June 1969.[39] At that meeting it was agreed to go ahead with the setting up of a body to be called the Federation of Mountaineering Clubs of Ireland (FMCI), to renew invitations to clubs which had missed this first meeting and to affiliate to AFAS.

There were further meetings of the Federation during the next eighteen months, with a wider representation of clubs.[40] There were some bumps along the road (amusingly recounted by O'Sullivan)[41] to full acceptance by all clubs involved and there was some dragging of feet, even obstruction, until it became clear that monies were available under the new government grants scheme for sports. Mountaineering was one of the few adventure sports which failed to receive a government grant from the 1970 budget. It received £350 in 1971 and £500 in 1972.[42] As Joss Lynam said to the author – perhaps being unfair to others who had committed themselves: 'Of course it was that money that started the FMCI too; without it, however hard you tried, I don't think you could have persuaded us all to federate.'[43]

Joss Lynam's club, the IMC, was understandably cautious about proposals which might weaken its dominant position as the senior and largest club. However, once it was assured of representation commensurate with its numbers,[44] it began to make the running and at a meeting held on 5 December 1970 in Newman House (attended by both IMC sections, Laune, Glenfoffany, QUBMC, UCDMC and Spillikin) it was agreed that within six months a constitution would be drawn up. The generally accepted history of its formation has it that the Federation was formed in 1971, but just as with the IMC and many similar organisations who drew up constitutions sometime after their inaugural meeting, it may be more accurate to date the Federation's beginnings to June 1969, or – with less justification – perhaps to that meeting in December 1970. (The original name proposed at the first meeting in 1969 was the Federation of Irish Mountaineering Clubs but that suggestion was quickly withdrawn when it was realised that its acronym, FIMC, might cause offence, being too similar to IMC.)

Within a short time following its establishment the FMCI was dispensing monies to individual clubs, arranging and sometimes financing training visits by young alpinists to ENSA in Chamonix and to La Berarde; it set up the Mountain Leadership Training Board and arranged public lectures by foreign mountaineers. It had eleven member clubs in 1972 with a membership of 712; by 1976 it had seventeen affiliated clubs with a combined membership of about 1,350.[45]

Government funds also enabled the Federation to publish several rock-climbing guides and to help with the Ramblers' publication of *Dublin and Wicklow Access Routes*. Members benefited from entitlement to mountaineering insurance through the agency of the BMC (British Mountaineering Council).[46] This access to insurance and, perhaps, the availability of government funds, may have influenced walking and rambling clubs to join an organisation set up for and by mountaineers. In turn, numbers mattered in approaches to government, so the FMCI felt it could not be too precious in considering applications for membership. Member-ship grew over the years so that by 2000 there were 102 clubs and a total membership of 5,500.[47] It revised its constitution on several occasions and underwent a change of name to Mountaineering

Joss Lynam. Influential administrator, life-long mountaineer.

Council of Ireland (MCI) in January 1990. All this, and what is outlined below, was achieved by voluntary individuals and committees without paid administrative staff until late 1989. Lynam's name figures prominently.

From then until the end of the century, as the workload increased substantially, AFAS's professional office staff undertook much routine office work on the Federation's behalf. Along with the change in name and a new constitution, the administration of the national body acquired a new dynamism as Stelfox, with authority derived from respect earned as a mountaineer, presided over an expanding and efficient organisation. This momentum continued under the chairmanships of Mike Keyes and Frank Nugent. In late 1999, with the aid of a Sports Council grant, a part-time MCI administrator became a full-time employee based in Dublin. The Northern Ireland Sports Council enabled the employment of an Access Officer whose duties were confined to the province.

Mountain Log

In January 1978 the first edition was issued of *Mountain Log* which was described as the newsletter of the FMCI. Edited by Joss Lynam and rather flimsy at first, the *Log* gradually widened content beyond the internal doings of the FMCI. It and its expanded version, *Irish Mountain Log*, which came into being in 1986, was to keep members informed on the growth of environmental and access problems in the hills, act as a sounding board through its letters pages and maintain some coherence between the various elements of the mountaineering world, from Sunday walkers to expedition mountaineers. That coherence was sometimes weakened, perhaps inevitably given the very different perspectives and needs of those elements. Among the more important sources of dissension were different approaches to the topics of Access and Conservation.

Access and Conservation

Until the 1960s there was scarcely an awareness of environmental or access problems in the Irish hills. In the early 1950s the unsurfaced road from Glenmacnass to Sally Gap, the Wicklow Gap road, and the road through Connemara's Inagh valley all ran through open, unforested areas. The TV masts on Kippure, Truskmore, Mount Leinster and elsewhere, with their approach roads, were not there until the early 1960s. Turlough Hill power station, its associated power lines and hilltop reservoir did not exist until the late 1960s and early 1970s. Wind farms would not appear until the 1990s. Access problems hardly existed.

However, as the population became more mobile, as participation in outdoor recreation grew, the FMCI became embroiled in conflicts to do with access and damage to the hill environment. There were strong opposing views among mountaineers on such things as the building of a footbridge over the Glenmacnass river. There were internal conflicts to do with the damage to the hills perpetrated by climbers and walkers themselves, especially through path erosion, through infringement on the remote tranquillity of the hills. Such violations, it was argued, were carried through by large groups on club outings,[48] organised mass traverses such as the Lug and Maamturk walks,[49] and the funnelling of recreationists through a limited number of easy access routes in the Mournes.[50] There were also differences in the approach members adopted towards dealing with farmers and access. There were external conflicts with various public bodies because of the environmental damage they inflicted or intended to inflict on the hills.

Environmental effects of recreation

The direct effect recreational users had on hilly environments was sometimes exaggerated. Compared to the large swathes of territory taken up by natural peat-hag erosion, turf cutting, forestry, water reservoirs, TV and communications masts, as well as electricity generation schemes with their various approach roads, the thin ribbons of hilltop paths seemed innocuous enough. But these very routes impacted directly on the experiences of the walker; they affected one's progress, one's desire to experience wild places and a degree of solitude. A well-beaten trail – worse, a badly eroded one – took from that sense of exploration, of isolation, of mild adventure (however illusory) which one hoped to find in the hills. By the late 1980s there were at least 115km of these ridge-top and approach paths at altitudes greater than 320m in Wicklow alone,[51] and there were places such as the Devil's Ladder on Corrán Tuathail and Mám Eidhneach in the Twelve Bens which had been rendered dangerous through overuse. Concern was being expressed about footpath braiding and erosion in the Mournes.[52] The FMCI, it seemed, could do little to ameliorate the situation. Attempts by some clubs to have the FMCI voice its disapproval of annual organised hill traverses or of excessive numbers on club outings were opposed by members of other clubs,[53] despite ample researched evidence that such concentrated usage had more impact on vegetation loss than dispersed use by similar numbers.[54] However, the kind of overcrowding already described in relation to the annual Mourne Wall Walk, and the responsible attitude of organisers of the Reeks Walk and others, eventually led to cancellations, to limitation of numbers, or to biannual walks.[55] Some clubs, however, continued to bring large numbers on individual outings, not realising that numbers alone, regardless of their effect on paths, were a visual and auditory assault on the solitude of the hills. (See hillwalking sections in chapters 8 and 10).

In 1982 the Federation agreed on a policy in relation to 'long walks' which laid down five recommendations which had to do with numbers, litter, the varying of routes, the avoidance of peak growth season and of permanent markers. It felt moved to publish this policy again in 1985 as it believed that many of its members were still unaware of 'the problems in relation to access and conservation'.[56] This dichotomy, between concern for environmental degradation on the one hand and the promotion of organised long walks on the other, would continue into the early years of the twenty-first century. *Irish Mountain Log* would simultaneously urge good practice among hillwalkers and give very detailed information about 'mountain challenge walks'.

The Federation's interaction with other entities

Access

The story of FMCI/MCI's dealings with public bodies, farming organisations and individual landowners on questions of access and the upland environment is worthy of a separate study. This brief outline gives some idea of the scope of the various issues with which the Federation had to contend and of its more notable successes and failures. The national body or individual clubs became involved from time to time in questions of access, as happened when military in the Republic tried to block access to Camara Hill,[57] and the army north of the border attempted to limit access within the Water Commissioners' wall in the Mournes.[58] However, little was done until late in the century to have access to uplands legally established as of right or even to consult with farming bodies on alternative proposals. The Wicklow IFA representative said at an environmental conference in Tiglin in 1989 that this was the first time she had officially met with upland recreationists.[59] The inhibiting effect of reliance on government funds may have accounted for a certain lack of vigour in pro-active efforts to ensure access to the uplands. Besides, FMCI/MCI had to rely on voluntary officers who were engaged in their spare time in numerous 'firefighting' duties as access and environmental problems arose throughout the country, this in addition to their normal mountaineering activities. Thus the field was left open to other bodies. The Northern Ireland Sports Council had been the main body representing recreational interests in settling the Mourne access problem outlined above. A campaign to prevent the fencing of upland commonage in Mayo resulted in the formation of a new body, Keep Ireland Open (KIO) in 1995. KIO was more forceful, some said confrontational, in its dealings with farmers and their organisations.[60]

The campaign in Mayo was indicative of a rapid geographic shift of access problems from east to west. Cooperation between recreationists and hill-farmers in the Wicklow–Dublin area began to achieve mutually beneficial results – cooperation in which the MCI played its part – while along the western seaboard tensions grew in areas unused to such problems. A Wicklow Uplands Council was set up in 1997, and was galvanised in the following year by a far-sighted grant of £25,000 from the Heritage Council.[61] With representation of a wide range of farming, tourism, community and recreational interests it would have its successes in the first years of the new millennium. A somewhat similar organisation, The Mourne Heritage Trust, was set up in 1997.[62] As with environmental issues, it is difficult to measure the MCI's influence on decisions taken by either of these bodies. The passing of the Occupiers' Liability Act, 1995, which was supported by farming and recreational groups, was supposed to ease farmers' fears of litigation by those encroaching on their land but, contrarily, led to further restrictions on the part of many farmers, possibly because of a new awareness brought about by the use of the term 'liability'. This seemingly intractable problem of agreed access to the uplands and what the MCI could pro-actively do about it was still very much to the fore as the millennium ended.

Environmental encroachments

The Federation was involved in environmental issues from a very early stage of its existence but as other bodies, statutory and otherwise, were also involved, it is difficult to ascertain how effective its overall contribution was. These other bodies acted sometimes as adversaries, occasionally as collaborators. Successive MCI Environmental and Access Officers did a good job of keeping members abreast of the issues but they could hardly be expected to be present at county council meetings, planning appeals or other forums at which decisions affecting the uplands were made. Trust in the Republic was placed in bodies such as An Taisce and Bord Fáilte which had statutory standing. That such trust could some-times be misplaced was shown at a planning appeal hearing in 1988 against a hydroelectric scheme at Coomasaharn near Glenbeigh, County Kerry. A joint presentation by the FMCI and Bord Fáilte was almost scuppered at the very door of the hearing chambers when the Bord Fáilte representative revealed that the government had ordered that the Bord's objection be withdrawn. It says much for the commitment of the Federation's representatives, who came mainly from the Limerick Climbing Club, that they went ahead with their case against a powerful body such as the ESB and, with the help of various experts, succeeded in their appeal. Similar expertise was available to the MCI in the influential part it played in relation to the refusal in 1992 of planning permission for National Park interpretive centres at Luggala and Mullaghmore in counties Wicklow and Clare, respectively. It was also prominent in resisting Dun Laoghaire–Rathdown local authority's plans to place a travellers' halting site in Dalkey Quarry.

At the millennium's end, as the Celtic Tiger emerged from the stifling undergrowth of what had been a backward economy, and following the formation of a new, dynamic and well-funded Sports Council in 1997, the MCI was well set for expansion and professionally implemented approaches to the issues raised in this chapter.

12

Winter on the Eiger Nordwand

The summer of 1990 was, according to *Irish Mountain Log*, the best one yet for Irish alpinists.[1] Perhaps so, but there was little of the initiative, the venturing onto ground not previously trodden by Irish climbers which took place in the early 1980s and prior to that. The practice continued of most young Irish alpinists measuring their abilities against what they knew of the capabilities and accomplishments of their predecessors, and applying this knowledge to decide on their climbing itinerary. There were no important breakthroughs except, to a very significant extent, in winter climbing.

Of those older predecessors, Somers was again in the van and chose new ground. With Fenlon he was in the Massif des Écrins where they climbed the Coup de Sabre, the North Face of the Col Est de Pelvoux and a TD route on Les Bans, but they remembered best their ascent of the South Pillar of the Barre des Écrins. At the time, they felt this to be one of the best routes they had done despite its dangerous looseness and uncertain line. Somehow – and every mountaineer will relate to this – other factors lent a certain magic to the route which was beyond its intrinsic merits. The lack of the kind of development so jarring in more fashionable Alpine areas, with their railways and cable cars, imbued the climb with a traditional air. The pair (they were both of an imaginative bent) somehow created a fanciful history of the first ascent which was inspired by what may have happened in this area of French Resistance during the German occupation.[2] Climbers will be familiar with the aura which can encompass a climb because of its history: in this case that history was imagined! If Somers's recall is accurate, they also did the east face of Olan at about this time.[3] They moved to the Mont Blanc area where they climbed the left-hand Brouillard Pillar, a remote, difficult-to-reach bastion on that peak's southern flank, the quality of which is suggested by the identity of the first ascensionists, the great Bonatti and Andrea Oggioni. They went on to do, among other things, the Direct Start to the North-East Spur of Les Droites,[4] described by Lindsay Griffin as one of the greatest climbs in Europe.[5]

Irish Mountain Log, in its round-up of Alpine happenings, may have been referring to the number of high-quality routes done but it missed the point that most were old Irish favourites and that these engaged the attention of just a handful of climbers, most of whom were well-known old hands. Among the more notable ascents were those completed by Clare Sheridan who was the first Irishwoman to climb the Walker Spur, on which Robbie Fenlon was her partner, as she was also on the American Direct on the Dru with Andy McFarlane. Accompanied by Harry O'Brien, she also climbed the South Ridge of the Aiguille Noire de Peuterey, the first complete Irish ascent. Back in the Écrins, Dawson Stelfox and Willie Brown-Kerr were with a large party from Tollymore Centre who climbed many of the standard routes. Frank Nugent and Martin Daly were also there, as were the Reas who then went on to Chamonix where they did some of the usual if harder classics, as did Cooper, O'Brien and Calvin Torrans. Fenlon rounded off an exceptional season by effecting an ascent of the American Direct on the Dru with Torrans and, moving to the Bregaglia, by climbing the Cassin line on Piz Badile with Breeda Murphy. That route was also completed by Phil Holmes and Gary Murray. Torrans climbed the Walker Spur. A group from QUBMC was in Chamonix climbing the usual favourites.[6] A particularly poignant accident occurred in the stone-threatened couloir which is crossed on the way to the Goûter hut and Mont Blanc, when Ian Travers was killed by a rockfall. Ian, father of two young girls, was widely known for his mountain training work with the Scouting Association and his insistence on safe practices.[7]

In Zermatt, Moss, Emily Hackett and Vera Kelly, joined by Deirdre Ní Choileáin, had their habitual busy season including one of Gerry's trademark traverses: Nadelhorn, Stecknadelhorn, Hoberghorn and Dürrenhorn.[8] John Breen was also in the Saas-Fee/Zermatt area where, in 1989–90, he continued his ski moun-taineering traverses, taking in the summits of Allinhorn, Breithorn, Monte Rosa and Cimedi Jazzi, besides crossing the Alphubeljoch. He continued breaking trail throughout the 1990s in this aspect of mountaineering, until then largely ignored by the Irish (except for the Mastersons), repeating the Chamonix–Zermatt haute route, doing traverses in the Klosters area, in the Zillertal and Stubai areas of Austria, and in the Bernese Oberland where his traverses brought him to the summits of Grünhornlücke, Fiescherhorn, Wannenhorn and Scheuchzerhorn, almost all being in the 3,500–4,000m range.[9]

An expedition in 1991 to Manaslu in Nepal removed from the Alps most of the climbers operating habitually at an advanced level and written sources record very little activity. UCDMC had a meet based in La Bérarde in the Écrins.[10] Ian Dillon and American Rick Harlan managed the American Direct on the Dru.[11] Tim Neill on his first alpine trip hitch-hiked to Chamonix and with his partner climbed a number of the good rock routes popular with the better Irish climbers, and during bad weather had time to spend on sunny limestone crags.[12] An entertaining rescue effort, for spectators if not for the victim, occurred on the Petits Charmoz when Aidan Coughlan's knee became jammed in a crack he was leading. His climbing partners made strenuous efforts to release him but were forced to signal for a rescue helicopter which, when it saw Aidan's predicament, went to collect a doctor and some kind of lubricant. It then took the doctor and two rescuers to haul him free unharmed before he was evacuated to Chamonix.[13] Evacuation of a different kind was Shane Brogan's cause for concern as he tackled a nearby route on the Aiguille de l'M as part of an ENSA course. Plumbing problems of the inner man, rarely mentioned but not uncommon in mountaineers adjusting to altitude and change of diet, were exacerbated by the presence of instructor/guides and fellow participants. He led the crux of a pitch with a degree of urgency which was heightened by his condition and the knowledge that he was probably off route. Countless episodes of this nature occur in the mountains, sometimes with embarrassing conclusions, but rarely receive the humorous treatment afforded in Shane's account.[14]

In 1992 Moss was back in Zermatt with Bob Norton and Convery where, along with satisfying Gerry's fondness for traverses, they did the Weisshorn, a more worthwhile objective than the Matterhorn.[15] In Chamonix, Torrans and Cooper did the Albinoni Couloir on Mont Blanc de Tacul. Sheridan completed the Frontier Ridge on Mont Maudit in poor conditions.[16] Taking 1991 and 1992 together, Orla Prendergast and Breeda Murphy climbed some of the usual Chamonix TDs besides the Swiss Route on the Grand Capucin, the Contamine Route on Pointe Lachenal and La Marchand de Sabre on Tour Rouge.[17]

Even though the weather in Chamonix in 1993 was the worst for many years, Irish climbers managed to get a fair amount done. When the Petit Dru came into condition in early August Paul Harrington and Bill Murphy of UCDMC scaled the Bonatti Pillar, as did Joan Flanagan, Peter Owens and Alan Young, these three finishing in a snowstorm. Martin Daly and Willie Rock climbed the American Direct to the feature known as the 'jammed block', from which they abseiled down, an aspect of Alpine climbing which had gradually come into vogue and which recognised as valid the climbing of a route to the end of the major difficulties followed by a descent by abseil. Some of these routes even had regularly spaced, bolted abseil points.[18] On their way down the pair met Harrington and Murphy on their way to the top. The latter pair were delayed by thick snow on the upper reaches of Tacul's Gervasutti Pillar and had an uncomfortable bivouac near the summit. (Was it only the Irish who so frequently encountered problems with bivouacs and fraught retreats on Mont Blanc du

Tacul?) Paul Dunlop had a remarkable first Alpine season in 1993, further enhancing his home-grown reputation. Having traversed the Aiguille de Bionnassay to Mont Blanc, he completed the American Direct Route on the Petit Dru in just one day starting from the Grands Montets téléphérique station, and then went on to do the Central Pillar of Freney as well as other routes.[19] Cooper and Torrans made what was almost certainly the first Irish ascent of the Nant Blanc Face of the Aiguille Verte, one of the finest mixed routes in the Mont Blanc range. Sheridan then joined Cooper to do the Boccalatte Route which is just to the right of the Gervasutti Pillar on Mont Blanc du Tacul.[20]

Gerry Moss was in Saas-Fee and Arolla. With Bob Norton and Hugh Sharkey he climbed the Jägihorn, Weissmies, Lagginhorn, Pigne d'Arolla and did several other routes besides a traverse of Mont Blanc de Cheilon. Liam Convery was on the North Ridge of the Piz Badile and also did the Matterhorn by the Italian Ridge (a better choice than the Hörnli), and traversed the Meije.[21]

In 1994, Gerry Moss and friends showed lesser mortals how it is done by completing the traverse intégrale of Monte Rosa, Lyskamm, Castor, Pollux and Breithorn, a committed undertaking, especially on the long and sometimes quite difficult arête of the Lyskamm. His companions were Vera Kelly, Hugh Sharkey and Terry O'Neill who also accompanied him on several others of that season's outings.[22] Joss Lynam, now aged seventy, did the Spigolo Delago in the Dolomites with equally old stagers Mike Banks, Bill Hannon and Frank Winder. That pocket dynamo, Eddie Gaffney, was back in the fray, soloing the Grand Marmolata in Italy, Grossglockner in Austria and the Hörnli Ridge of the Matterhorn. Tony Farrell, Robert Dollard, Joan Moynihan and Carolyn Read were descending the South-East Ridge of the Oeschinenhorn in the Bernese Oberland when all four were caught in a fall in an area of loose rock. Shaken, they abseiled, but then ran out of abseil loops and felt they had to be rescued by helicopter, which they duly were. Margaret Pailing was one of a party which completed a traverse of Mont Pelvoux. Paul Keogh and Alan Chambers climbed the Cassin Route on Piz Badile, as did Joan Flanagan and Peter Owens.[23]

In Chamonix, there were heavy snows in the spring which remained on the mountains well into July, curtailing climbers' activities. Then temperatures shot up, clearing many routes, including the Walker Spur, of snow and ice and making even the approaches to some of the higher huts much trickier. Climbers' growing concerns about global warming and its effect on glaciation seemed justified. Most people opted for shorter day-long routes such as the Cordier Pillar on the Charmoz. There were six Irish climbers in one day on the Frontier Ridge. Donie O'Sullivan made the best of the shortened season, climbing the Freney's central pillar with Torrans and Rea, the Bonatti Pillar on the Dru with O'Brien and the Swiss Route on the Grand Capucin with Sheridan. Young climbers James O'Reilly and Ralph Hanse did the American Direct on the Petit Dru's west face.[24] Chris Martin and his climbing partner had an unfortunate first Alpine season, when a fall on the Cosmique Arête of Aiguille du Midi resulted in serious injuries and Chris's evacuation by helicopter.[25]

Gerry Moss and Vera Kelly climbed the Eiger's Mittellegi Ridge in the summer of 1995. The pair were part of an IMC group visiting the Bernese Oberland which also included Mike Scott, Sharkey, Convery and Hannon. Other routes included the Wetterhorn, Jungfrau, Kleines Schreckhorn and traverses of the Mönch, of Gross Grünhorn and of the Engelhörner.[26] An interesting and exposed traverse, that of the Grandes Jorasses, was completed by O'Brien, Torrans and Sheridan. Orla Prendergast and Breeda Murphy were on the Swiss Route on Grand Capucin. Peter Keane did the Dru's Bonatti Pillar with an American friend.[27] O'Brien went on to do Mont Dolent with his family and the Old Brenva Route with Torrans.[28] Traverses seemed to be *de rigueur* that year and a particularly notable one was in an area which is outside the normal scope of this history: Catherine Jordan, Penny Bartlett and Breda Farrell completed a 450km-long traverse of the Pyrenees in thirty days. Originating at St-Jean-Pied-de-Port, the traverse took them to Mont-Louis, an achievement only slightly diminished by their use of the word conquer in a mountaineering context.[29]

Fenlon and Stelfox were almost skyborne for three days, so airy was the traverse they completed – the combined wonderful ridges of the Aiguille Noire and the Aiguille Blanche de Peuteret soaring to the summit of Mont Blanc. A spell of fine weather broke just as they reached the summit. This was the kind of undertaking – challenging, committing, a line of the utmost beauty and remoteness – which ought to have inspired those young tigers dealing with the well trodden faces of the overrun Aiguilles. The route had perched there in its tantalising aloofness since the aborted attempt by Goulding and O'Leary twenty-nine years earlier. The choice of route is illustrative of the imaginative flair of Stelfox and Fenlon and its completion a confirmation of their mountaineering maturity. In Stelfox's case particularly, their success serves as an opportunity to look closely at a figure who had figured prominently in high-profile doings in high ranges in recent years (see next chapter) but whose success in those arenas was built on long experience in the Alps, and at home on Irish granite and Scottish ice.

Dawson Stelfox's career in the years leading up to Everest 1993 shows the kind of progression experienced by a leading mountaineer and, indeed, by the average mountaineer, albeit at a less exalted level.

Aiguille Noire and Aiguille Blanche de Peuteret. The traverse intégrale is one of the Alps' great courses. Starting at about one third the height of the picture's left edge, the ridge rises in dramatic bounds to the summit of Mont Blanc at the upper right edge. ROBBIE FENLON

Stelfox, while he was still under ten years of age, was taken into the hills by his grandfather who lived in Newcastle, County Down, where the boy spent his summer holidays.[30] Already committed to the hills when he first appears in this history at the age of eighteen as a rock climber (see chapter 6), he would gradually expand his horizons. He would learn some of the basic skills as a client at Tollymore Centre and would develop these as a voluntary instructor at the Centre and then as an occasional professional. As a student of architecture at Queen's University Belfast, he was on that 1977 trip to Iran's Alum Kuh and not long afterwards he was in Peru, then to the fateful climb on Bhagirathi when he was just twenty-three. He was already a highly skilled and experienced performer on rock, on ice, on mixed routes winter and summer, before he put his career as an architect partly on hold to become a professional guide with all the extra training and skills acquisition that entails.[31]

Mountaineering was, and is, at heart an activity which at its best is undertaken for its own sake and without a desire for public acknowledgement or gain. A climber might wish for the approbation of his or her peers, but the real pleasure lies in the act, the ambience, not always the attainment although the top must ever be striven for. Yes, ego enters, but almost all climbers would climb even if their successes were known only to a few (as indeed was the case on the Peuterey ridge). It is not necessary to explain this to mountaineers and it is very difficult to elucidate to those who do not climb. The kind of hardiness, of honed reflexes and judgement that comes from a long build-up is acquired well away from the limelight by expert and journeyman alike. Stelfox's other qualities, those that made him such a successful leader and exemplar, were possibly innate, but may also have sprung from the confidence acquired through overcoming mountaineering adversities. Too many events will intrude on the Himalayan narrative in the next chapter to do sufficient justice to Stelfox's mountaineering journey towards that particular sphere. Consequently, it is best to impress here on the reader that his journey was a long one which will be contrasted with a new type of mountaineer who had already begun to appear on the Himalayan and world scene.

It needs to be reiterated that record keeping was extremely poor, with neither the *Mountain Log* nor the *IMC newsletter* having a regular section devoted to doings in the Alps and higher ranges, although occasional informed contributions by Sheridan or Harrington were valuable. The short-lived *Rock Climber* extensively covered the Irish rock-climbing scene for a few years in the 1990s. No journal of record existed comparable to the IMC journals of the 1950s and 1960s. While most of the important events did find their way into print, there were now so many Irish climbers engaged in activities throughout the world that it would have been impossible to keep track of them all; neither can this history.

Long-time IMC members Mike Scott and Des Doyle, with Helen Condon and Seamus Fitzpatrick, were in the Bregaglia in 1996 where they climbed Piz Cambrena by its north ridge and Piz Morteratsch by the Biancograt besides traversing Piz Palu. Moving across to Italy in search of better weather they did the north ridge of Monte Disgrazia. Bad weather hit much of Europe that summer causing huge floods in Chamonix and dismay in campsites. Before the floods, Phil Holmes and John Armstrong did the Swiss Route on the Courtes and Mont Maudit's Cretier Route. A Belfast climber at college in London, Dave Hollinger, climbed the Central Freney Pillar, Route Major and the Bonatti Pillar. That Bonatti Route was also climbed by Sheridan with Malcolm Wakefield, son of Brian who had been Goulding's partner on many 1960s climbs.[32] Also on the Pillar were O'Brien and Donie O'Sullivan.[33] Gerry Moss was back in Grindelwald, from which, with Peter Britton, he did the Mönch, Gross Fiescherhorn, Finsteraarhorn, Schreckhorn and Aletschorn, several of these, needless to say, as traverses.[34] Some UCDMC members were in Zinal and Chamonix. Orla Prendergast and Avril Tormey were in the Écrins, the highlight of their stay being a traverse of the Meije.[35]

Eddie Gaffney, that live-wire activist of the 1960s and 1970s, record breaker on Hart's and Lug walks, route pioneer in Glendalough and Donegal, and old friend, fell to his death while descending solo from Monte Disgrazia at the age of fifty-three.[36]

Eddie Gaffney *(left)* and Gareth Jones in 1993. GARETH JONES

EIGER NORDWAND IN WINTER

Without fanfare, two experienced climbers approached the North Face of the Eiger in early March 1997, still well within what is considered to be the Alpine winter season. The pair, from their Dublin base, had carefully watched weather predictions and, with the help of a contact in Zurich, decided that conditions would be suitable for at least a few days. They flew out and made their way to Kleine Scheidegg. The reader will have followed one of that pair, Paul Harrington, in these pages, as he progressed to hard Alpine routes. That progress can be further seen in the next chapter as he tackles hard Andean climbs, a 7,000m Indian giant, and faces the hardships of Alaska. He was well prepared for the hardest climb of his life, as was Martin Daly, a seasoned mountaineer.

The climb was not only their hardest, it was one of the finest achievements of Irish mountaineering, not directly comparable to the successful Everest climb but technically far harder and in different ways as committing as Stelfox's lone day on that mountain's summit ridge. Naturally apprehensive at the start of this most notorious of Alpine walls, they eased into remembered rhythm on the less difficult lower parts of the face, allowing bodies and minds to adjust following a lengthy absence from hard winter routes. Bivouac ledges were tricky to find under snow layers so they hacked out their first night's resting place in a small snowfield beneath the pivotal and historic Hinterstoisser Traverse. Next day the climbing became progressively harder as they passed or dealt with landmarks which feature in every Eiger Nordwand story since it was first climbed in 1938; the Swallow's Nest, the First and Second Icefields, the Flat Iron and Death Bivouac where they spent the second night.[37]

> We felt warm in the evening sun and those minutes before the sun set were some of the most peaceful I'd ever experienced on a mountain. This was some bonus! The human animal was happy! Nobody had ever told us about winter sun on the North Face of the Eiger.[38]

On the third day, as they dealt with The Ramp and the approaches to the Traverse of the Gods, they encountered climbing more difficult than they had expected – Scottish grade VI, 6, they agreed. 'Complete absorption,' thought Harrington. 'This is mountaineering in its most artistic form.' A third night was spent on another hacked-out ledge which was large enough for them to lie down. Tired, muscles aching, they pondered on what lay ahead, especially the Exit Cracks which were reputed to have the face's most difficult climbing.

Paul Harrington at dawn on the Hinterstoisser Traverse, Eiger North Face, March 1997. MARTIN DALY

Martin Daly belaying at Brittle Crack, Eiger North Face, March 1997. Note rope management. PAUL HARRINGTON

My darkest moments on the climb probably occurred that night ... We just had the most difficult climbing of our lives. We had to dig deep into ourselves to get where we were ... We were wondering how much harder we could actually climb.

The Traverse of the Gods and The Spider were dealt with efficiently and they tackled the Exit Cracks. Harrington led the first pitch and Daly led through. Harrington's turn again:

It was a narrow 70° ice filled groove. I started working my way methodically up it, planting my ice hammer towards its left side and my ice axe to its right. The ice was generally good but never thicker than a few centimetres. The rock on either side of the ice runnel was compact and featureless. There wasn't a single piece of in situ gear to be found. It soon became apparent that the groove would have to be climbed without protection. I wasn't particularly worried as I was making good progress. As on the third pitch of the ramp, I became completely absorbed on the moves in hand. Nothing else in the world mattered. About 15 metres up from the belay the ice disappeared in the right hand side of the groove. With my axe I struck the ice on the left about a foot or so above my hammer. Above this the ice was too thin on the left but better on the right. With my hammer in my left arm, I had to swing diagonally across my right to get a placement. I swung and the ice shattered. At this stage of the climb the pick was blunted and with the awkward angle I couldn't grip the shaft as firmly as normal. I aimed again a little higher and saw the ice fall away. There was no good ice left within arm's reach. The walls on either side of the groove were bare. Featureless. I envisaged desperate moves. Above protection, as on the ramp or access to the Gods, this is reasonable. Fifteen metres out from the belay, with nothing in between, it's not. I looked down and saw little hope of successfully reversing the moves. Besides, there was no point. There was no other way out. I knew I couldn't risk moving up with only a couple of pick teeth biting in poor ice. I placed my hammer firmly, a few centimetres below my axe. I mantleshelfed up on both tools, keeping the body as close to the ice as possible. I removed the axe and reached high above the hammer. The body was alive! My arteries and veins felt like the walls of a gorge trying to restrain a raging torrent. Adrenalin was surging through me. I picked my spot, held the axe firmly and struck carefully. I heard a deep thud. The placement was solid. I was back on course. The spirit was on fire. It burned strongly. It burned brightly. It danced beautifully. It danced like never before. We had almost cracked the route. The Exit doors were opening.[39]

Summit Ridge on the Eiger where Harrington and Daly bivouacked.
PAUL HARRINGTON

They had just one more hard pitch to do before reaching the slopes leading to the sharp summit ridge, on the side of which they dug out a ledge where they slept rather than risk a descent in their tired state. That descent to the Eigergletscher station was tricky so it was not until they sat in the restaurant that jubilant tears were shed. Their feat went virtually unremarked at home but mountaineers recognised its significance.

Chamonix was hit with bad weather again in the summer of 1997, resulting in unstable snow conditions. There were more Irish climbers than usual in the area, as was the case in several other

venues with a number of clubs being represented including the
Comeragh MC, Club Cualann, UCDMC, and IMC. Vera Kelly,
Gerry Moss and fellow IMC members Hugh Sharkey and Terry
O'Neill had their usual busy season. Torrans did Bonatti's route on
the Grand Capucin with Malcolm Wakefield while Joan Flanagan
and Willie Rock were particularly active on good-quality routes.
Young climbers James Gernon and Joe Purser had a good first season,
sticking mainly to rock routes but also climbing the north face of
the Col du Plan. Other Dublin climbers swarmed all over the rock
routes behind the Envers Hut.[40] Most of these are of the sort
already mentioned which are not necessarily followed to a summit.
William Rattray from Cork died from a fall on Mont Maudit.[41]

Winter ascents

Winter ascents in the Alps had slowly become more popular during
the early part of the 1990s, satisfying a need for those who sought
something more challenging than, or different from, summer
routes. Continued improvements in gear, techniques honed at
icefall venues (*cascades de glace*) in Alpine valleys, or on less reliable
and riskier Scottish ice, enabled even climbers from an island
dominated by Atlantic depressions to test their mettle on ice-
bound alpine faces and couloirs. Munster led the way. Kerryman
Ivan Counihan soloed the Swiss Route on the North Face of Les
Courtes on 15 January 1991, taking eight hours from hut to top,
and followed up by climbing the Frendo Spur with Marcus Brown
in February 1992. Then, on 10 March 1994, he climbed a route
on the North Face of Les Droites with his Dutch friend Melvin
Redeker, taking three days in severe conditions.[42] These were the
first reported Irish winter ascents of all three routes.

In March 1998 Eddie Cooper and Malcolm McNaught
climbed the North Face of Les Droites. They shared a bivouac with
a French pair who fell to their deaths the next day. John Hawkins,
a talented Cork engineer who lived in Mannheim in Germany, was
very active in this year, beginning in March by making an ascent
– following two failed efforts – of the 700m Swiss Route on the
Courtes in 7 hours. Alan Sarhan and James Gernon repeated the

Counihan tackling difficulties on Les Droites. MARTIN REDEKER

route shortly afterwards.[43] Hawkins also did the Albinoni-Gabarrou and Gabarrou-Marquis Routes on Mont Blanc de Tacul.

The most notable winter ascent, indeed the most remarkable Irish Alpine ascent of 1998, was the climbing of the North Face of the Matterhorn in March by Peter Owens and James O'Reilly. Somewhat riskily, this was their first Alpine winter trip and their first on a big mixed face. But their enterprise paid off. Following an initial ice slope, they encountered the usual downward sloping strata which exists on the north side of the Matterhorn in addition to poor protection and loose rock, unbound because of the abnormal sparsity of snow and ice. There was enough ice, however, to obscure possible belay ledges so they had to keep moving until 9 p.m. to find one, having been on the move since 4 a.m. The weather deteriorated as they climbed higher on the face next day, tackling some hard, poorly protected pitches and difficult route finding before following a gully which a Czech pair had also used to get off the storm-lashed face. Once on the ridge they were some 150m from the summit. Given the conditions they decided to descend to the Solvay bivouac hut where they spent the night. A long series of abseils next day got them to the Hörnli hut as darkness fell.[44] Fenlon and Chris Staunton had attempted the face in January but were forced to retreat in biting cold.[45]

There was a sizeable Irish contingent in Chamonix in the late summer with Joe Purser, Daragh Flanagan, James Mehigan and

Willie Rock showing their paces on some of the harder rock routes favoured by the Irish. Purser and James Gernon also did 'O Solo Mio' on Grand Capucin, a fine route in the modern idiom with pitches of E4.

John Hawkins continued making imaginative weekend raids from his Mannheim base and as early as mid-May was in Zermatt where, with Scot Bruce Normand, he made fast ascents of the North-East Face of Lyskamm and the Cresta Rey on Monte Rosa.

John Hawkins, who had remarkable Alpine success from his Mannheim base, with North-East Face of Lyskamm behind him. BRUCE NORMAND

In mid-July, again with Bruce and during an extended holiday, he made what was thought to be the first complete Irish ascent of the North-East Spur Direct of the Droites; but note the earlier claim of Somers and Fenlon. The two-day route provided hard mixed climbing on the upper half, entailing much dry tooling, and relying on ice smears and breakfast-bowl-sized lumps of snow frozen to the rock in which to plant crampons and tentatively placed tips of their ice axes. A following Chamonix guide was glad to avail of a tied-off rope to tackle a hard pitch which had been led by Bruce. There had been several unsuccessful Irish attempts on the route, including one by Hawkins himself, and it was climbed again by Willie Rock and a Welshman some weeks after this first success. At about this time, Hawkins and Normand were also in the Bregaglia where they did the Biancograt and the West Face of Piz Bernina. Vera Quinlan joined Hawkins for ascents of the North-West Face of Piz Palu and the long North Ridge of the Badile. An attempt on Badile's Cassin Route by Hawkins and Dara Owens was aborted in bad weather. Later, in August, Hawkins and Normand made a rapid one-day ascent of the Central Pillars of Freney. Leaving the remote Eccles Hut at 3.30 a.m. they bivouacked near the summit of Mont Blanc de Courmayeur at 9 p.m., a tour de force which held out much promise for Hawkins' future Alpine career.[46]

Sadly for Irish mountaineering and tragically for their families, John Hawkins and Englishman Andy Picken were killed in October of that year (1998) while climbing the Frendo Spur.

The first MCI Alpine Meet was held at Ailefroide in the Écrins in July 1998. It was a resounding success with eighty members attending. Many routes were done, sometimes by several parties simultaneously with the best route being the South Pillar on the Barre des Écrins which was done by Purser and Gannon. Their reaction to the quality of the climb could hardly have been more different from that of Fenlon and Somers eight years previously and is amusingly (and wistfully?) described by Somers in 'South Pillar'.[47]

That year was an exceptionally active year for Irish mountaineers in the Alps and further afield, and a gratifying one from the historian's point of view because of the detailed information compiled by Paul Harrington in *Irish Mountain Log*. It can be assumed, as Harrington himself did, that alongside the more high profile or well-chronicled happenings there was an amount of Alpine activity on the part of the members from various clubs. The same thing can be said of the millennium's last year, 1999, when very little Alpine activity was recorded apart from the second MCI meet in Arolla. Large numbers attended and many good mountain routes were done, the best of these being a traverse of Dent Blanche by Frank Nugent and Kevin Yallop. Some of the participants met Kevin Byrne and Sean Barrett of the IMC who were having a busy fortnight in Zermatt.[48]

Irish alpinists in that last decade of the millennium had demonstrated their abilities as more climbers than ever before tackled hard routes, although many of these had many previous Irish ascents. Winter routes, in particular, elicited examples of flair, daring, technical ability and resolve. Irish mountaineers had come a long way. The Alps, despite excessive development, remained as perhaps the greatest of mountain playgrounds, combining accessibility, variety, beauty, history, facilities and inspiring traditions. However, the focus of initiatives in world mountaineering had moved elsewhere. It remained to be seen if the Irish would respond to that challenge.

13

Ama Dablam, Manaslu, Everest

THE AMERICAS

In 1990, prompted by Kevin Higgins' interest in the history of Irish-connected nineteenth-century mountaineers, a six-person team from Kilkenny's Tyndall Mountain Club (Higgins, Don Roberts, Ned and Nuala Mahon, Gerry Herlihy and Martin O'Reilly) were in British Columbia where they climbed in the Purcell Range, one corner of which contains the Bugaboos. The range was named by the Palliser exploratory and scientific expedition of the late 1850s led by Dublin-born John Palliser. Its eponym was a Professor Purcell at Queen's University Cork. Higgins' team climbed Mount Leitrim (3,520m) and Mount Carmarthen (3,040m). A fall occurred on descent from the latter peak which entailed a long haul down the mountain with one injured climber, a lengthy trek by another from their remote camp to alert rescue teams and a helicopter rescue from the accident site of a more seriously injured team member.[1]

Paul Harrington moved from Ecuador, where he climbed a 5,000m peak called Tungurakua with Declan Doyle, to Peru's Cordillera Blanca where they climbed Alpamayo (5,947m), one of

South America's most beautiful mountains. Paul then teamed up with a Spanish climber to do the second ascent of a line on the West Face of Cayesh (5,721m). This mixed route, which had rock pitches of UIAA grade VI and ice run-outs of Scottish grade IV, took two days and stopped just 15m short of the summit when they were confronted with that sort of impossibly steep, sugary snow so typical of ridge tops in the Peruvian Andes. They descended in darkness.[2]

In Yosemite that year, Ian Rea and John McDonald did Half Dome and the East Buttress of El Capitan while Paddy Mallon and Martin McNiff climbed a route on Middle Cathedral and Snake Dyke on Half Dome.[3]

HIMALAYA AND THE ARCTIC

Orla and Maurice Prendergast, with Tomas Aylward and Damien Cashin, were in Pakistan's Naltar valley where the first-named three climbed the south summit of Sentinel (5,260m) and an unnamed peak. Such lightweight trips had become possible and fairly popular with the opening of a road from Rawalpindi to Gilgit as part of the Karakoram Highway, this road replacing the risky flight made necessary in the 1960s when partition from India had made the previous approach from Srinigar impossible.[4]

In the Arctic, Paddy Barry, the well-known sailor with Tilman-esque aspirations, recruited Dave Walsh and Dónal Ó Murchú for a trip to Spitzbergen where they climbed several peaks including a virgin peak of something more than 700m.[5]

In 1991, in India's Garhwal, Paddy O'Leary and Joss Lynam were on a second Anglo-Irish attempt on Jaonli's South Ridge (6,632m), having failed on avalanche-prone slopes in 1989. O'Leary and Jim Milledge, going well, turned back at about 6,400m to avoid an impromptu bivouac in bitter mid-October cold. Before they could launch a second attempt a severe earthquake hit the region and opened up a crevasse on the ridge which they could not pass because of the instability of newly thrown-up huge and teetering ice blocks. The elderly team included a 1953 Everest

Paddy Barry's *St Patrick* at anchor in Magdalena Fjord, Spitzbergen. The encounter with kayaks in the foreground led Dave Walsh to an adventurous career in sea-kayaking. DAVE WALSH

Donal Ó Murchú *(left)* and Dave Walsh ashore on Spitzbergen. DAVE WALSH COLLECTION

veteran; a medical man from the famous Silver Hut scientific-mountaineering expedition of 1960–61; a noted polar explorer; and our co-leader, ex-marine Mike Banks, who was a first ascensionist of Rakaposhi, and had also been an aide-de-camp to the governor of Hong Kong, a member of Mountbatten's staff, a

Liberal candidate in a general election, the recipient of an MBE for his crossing of the Greenland ice cap, and an author and broadcaster.[6] The piquancy of conversation at Base Camp and on the approach march can be guessed at.

Aftermath of 1991 earthquake in Gangi village. AUTHOR'S COLLECTION

All these ventures of the early 1990s pale in contrast with two big endeavours in 1991, the results of which would profoundly affect the history of Irish climbing in the decade. Attempts at Manaslu and Ama Dablam had quite different outcomes.

AMA DABLAM

The effort on Ama Dablam (6,856m), led by Con Moriarty, was carried out by climbers from Kerry, Cork and Dublin. The peak, one of the world's most beautiful, was first climbed in 1961 by climbers engaged on the groundbreaking Silver Hut expedition and since then had had quite a number of ascents by various routes, but had experienced its second British ascent only in 1990.[7] Fixed ropes and numerous guided parties have since demeaned the South-West Ridge but when the Irishmen climbed it there was still

Ama Dablam, the highest Himalayan peak climbed (in 1991) by an Irish team until Everest in 1993.

much free climbing, a few pitches being of VS/HVS standard with ice at about Scottish III grade or harder. The peak was meant to be done in alpine style (how often would we hear of such intentions on other big peaks?), but the two Kerrymen who were destined for the summit, Moriarty and Mike Shea, were laid low at Camp I by an out-of-date tin of Indian fruit which resulted in an escape to base – and hospitalisation in Pheriche for Shea. Weather caused several retreats to lower camps.

Tony Farrell, a Dublin man, and Corkonian Pat Falvey found that they had to fix ropes on the loose pitches above Camp II where they were joined by Mick Murphy who was a carpenter and sometime teacher, and Ciaran Corrigan. The former pair descended to rest for a day or two while the others advanced along the heavily corniced Mushroom Ridge to a planned bivouac somewhere near the normal site of Camp III. Corrigan had serious difficulty with his chest which transpired to be pulmonary oedema. Murphy, lightly laden, went for the summit, leaving Corrigan to his own devices (by mutual agreement according to Falvey).[8] Having descended part of the way, Corrigan was evacuated to base by an American team and from thence to hospital. Murphy's single-mindedness and toughness got him to the top, the only successful ascent of the peak in that season and the highest Himalayan summit yet reached by a member of an Irish team. He was overtaken by nightfall on descent and endured a long night without bivouac gear in a bergschrund at about 6,500m, suffering a badly frostbitten foot. He somehow managed to get back along the ridge and to Base Camp into which he hobbled two days after he had topped out. Following treatment by the doctor of the American team he was evacuated to hospital. Moriarty and the remaining fit members made another attempt but were forced to retreat in poor weather, with Moriarty suffering a debilitating spinal injury on descent.[9]

There was a natural temptation to make too much of the Ama Dablam success, losing sight of the fact that the peak was surrounded by greater giants, including four of the world's highest, all of which had been climbed many times. But the success must be seen in an Irish context. There was a reluctance in some urban climbing circles to fully acknowledge either Moriarty's imaginative leap in getting the venture under way, or the significance of the ascent for climbers outside the major cities, and indeed for Irish mountaineering. Frank Nugent generously recognised the Munster men's feat, saying that it 'must surely rank as the best Irish climb in the Himalaya to date'.[10] Given the mountain's steepness, its height, a very exposed ridge, the fact that few peaks of that height, and none in the Himalaya, had yet been climbed by Irish-based mountaineers, the team's success was noteworthy. The Irish success led to Mike Murphy being recruited to the team which would climb Everest two years later, to Corrigan's lifelong respiratory problems as well as Moriarty's spinal injury and the consequent curtailment of that pair's promising climbing careers. This trip was also the beginning of Pat Falvey's game-changing high-altitude career.

MANASLU

Manaslu is the seventh highest peak in the world at 8,156m. It was first climbed by a Japanese team in 1956 and was climbed fairly frequently before an Irish team arrived at Base Camp in 1991. Since then it has been advertised by several commercial climbing companies as being the ideal training peak for Everest, and that is how it was regarded by the team led jointly by Nugent and Stelfox. In order to end up with the strongest possible team for an eventual attempt at Everest, and to make that undertaking a North/South affair, the Manaslu team, besides the joint leaders, consisted of Phil Holmes, Calvin Torrans, Harry O'Brien, Robbie Fenlon, Mick Murphy, Mike Barry, Gary Murray, Martin Daly, Dermot Somers and Donie O'Sullivan who was a doctor as well as a climber. That particular mix was not conducive to harmony. None of the women approached felt that they could commit.[11]

Manaslu is not technically very hard, although it has a few tricky bits, and its main virtue, from the Irish point of view, lay in its height and the opportunity to learn, as a team, how to organise, carry loads, survive and work as a team at high altitudes. The peak is subject to devastating avalanches, even on the easiest route, and would provide the younger members of the team with the experience of operating in these conditions. There were tensions and differences of opinion, especially between those who sought something akin to an alpine-style ascent, a term whose ambiguity allows for all sorts of gradations, and those who felt that limited compromises were necessary in order to ensure an Irish eight-thousander success on the run-up to Everest. Other factors contributed to the ensuing estrangements which are not strictly pertinent here. What is relevant, if various reports are correct, is that nearing the end of the failed attempt some of the climbers asserted that the further progress was now impossible given the conditions they had battled with from the outset, and they retired to base.

A group of five – Stelfox, Somers, Fenlon, Nugent and Barry – having yet again dug themselves and their tents out of deep, freshly fallen snow, floundered ahead in an effort to establish Camp III. They ground to a sad stop at 6,100m where the steepening slope made the deep snow unstable.[12] That shared experience by the five, driven by a common outlook, further widened the rift which already existed between the two factions which formed around Stelfox and Torrans. According to some, the rift was further widened by newspaper articles and statements to the press which seemed to

Manaslu, 1991. Conditions were difficult and dangerous. DAWSON STELFOX

blame those who had retired to base for the failure to establish Camp III.[13] It also determined the future mountaineering careers of most of those involved in the expedition. None of the individuals on either side would take part, before the century ended, in similar projects with anyone from the other camp.

Other Achievements 1992–93

There is an article in *Irish Mountain Log* of summer 1992 which describes a group outing to Kilimanjaro,[14] the forerunner of mass ascents over the years by people who probably would not consider themselves to be mountaineers. These ascents were all indicative of a change in the way Irish people regarded mountaineering, a change of which professional expedition organisers took full advantage. In contrast that same summer, what was described as eighteen superannuated members and ex-members of the IMC spent almost three weeks in Wyoming's Tetons. Nine unguided ascents and one guided effort were made on peaks varying from easy scrambles to a climb to the summit of Grand Teton (4,197m) by the Upper Exum Ridge. The Exum was done by sexagenarians Frank Winder and Bill Hannon while fellow oldies Noel Brown,

Lynam, Noel Masterson and Sean Rothery were also particularly busy.[15] In Nepal, Gary Motyer and Ciaran Clissman separately led groups up popular trekking peaks.[16]

Ian Rea and Gary Murray, with Britishers Andy Cunningham and Richard Mansfield, having been prevented by heavy snow from a try at their other objectives, made a first ascent of Manda III (6,529m), in Garhwal in a six-day alpine-style push.[17] This was the third or fourth time that Irishmen had made a first ascent of a Himalayan 6,000m peak. In the Andes, Mike Shea summited on Aconcagua in February despite being held up by bad weather.[18]

In 1993, Irish doings in distant places were in danger of being overlooked because of important happenings on Everest and because, by now, trips afar had become fairly common. Joe Lyons climbed the Polish Route on Aconcagua in Argentina. Pat Lynch and friends were on Mont Elbruz (5,462m), Europe's highest peak, and Mont Gumachi (3,805m) with a commercial group.[19] Shane Brogan did the Nose on El Capitan with an American friend. Orla Prendergast and Breeda Murphy were also in Yosemite where they did several classic rock routes, including the Central Pillar of Frenzy on Cathedral,[20] which taken together with those climbs done in the Alps by Sheridan and Flanagan made 1993 a good one for Irishwomen.

O'Leary was in Garhwal, India, helping students of the Mountaineering Institute at Uttarkashi to the top of Draupadi Ka Danda (5,700m), before leaving to do solo crossings of high passes and explore routes into unclimbed mountains which had not been seen by outsiders since the Indo-Chinese war of 1962.

In Greenland, Lynam and Banks were on yet another *Saga*-sponsored trip, this time to Sermersoq island near Cape Farewell. With Bill Hannon and a Briton, Roger Birnsting, they climbed a total of twelve peaks, seven of which were first ascents.[21]

EVEREST

There is a traverse just below the crest of the North Ridge high above the last camp on Mount Everest where 'easy ground becomes serious'[22] as the climber finds himself 'teetering on the roof tiles of

Gramang Bal in Kinnaur, one of several peaks there and in Spiti reconnoitred by O'Leary in 1993–94 and later climbed or attempted by Irish teams. AUTHOR'S COLLECTION

the planet'.[23] Here, above a ghastly 3,000m drop to the Rongbuk Glacier, the stratification of the rock slopes outwards at an angle which, taken with care, is just about feasible. Covered with loosely adhering snow it demands concentration and steadiness. Encumbered by bulky boots, crampons of doubtful help, vision usually impaired by goggles and oxygen masks, those who have gained this point since it was first reached in 1922 have been aware that a slip here would be disastrous as, indeed, it seems to have been for that 'golden boy' Mallory and his partner Sandy Irvine. Roping-up here is a psychological crutch, a friendly bond rather than a safety line, as even the most experienced would find it very difficult to arrest a fall. At about midday on 27 May 1993, Frank Nugent – stalwart on Zhangzi, determined on Manaslu, a driving force throughout – stopped here at about 8,680m, his rapid breathing under physical and nervous strain having severely depleted his oxygen supply. It was easy to calculate that he and his climbing partner Dawson Stelfox would not make it to the summit and back to their last camp before running out of oxygen; in Frank's case much earlier than that.[24] Frank decided to turn back, a decision which was probably influenced by several factors: a desire not to hinder

Dawson whose technical expertise was superior; a sensible caution; the simple fact of his having a bad day; thoughts of his family. It was a decision which must have been galling in retrospect, bearing in mind that it was doubtful that an Irish effort would have been made on Everest at that time were it not for his initiative and drive over a period of six years or more.

Stelfox's lonely climb to the summit is well chronicled, described in several books and numerous articles. There have been about a dozen Irish ascents between then and now from this north side. But, if there is one underlying theme in this history, and in a particular approach to mountaineering, it is that the psychological barriers confronting the first person to overcome a mountaineering problem are at least as important as the physical ones, and make the total effort considerably more difficult and worthy. Stelfox was not the first person to reach the earth's highest point from its north side but, being the first Irish or British person to do so, he had almost no yardstick by which to measure his capabilities other than his own long build-up of experience. That experience, that resultant faith in himself was shown to near-perfection on his descent in gathering darkness, without oxygen, with faculties blunted. He had difficulty finding the top of the rickety ladder on the notorious Second Step and somehow coped with those 'steeply sloping, evilly smooth slabs'[25] as he approached the final section where the narrow North-East Ridge merges into the ill-defined slopes of the North Ridge leading down in darkness to the highest tents and safety. Radio communication with his friends below were of incalculable value.

Next morning the two youngest members of the team, Burke and Fenlon, leaving Nugent and Stelfox to rest at Camp III – insofar as rest is possible at 8,200m – made their attempt on the summit and were making good progress. They halted at the first step when it became apparent that Burke had but one hour's oxygen left and that the narrow weather window was closing, that window which usually appears for two or three days near the end of May and upon which climbers of Everest depend so much. Fenlon, who was going well and seemed eminently capable of

Everest team (1993) departing from Dublin Airport. Somers and Stelfox were already in Nepal. JOHN BOURKE

reaching the top, weighed his chances against these factors and decided he did not wish to proceed alone on a mission already accomplished.[26] They turned and, as he later wrote, 'backs to history we descended into footnotes'.[27]

The team's achievement was remarkable and done in good style. They had opted for oxygen at and above the highest two camps and that was sensible given that none of the team had previously been above 8,000m. The first ascent of this route without supplementary oxygen had been made only three years before, and the length of time to be spent on the long, high, final ridge to the summit would be considerable. Altogether the effort was an admirable one by the team and its backup staff and friends: admirable in the readiness to dispense with a strong Sherpa team in favour of just two of that tribe, one of whom happened to be the camp cook. It was praiseworthy in that members hauled most loads themselves, even carrying loads for a Chinese team which had its own Tibetan porters, in return for being allowed to use that team's fixed ropes up to the beginning of the North Ridge at the North Col. It was exemplary given the loyal group decision that co-leaders

Stelfox and Nugent should be supported as the summit team when there were others technically able and acclimatised. And then there was the conscious decision by Mick Murphy (and a similar one earlier by Mike Barry) to miss out on his own summit attempt so that Fenlon and Burke would have sufficient oxygen. Richard Dean (now O'Neill Dean since meeting Frida on a Tiglin course) had made a heroic effort without oxygen on the team's first carry to near the 8,000m mark, and had exhausted his resources in doing so. Somers, who had also carried high, was laid low with a suspected blood clot. This group effort was done in good spirit and it was patently obvious that this was a compatible team. Their individual contributions and self-sacrifices are well described in Lorna Siggins' two books.[28] But their success was an inspirational boost to Irish mountaineering and, now that this arduous and painful challenge had been met, climbers could get on with the exploration of the infinite possibilities offered by unclimbed routes and peaks in the Himalaya and other high ranges. Or so it seemed at the time.

There was already an increase in activity in higher ranges as evidenced in the previous three years. Later that summer of 1993 an attempt was made on Masherbrum II in Pakistan's Karakoram Himalaya. The team, led by Mike Keyes, paid the appropriate peak fee for what they thought was a 7,000m peak which had first been climbed by Italians in 1988. However, their observations led them to believe that it was considerably lower than the Italians had estimated, being somewhere in the 6,600m range. Members Shay Nolan, Dermot Fleming, Noel Clarke and Kevin Yallup established Camp I on a col at 4,900m and set about establishing Camp II on a plateau at the top of a steep slope. Bad weather prevented this and they were forced to retreat from the mountain.[29]

A little earlier, at about the time the Everest team were making their way home, an Anglo-Irish group showed considerable initiative in choosing as its objective unclimbed Koz Sar some 250km west of Masherbrum II. The peak is variously given as being 6,677m or 6,492m in height and is very near Kampire Dior, the original objective of our expedition in 1964, but which, although we were never told this, was in a prohibited area from

1951 until 1991. The group led by Andy Creagh, with P. Williams, Declan McMahon, S. Richardson and I. Wolton reached 5,800m, fixing ropes along the way, before retreating because their climbing permit had run out.[30]

Later that year, Corkman Pat Falvey joined a commercially run post-monsoon attempt on Everest via the same route used by the previous Irish team. He reached Camp II before retreating because of the threat of avalanche. Then, when he was set to leave the North Col on a further attempt to reach the summit, he found himself replaced by the team leader and company representative who eventually reached the top.[31]

In Alaska in June 1994 Mick Murphy, Con Collins, Pat Falvey and Finbar Desmond reached the summit of Denali (Mount McKinley) via the West Buttress. They suffered, as almost everyone does, on this, the tallest mountain in North America. The rest of the ten-person team led by Murphy felt unable to climb higher in the rough conditions. This was the first top to be reached by Falvey in his effort to complete ascents of the Seven Summits, the highest mountains on each continent. At about the same time, and thousands of kilometres to the south, Kieran O'Hara and friends completed an ascent of Ancohuma (6,427m) in Bolivia.[32]

In the Garhwal Himal, a group with some UCDMC connections and organised by Ciaran Clissman was on a post-monsoon effort on Satopanth (7,075m), a peak first climbed in 1947 and which had a number of subsequent ascents. Clissman had astutely sought out a mountain of some substance which was objectively safe and technically interesting without being too difficult for a group of young climbers, most of whom were fairly inexperienced. Three members decamped to Delhi because of chest infections while the others, starting from Base Camp at 4,850m began the task of establishing camps at 5,400m, 5,800m and 6,400m. The route was rather more difficult than expected, but not overly so, and involved a heavily crevassed serac barrier and a 40–60 degree ice slope below the second camp. Within seven days of reaching Base Camp, Clissman and Alan Conway tried for the summit from Camp III but turned back about 100m short of their goal. This was because of avalanche risk and a route-finding error, they said, but it also seems probable that they had not allowed time for acclimatisation and were thus unable to try a safer variant to their line. Paul Harrington who tried on his own the next day, taking the variant recommended by the others, reached the summit in three hours and descended to Camp II. The team were helped at times by fixed ropes left by a Japanese team.[33]

In Yosemite, Ian Rea, Andy Cunningham, Willie Rock and Tom Ryan followed the usual Irish itinerary, while Breeda Murphy and Orla Prendergast were the first Irishwomen to climb the west face of the Leaning Tower, besides doing the South Face of Washington Column and several other routes. Dermot Fleming and Shay Nolan were also there doing classic short routes.[34]

In 1995, Lynam and O'Leary, on this occasion with Phil Gribbon, were on yet another *Saga*-sponsored trip, this time to Bogda Ola, an Alps-like offshoot of the Tien Shan range in the Chinese province of Xinjiang. Between them, the five-member team, which also included Britons Mike Banks and Barrie Page, reached summits on seventeen occasions, climbing four 4,000m peaks including one or two first ascents as well as some minor

Mike Banks, leader of a number of Anglo-Irish expeditions on his last Himalayan trip in 1995. He is sitting beneath Rakaposhi of which he had made the first ascent in 1958. AUTHOR'S COLLECTION

summits. The team visited Eric Shipton's old consulate (since demolished) in Kashgar, along with the Turfan Depression, the second lowest continental point on the planet, and travelled home via the Karakoram Highway to Pakistan, on the way passing by Rakaposhi, focus of long-ago ventures by Lynam, Banks and O'Leary.[35] For the septuagenarians Banks and Lynam it was to be the last trip to the great mountain ranges in which they had explored and climbed extensively over a span of fifty years.

Kevin Quinn and Banjo Bannon reached the summit of Denali/Mount McKinley in fifteen days via the usual West Buttress Route. Snowfall was even worse than usual.[36] On 6 August 1995, Jack Bergin and Maire Keenlyside reached the summit of Kuti Dorkush, c. 6,000m, in the Batura Muztagh of Pakistan. They had coped with the heavily corniced South-West Ridge to complete what they insisted was the first ascent of this peak. However, a few years later an article in the *American Alpine Journal* suggested that there may have been a previous success on this peak by a German 1959 expedition.[37] In any case the Irish pair's achievement was a noteworthy one for a two-person team.

In May 1995 Pat Falvey achieved his long-held ambition of reaching the summit of Mount Everest. He, and other members of a commercially organised expedition which had ample Sherpa support, left their camp at 8,200m at midnight on 26 May and made their way, without Sherpas, up the same route followed by the Irish 1993 expedition. Pat's oxygen ran out at the summit and the descent was a hard struggle with one of his friends also running out of oxygen. Pat found a half-full bottle of oxygen at the Second Step and managed to get something from another bottle to help his friend down the step. The three had coped with all this without Sherpa support but were now joined by Niama who carried extra oxygen to just below the Second Step and by Dorgi further down. It is doubtful if the ill climber would have made it back without their help.[38]

Pat Falvey was a new phenomenon in the mountaineering world. The author must confess to sharing scruples, felt by many traditional mountaineers about the direction in which Falvey steered an aspect of our shared avocation, and would probably be as severe in his condemnation of the person himself were it not for very favourable impressions of Pat formed during his early training and ample evidence that he was a very able high-altitude mountaineer. Pat Falvey started climbing in his late twenties when he turned to the hills following the collapse of the building business which had made him a millionaire and then left him almost penniless. Following one of his earliest outings in the Kerry hills he determined to climb Everest and it reflects well on him that within eight years he had succeeded. There was no doubting his toughness, self-reliance and ability to operate at high altitudes but the brashness of his approach to mountaineering was at odds with that of those mountaineers who then considered themselves in the mainstream. The vocabulary he used – 'death zone', 'assault' – the emphasis on high-profile objectives such as the Seven Summits, all these were strange new ideas, or new forms of mountaineering expression. Many mountaineers were reluctant to give due credit to his achievements, his improving technical ability and to his rapidly expanding knowledge of high-altitude mountaineering. They were slow to admit that the usual extended build-up of expertise and judgement, of high technical attainment, could be to some extent bypassed by someone who was obviously capable of dealing with the rigours of high altitude. Of course, Falvey was not an untrained mountaineer, although much of his early experience acquired in Kerry and elsewhere was completed outside the fairly tight circle then known to urban-based mountaineers.

Irish mountaineers, particularly cragsmen, would have to adapt to a new era in which extreme technical skill was considered less important on big mountains than the ability to put up with prolonged hardship, to endure cold, shortage of oxygen, back-breaking carrying of loads; to trust in self-reliance and an ability to perform at an appropriate technical level for weeks, even months on end. Entrepreneur and businessman as he instinctively was, it was on the cards that Falvey would make a career out of his high-altitude endeavours, and in this he was following, in his unique way, a long tradition of activists turning professional. Mountaineers, even those who regarded his achievements with respect, were dismayed at this commercialisation of the big peaks. But it was not Falvey's doing that led so many people, including some Irish, occasionally with minimal mountaineering experience, to allow themselves to be shepherded by teams of Sherpas who had prepared the way to the summits of some of the world's great peaks, sometimes passing corpses or the dying; so many people indeed that they presented a danger to themselves, to their handlers, and to what had been one of the few unsullied environments in the world.

Falvey ended the year 1995 with his ascent of Aconcagua with Con Collins.[39] During subsequent ventures, he picked up techniques of survival and more experience at high altitude than any other Irish mountaineer of the time. His particular approach to the ventures gradually became accepted by a wider public who, in all likelihood, regarded the reservations of other mountaineers with some puzzlement, especially when it saw them seeking much publicity when they were engaged in fund-raising for their more ambitious projects.

The most interesting outing in 1996 was that by Torrans, Cooper, Rea and Harrington to Alaska. Their original goals had been to climb Mount Hunter and to put up a new route on the south side of Mount Foraker but poor snow conditions diverted them to the Sultana ridge of Foraker. They spent six and a half days getting to the summit from the glacier landing strip, losing time in bad weather and white-out. Following several days' rest they climbed the West Rib of Denali/Mount McKinley, taking six and a half days here also. Both routes were first Irish ascents.[40] A daunting feature of the ascent to Foraker (11km distance and 3,810m height gain) was the number of times team members fell into crevasses – about twenty. Harrington was impressed, even taken aback by the intense dedication of his partners which extended to cutting down on rations.[41]

As part of his Seven Summits quest, Falvey climbed Mont Elbruz in winter conditions.[42] Moira Rea, Irene Bankhead, Sheila Willis and Helen McKeeman were in Bolivia where they did several

5,000m peaks and the last two named did Huayna Potosi (6,088m), a popular mountain not far from La Paz. An account by Willis in *Irish Mountain Log* was an interesting and engaging contrast to the more usual macho mountaineering style.[43]

The year 1997 began with Pat Falvey's January ascent of Mount Vinson (4,899m), Antarctica's highest peak and accessible only to those who could afford the costly arrangements including the long flight from Chile. There were mutterings in 'elite' circles, according to Pat, about his hogging of such a large chunk of the limited government funds available to expedition mountaineers. He went on to climb Mount Cook (3,724m) in New Zealand with Mike Shea, and then to Mount Kosciuszko (2,228m), Australia's highest peak, where he completed his Seven Summits venture with his three Kerry friends Moriarty, Shea and Gene Tangney.[44] Previously, Moriarty and Tangney had climbed Mount Cook's North Ridge.[45]

Another, much earlier, Irish Antarctic adventure was emulated in February when, following a failed attempt to repeat Shackleton's remarkable voyage in the *James Caird*, four members of the South Arís expedition – Nugent, Mike Barry, Jamie Young and Paddy Barry – completed a mountaineering traverse of South Georgia.

In China, Robbie Fenlon was co-leader of a UIAA-arranged international camp in the Chola Shan range. Liam Reinhardt went along as a participant on the five-week long summer outing. A few 5,000m peaks were climbed.[46]

Broad Peak

In 1998 Eddie Cooper chalked up what was the best Irish ascent of the year in the great ranges when he reached the fore-summit of Broad Peak, the world's twelfth highest mountain on 8 July. (Broad Peak is 8,051m in height. The fore-summit is variously given as 8,028m or 8,034m, which would make it the thirteenth highest). The mountain was regarded by the team as a secondary objective and as acclimatisation for an attempt on K2, but that peak was not possible due to poor conditions. Broad Peak was done in what is known as lightweight style, without an extensive build-up, porters or bottled oxygen, but the team openly stated their intention to rely on existing protection such as fixed ropes when on K2.[47] This was understandable and normal procedure on such a crowded and well-used route but is a testament to the subtleties and ambivalences of the ethics of alpine or lightweight ascents. Other members of the exceptionally strong team – Torrans, Rea, Donie O'Sullivan, Martin Daly and Paul Dunlop – failed for a number of reasons to reach the top of Broad Peak, and when they were again ready, bad weather had set in.[48] Although regarded as one of the easier 8,000m peaks, this was a great showing by Cooper and was probably seen as a vindication of their approach by those members who had been on Manaslu in 1991.

Broad Peak team 1998. *(L–r)*: Paul Dunlop, Eddie Cooper, Ian Rea behind Calvin Torrans, Donie O'Sullivan *(rear)* and Martin Daly. CONOR O'CONNOR

Pat Falvey and Gavin Bates had already become the first Irish mountaineers to reach an 8,000m peak without bottled oxygen or high-altitude porters. They reached the summit of Cho Oyu, the world's sixth highest peak at 8,201m on 20 May 1998. Pat and Gavin, along with Con Collins and Eoghan Sheehan had bought their way on to an international team with a permit to climb the mountain from the Tibetan side. This payment covered permit, transport to Base Camp and for yaks to carry to Advanced Base Camp. They paid a porter to help carry a large tent to Camp I but otherwise carried everything themselves.[49] The mountain is not one of the harder 8,000m peaks; some would say it is the easiest, but that does not alter the fact that this was the very first time Irish climbers had reached a summit of this height without aid beyond Camp I, nor does it take from Falvey's feat in being at that time the only Irish person to have reached the summits of two 8,000m peaks.

An attempt on Jonsang Peak (7,383m) in the Kanchenjunga region, a venture which could have been the hoped-for post-Everest breakthrough to hard technical climbing on high Himalayan peaks, came to an abrupt halt in mid-May. A youngish team of able climbers were denied sufficient time on the mountain because of two weeks' delay waiting for gear at Kathmandu and a further two weeks on a long walk-in. The chosen route on the South Face was unclimbed and transpired to be harder than expected. The team, led by Kieran O'Hara of Tollymore Centre, had little experience of the Himalaya, with the important exception of Robbie Fenlon and, to a lesser extent, Malcolm McNaught and Tomas Aylward. This rawness may have told against them. By the time they felt sufficiently acclimatised they had just seven days to reach the summit and return. O'Hara, Aylward (of Tiglin Centre), Garth Henry and Shane Brogan were forced to bivouac on a steep snow slope on their very first day on the face and, though one pair opted to try further progress, it had become obvious that with deteriorating weather the sortie would have to be aborted. The highest point reached was about 6,650m.[50]

Also in the Kangchenjunga region were Roger McMorrow and Nigel Hart, two final year medical students at QCB who were engaged in research into high-altitude sickness, doubtless much to the chagrin of less fortunate students south of the border. The pair managed to fit in an ascent of the east summit (6,400m) of Ramtang Peak which had been attained only once before.[51]

Mary Nash of UCDMC, with Welsh friends, was probably the first Irishwoman to reach the summit of Aconcagua. Many kilometres to the south Johnny Gillmor made an attempt on Cerro Torre which was foiled by the usual Patagonian weather after he and his

English partner had completed the first five rock pitches.[52] Orla Prendergast, Joan Dineen and Anthea Packer were in Bolivia on Huayna Potosi and Condoriri.[53] In Greenland, Vera Quinlan, despite long delays which are typical of that region, was helicoptered to the Champs Elysées Glacier where, with members of a British group, she made good use of an eight-day break in the weather to do four first ascents of reasonable standard.[54] Gerry Moss and Terry O'Neill were in the USA where, typically, they climbed on every day but two of their 22-day stay in California and Nevada. They ranged from Joshua Tree and Suicide Rock to Yosemite and on to Red Rocks where they delighted in the climbing and in the uncrowded space, sky and smell of the desert evenings.[55]

In Nepal, following some adventures on the Mera La, Pat Falvey and Con Moriarty, self-sufficient but for a support party of two Kerry friends, were back, in 1999, on Ama Dablam which, by now, was approaching in popularity those Chamonix routes so favoured by the Irish. Moriarty developed quite severe altitude sickness at Camp I, leaving Falvey to try for the summit himself. Falvey skipped Camp II and from Camp III gained the summit on 28 October, providing further proof, if any was needed, that he was well capable of tackling even a quite technical Himalayan peak in alpine style, relying only on his own resources.[56]

In India's Spiti, Paddy O'Leary and Mike Scott were on an exploratory

Pat Falvey on Ama Dablam in 1999.
PAT FALVEY COLLECTION

trip, being the first westerners to penetrate the Debsa valley, in order to find a way into nearby Kangla Tarbo I (6,315m), on which Indian teams had failed twice. As part of their exploration they climbed Kangla Tarbo II, an easy peak of about 6,200m, which had its first ascent in 1998. In the following year an IMC team would make a first ascent of the higher peak.[57]

Michael Scott crossing Khamengar River, Spiti, in 1999 en route to Debsa valley.
AUTHOR'S COLLECTION

The most technical climbing done by Irish climbers in the greater ranges in 1999 was in Peru where Joe Purser and Conor Reynolds spent six weeks in the Cordillera Blanca as part of a several months' long climbing trip, concentrating on routes neglected by previous Irish visitors. They climbed the south face of Churup (5,493m) by the original 1972 route, spending seventeen hours getting up and down this line of about Scottish Grade IV/V in its lower part. They went on to do two more peaks of considerable difficulty – Chacraraju (6,001m) and Ocshapalca (5,881m) – before doing the Ferrari Route on the South-West face of Alpamayo (5,947m). Four Irishmen, Philip Brennan and Dave West along with Mick Mangan and Jarlath Keogh, reached the summit of Aconcagua by the normal route.[58]

There were quite a few Irish in Yosemite in September where Alan Sarhan demonstrated his ability and speed by climbing each of his chosen routes in one day. He did Astroman and Rostrum with Niall Grimes in ten hours, and with Joe Purser managed the West face of Leaning Tower – normally a two-day route – in just one day. Sarhan, with James Gernon, and Joe Purser who had come up from Peru via Ireland [*sic*], made a one-day ascent of the long West Face of Half Dome which is normally considered to be a two- to three-day venture. The route was climbed on the same day by Grimes and a Welsh partner. Purser went on to do Lurking Fear on El Capitan over three days.[59]

Epilogue

During a winter of the early twenty-first century, three elderly walkers descending from a snow-capped Lugnaquilla fought through the debris of a felled forest beside the waterfall in the Fraughan Rock Glen or the Baravore valley. The oldest of the three remembered when there was no forest here and marvelled, as he so often did these days, that he had lived through so many changes, outlived an entire ecosystem. Mountaineering and national history walked with them as they moved downhill. Up on their left was the gully climbed by Harold Johnson and also, almost a hundred years ago, by that bright young officer and Trinity professor, E. L. Julian. Near the extreme left of the crag was Great Gully Ridge put up by Kopczynski and Morrison in 1951. This oldest member had been on that latter route the previous year and had looked across a narrow gap at a nest of peregrine fledglings. Were those nestlings of the same lineage as the bird whose nest Julian had solicitously avoided before he went off to be killed in Gallipoli?

Further down, on a forest road, two weary young women and a lad came out of a side track and asked: 'How far is it now?' As the drift of their query was sorted out it was realised that today was when the annual Art O'Neill Walk was held on some charitable or commercial basis. These clueless unfortunates had, they claimed, been sent down this off-route way by 'them' as indicated by a vague wave in the direction of Table Mountain. They gradually dropped behind as the older group guided them down. At a viewpoint on a bend in the track the head of Glenmalure came into view. Had Fiach McHugh O'Byrne watched near here 400 years ago when his clan routed the Lord Deputy and his troops as they came over the hill?

On reaching the valley floor, the tiny youth hostel was passed, housed in what was said to be the isolated hill-cottage which featured in Synge's *Shadow of the Glen*. It had once been owned by Kathleen Lynn, feminist, benefactor of Dublin's poor, medical officer to the Citizen's Army during the 1916 Rising. Prominent political activists of the time, including Éamon de Valera, were reputed to have visited her here. A little further down was the field in which the oldest walker had camped on the day that Dev himself had come to open the new hostel. As the elderly 21st-century trio splashed across the ford to the big car park there was a hubbub: smiling, welcoming faces appeared and then turned away as they realised that these old people with their walking poles were not participants in this re-enactment of O'Neill's fateful escape from Dublin Castle. There were scores of onlookers here and a big tent with, presumably, soup and awards for those who had made it. No one seemed to be aware that it was still almost a two-hour walk to the fugitive princes' true destination.

At the back of the car park, not far from a large granite boulder carved with the names of men from these valleys who had fought in the 1798 Rebellion, the three senior walkers removed their boots beside their waiting car. Cheers broke out for the three tired youngsters who had followed them down.

————

Of course, I was the old man of the three who had spent the day on Lug, the others being not too much younger. This was the car park at which I was surprised by the class of car parked there in the 1990s. Apart from the obvious contrast with the Art O'Neill walk as described in the prologue, I was not on this occasion consciously thinking of all the changes which had affected mountaineers and the mountains in the intervening fifty years.

However, as a matter of course, I was aware that the growth in outdoor recreation had brought a modicum of prosperity and jobs to some in this valley, to the thriving hotel down the road and nearby B&Bs. New homes had been built. I was aware that well-surfaced roads and a motorway had brought Dublin closer. Conveniently situated beside the M50 which now encircles the capital there were several large outdoor stores and a new climbing wall, one of the country's biggest. Other motorways now brought climbers and walkers on one-day trips to the Mournes or even Connemara and back.

I was further aware that the section of the Wicklow Way which linked Glenmalure and Glendalough through the Wicklow National Park was a boardwalk for much of its length. We had seen the results of 'wheelies' by quad-bikes on Lug's vulnerable summit. Access to the hills had become problematic, entangled with politics and upland farmers' desperate efforts to protect their way of life.

I was aware, following the Everest success of 1993, that optimistic expectations of the progress the Irish would make on hard faces on the high Himalayan and Central Asian peaks had not been met. Yes, some forceful attempts had been made early in the new millennium on some of Patagonia's already-climbed big rock faces, and several lines had been pioneered on a difficult Greenland face; there were indications of fast winter times on hard Alpine faces. All admirable, but not quite the anticipated breakthrough. The main focus of attention in this first decade were attempts and successes on overcrowded Everest, K2, Broad Peak and completions of the Seven Summits. One cannot begrudge the success of any of these endeavours, some of which were extraordinary personal triumphs, some needing Sherpa assistance to the very summit. These were all fine, even courageous, personal efforts. Ger MacDonnell's quite remarkable heroism on K2 had reminded us of the best moun-taineering instincts,[1] while Clare O'Leary's successes on Everest and elsewhere gave an indication of potential female talent.[2] But, apart from the doings of these untypical exemplars, how had Irish mountaineering been advanced? There were ongoing smaller endeavours – let's drop the term expedition – on unclimbed 6,000m peaks of varying difficulty, mainly in India. Was that the future for Irish big-range mountaineering?

At home, there were further advances in technical expertise and more participation at a high level, especially in sport climbing, so much so that it was difficult to see where Irish rock-climbing would proceed. Apart from new lines on already densely developed faces what historically significant breakthroughs would occur?

We piled into my friend's FreelanderTD4 and drove down to the hotel. There, in the ageing company of many of those whose names appear in these chapters, we would dine, as we did annually, in the room which had probably been used by Hart, perhaps by Julian and Kirkpatrick, all those years ago.

Endnotes

Abbreviations used

IMCJ	*Irish Mountaineering Club Journal*
IML	*Irish Mountain Log*
UCDMC History	*UCD Mountaineering Club 1961–2011: an incomplete history*

Prologue

1 J. B. Malone, *Walking in Wicklow* (Dublin, Helican, 1964), p. 74
2 L. M. Cullen, 'Politics and rebellion: Wicklow in the 1790s' in *Wicklow: history and society*, eds., K. Hannigan & W. Nolan, (Dublin, Geography Publications, 1994), p. 483.
3 Conversation with Noel Kavanagh, 1963.
4 Tomas Ó Cuinn, 'Glenreemore or Glenmalure. Where does the Fugitive Prince lie' in *Irish Mountaineering Club Journal* (henceforth *IMCJ*), 1964.
5 *Ibid.*

Chapter 1: A Break in a Day's Walk

1 Richard Barrington, 'Henry Chichester Hart' in *The Irish Naturalist*, vol. xvii, no.12, December 1908, pp. 249–54.
2 Frank Nugent, *In Search of Peaks, Passes & Glaciers* (Cork, The Collins Press, 2013).
3 John Tyndall, *Hours of Exercise in the Alps*, (London, Longmans, Green & Co.,1871), pp. 415–20.
4 D. A. Webb, 'The hey-day of Irish botany' in *The Scottish Naturalist* 1986, pp. 123–34; *The Irish Naturalist*, December 1908.
5 *The Irish Times*, 'Irishman's Diary', 9 November 1932
6 Robert Lloyd Praeger, *The Way That I Went* (Dublin, Allen Figgis, 1980), pp. 57–58.
7 Nugent, *In Search of Peaks, Passes and Glaciers*, p. 187.
8 Robert Lloyd Praeger, *Some Irish Naturalists* (Dundalk, Dun Dealgan Press, 1949).
9 Lynam, Introduction to Haskett-Smith, *Climbing in the British Isles* (London, Longmans, Green & Co., 1895, reprinted Dublin, 1974).
10 H. C. Hart, 'Ireland' in W. P. Haskett-Smith, *Climbing in the British Isles*.
11 Praeger, *The Way That I Went*.
12 Geoffrey Winthrop Young, *On High Hills* (London, Methuen, 1944).

13 Con Ó Muircheartaigh, *Irish Mountain Log* (henceforth *IML*), 44, autumn 1997; interview October 2013.

14 Alan Hankinson, *Geoffrey Winthrop Young: poet, mountaineer, educator* (London, Hodder & Stoughton, 1995).

15 G. W. Young, *Mountains with a Difference* (London, Eyre and Spotiswoode, 1951).

16 Judith Hill, *In Search of Islands: a life of Conor O'Brien* (Cork, The Collins Press, 2009).

17 *The Irish Times*, 12 February 1895.

18 Nugent, *In Search of Peaks*, p. 201.

19 *The Irish Times*, 28 February1895

20 *Ibid.*, 11 September 1902.

21 *Ibid.*, 18 April 1933.

22 *Ibid.*, 21 October 1911.

23 Nugent, *In Search of Peaks*, p. 221.

24 Christopher Harvie, *Bryce, James, Viscount Bryce* (1838–1922) Oxford Dictionary of National Biography 2004, online ed. January 2011. http://www/oxforddnb.com/view/article/32141 accessed 14 March 2012.

25 Joss Lynam, 'A history of Irish mountaineering' in *Peak Viewing 7*, (Belfast, 1979).

26 George Band, *Summit: 150 years of the alpine club* (London, Harper Collins, 2006), pp. 50–53.

27 W. T. Kirkpatrick, *Alpine Days and Nights* (London, George Allen and Unwin, 1932).

28 *The Irish Times*, 15 May 1941.

29 Page Dickinson, 'A Rock Climb in Co. Wicklow', in *Climbers' Club Journal*, vol. xi, old series, no. 41, 1908–09, pp. 8–13.

30 *Ibid.*; Frank Winder, 'Notes on early Wicklow climbing' in *Rock Climbing Guide to Wicklow* (Dublin, MCI, 1993).

31 Judith Hill, *In Search of Islands*, p. 18.

32 Patricia Boylan, *All Cultivated People: a history of the United Arts Club* (Gerrards Cross, Colin Smythe, 1988).

33 Hankinson, *Geoffrey Winthrop Young*, p. 118.

34 Young, 'From genesis to numbers' in G. Sutton, G. W. Young, W. Noyce, *Snowdon Biography* (London, Dent, 1957); Young, *Mountains with a Difference*, p. 4.

35 Young, 'From genesis to numbers'.

36 Page E. Dickinson, *The Dublin of Yesterday* (London, Methuen, 1929), pp. 67–70.

37 Harold Johnson, *IMCJ* 1952.

38 Anthony P. Quinn, *Wigs and Guns* (Dublin, Four Courts Press, 2006).

39 *The Irish Times*, 25 November 1911.

40 Conor O'Brien and Page L. Dickinson, 'Irish Mountaineering', in *Climbers' Club Journal*, vol i, new series, no. 1, February 1912, pp. 90–96.

41 Dickinson, *The Dublin of Yesterday* (passim).

42 Patricia Boylan, *All Cultivated People*; Kevin Higgins, 'The first Celtic Tiger' in *Journal of the Irish Mountaineering and Exploration Society*, vol. 3, 2012.

43 Hill, *In Search of Islands*; Boylan, *All Cultivated People*.

44 Boylan, *All Cultivated People*.

45 *The Irish Times*, 9 November 1932.

46 Dan Breen, *My Fight for Irish Freedom* (Dublin, Anvil, 1981); Tim Robinson, *Connemara; a little Gaelic kingdom* (Dublin, Penguin, 2011); Tom Barry, *Guerrilla Days in Ireland* (Dublin, Anvil Press, 1949); Jonathan Bardon, *A History of Ulster* (Belfast, Blackstaff Press, 2005), pp. 490–91; *Connacht Tribune*, various dates from 15 February 1913 to 11 November 1922; personal observation of memorial tablets in several mountain locations.

47 Robinson, *Connemara*, pp. 290–1.
48 Claude Wall diaries, National Library.
49 'Obituary', *IMCJ* 1968.
50 Harold Johnson, 'Introduction' in *Rock Climbing Guide to Scalp*, self-published, 1958.
51 *Ibid.*
52 Roy Foster, *Modern Ireland 1600–1972* (Harmondsworth, Allen Lane, 1988), pp. 436–8: Declan Kiberd, *Inventing Ireland; the literature of the modern nation* (London, Jonathan Cape, 1996), pp. 217–38.
53 Bardon, *A History of Ulster*, pp. 332–34.
54 *Ibid.*, pp. 427–30.
55 D. A. Webb, 'The hey-day of Irish botany'.
56 Foster, *Modern Ireland*, p. 538; Bardon, *A History of Ulster*, pp. 527–34.
57 *The Irish Times*, 29 May 1930.
58 *Ibid.*, 18 July 1933 and 12 September 1933.
59 Terry Trench, *Fifty Years Young: the history of An Óige* (Dublin, An Óige, 1981), p. 23.
60 Bardon, *A History of Ulster*, pp. 532–37; 570–92.
61 Trench, *Fifty Years Young.*
62 Wall diaries.
63 Pat Holland, unpublished initial draft of *Mountain Rescue in Ireland*, sent by email February 2014.
64 *The Irish Times*, 8 April 1933.
65 *Ibid.*, 28 December 1932.
66 *The Irish Times*, 17 July 1938 and 10 October 1932.
67 *IMCJ* October 1951.
68 *IMCJ* winter 1952.
69 J. W. Crofton, 'Connemara' in *Cambridge Mountaineering* 1934, p. 111.
70 E. C. Allberry, 'Lugnaquilla' in *Cambridge Mountaineering* 1934, pp. 110–11.
71 *The Cork Examiner*, 10 July 1935.
72 *Outdoor Kerry*, March–September 1987.
73 Lynam, 'A history of Irish mountaineering', in *Peak Viewing* 7; J. C. Coleman, *The Mountains of Killarney*, (1948, Dundalk, Dundalgan Press); Coleman, *Journeys into Muskerry* (1950, Dundalgan Press).
74 Joss Lynam, *IMC50, The Golden Jubilee of the Irish Mountaineering Club 1948–98.*
75 P. McAteer, *80 Years of Hostelling & the Story of the Mourne Wall Walk* (Belfast, 2011).
76 Charlie Brims in a letter to Des Agnew, 16 March 1962 (IMC archive).
77 R. H. Common, Record of group's doings from 1935 to 1939, owned by Bernagh Brims of County Down and Scotland.
78 Phil Gribbon (Montagnard), *IMCJ* 1955–56.
79 *The Irish Times*, 2 December 1948.
80 *Ibid.*; *Dalkey Quarry Rock Climbing Guide*, 2005.
81 *Dalkey Guide*, 2005.
82 *IMC50.*
83 'Obituary' in *IMC newsletter*, autumn 2005.
84 *Ibid.*; *The Irish Times*, 2 December 1948.
85 *Irish Independent*, 31 January 1950.
86 *The Irish Times*, 15 January 2011, obituary.
87 Aleck Crichton, letters and recorded interview 2010.
88 http://www.ww2talk.com/forum/irish-guards/28780-micks-2nd, accessed 8 February 2012.

89 Crichton, letters and interview.
90 *IMCJ* 1, August 1950.
91 *IMC50.*
92 *Ibid.*

Chapter 2: Comrade Lysenko and The Affables

1 *The Irish Times*, 26 January 2008; Dan Shipside, 'Pioneers', recorded conversations of early climbers. www.Danshipsides.com/DshipsidesWeb/pioneers.html
2 *The Irish Times*, 26 January 2008.
3 Frank Winder, interview in *IML* 50, spring 1999.
4 Perrott, *IMCJ* 1, 1950.
5 Joss Lynam, *IMC50, Golden Jubilee of the IMC*, 1998, p. 8; Aleck Crichton, letter, 18 May 2011; *Climbers' Club Journal*, vol. xvi, no. 1, 1969, p. 55.
6 Aleck Crichton, interview and letter, 18 May 2011. *IMCJ*, 1950.
7 *Climbers' Club Journal*, vol. xvi, no.1, 1969.
8 Frank Winder, 'Notes on early Wicklow climbing.' in *Rock Climbing Guide to Wicklow*, 1993.
9 Winder in Dan Shipside, 'Pioneers'.
10 Terence Brown, *Ireland: a social and cultural history 1922–2002* (Cornell University Press, 1981).
11 *The Irish Times*, 11 August 1988; Denis Helliwell, *North-West Mountaineering Club Journal*, 50th anniversary edition (2005).
12 Sean Rothery, interview autumn 2011; Rothery, *IMC newsletter* no. 5, 1970.
13 Bardon, *A History of Ulster*, p. 543
14 Dan Shipside, 'Pioneers'.
15 Padraic O'Halpin and Elizabeth Healy 'Impromptu' in *IMCJ* 1963.
16 E. Healy, *IMC newsletter*, spring 2008.
17 Winder, Lynam, *IML* 13, 1989.
18 P. Kenny, in conversation, mid-1950s; Winder, interview *IML* 50, spring 1999; obituary *IML* 13, winter 1989.
19 Shipside, 'Pioneers'.
20 *IMC newsletter*, no. 2, 1993.
21 Winder, Lynam, *IML* 13, 1989.
22 *Wicklow Rock Climbing Guide*, 2009.
23 Kenny, *IMCJ*, March 1951.
24 Colin Wells, *A Brief History of British Mountaineering* (2001, Mountain Heritage Trust), p. 74; Winder, Kenny obituary, *IML* 13, winter 1989.
25 *IMCJ* 1951.
26 Shipside 'Pioneers'.
27 *IMCJ* 1960; *IMC newsletter*, summer 2011.
28 *IML* 22, spring 1992.
29 *IMCJ* summer 1952; *Outdoor Kerry*, December 1988 – March 1989.
30 P. Gribbon, email 17 February 2011.
31 *Ibid.*
32 'Introduction' in *Mourne Rock Climbs*, 1973.
33 Gribbon, *IMC50*, Dublin 1998.
34 Gribbon, email 17 February 2011.
35 Gribbon, *IMC50*; Gribbon, email 17 February 2011.
36 *IMCJ* 1960.

37 Brian Rothery, in conversation, 1960s.
38 Gribbon, email 17 February 2011.
39 *Ibid.*
40 Lynam, *IMC50.*
41 *IMCJ*, October 1951.
42 George Band, *Summit*, pp. 97–100.
43 Sean Rothery, *A Long Walk South* (Cork, The Collins Press, 2001), p. 209.
44 Winder, *IMCJ* 1952.
45 Dublin Section minutes, IMC archive.
46 www.newsletter.co.uk 9 February 2014.
47 Gribbon, email 17 February 2011.
48 Sean Rothery, *A Long Walk South*, pp. 210–11.
49 Harold Drasdo, *The Ordinary Route* (Glasgow, Ernest Press, 1997), p. 95.
50 George Band, *Summit*, p. 106.
51 *IMCJ* 1954. Pat McMahon interview June 2011.
52 Drasdo, *The Ordinary Route*, p. 104.
53 Band, *Summit*, p. 100.
54 *IMCJ* 1955–6
55 John Morrison, *IMCJ* 1952.
56 Sean Rothery, in conversation 2011.
57 Lynam, *IMC50*, 1998.
58 Kenny, *IMCJ* 1955–56.
59 *Rock Climbing Guide To Wicklow*, 1993.
60 This paragraph is written from author's memory and those of friends, some of whom have seen Kenny's letter.

Chapter 3: Where Does the Fugitive Prince Lie?

1 Ciaran Mac an Fhaile, *IMCJ*, 1951.
2 Drasdo, *The Ordinary Route*, p. 152.
3 *IMCJ*, 1955–56.
4 Author's own experiences and those of friends.
5 Elizabeth Healy, *IMC newsletter*, spring 2008; author's personal experience.
6 An Óige *Review*, August 1956.
7 Nora Hall, letter, 21 July 2011.
8 Uinseann Mac Eoin, *Peaks and Summits.* (Privately produced monograph, 1996).
9 *The Irish Times*, 19 October 1954.
10 *Ibid.*
11 H. C. Hart, 'Ireland' in Haskett Smith, *Climbing in the British Isles*, p. 37.
12 Praeger, The Way That I Went, p. 173.
13 MacEoin, *Peaks and Summits.*
14 Lynam, *Mountain Log* 26, (later to become *IML*), spring 1986.
15 Mac Eoin, *Peaks and Summits.*
16 *The Irish Times*, 11 August 1988; conversation with Calvin Torrans.
17 Pat McMahon, interview 2011; Noel Brown, conversation 2012.
18 IMC meets list October/April 1953, IMC archives.
19 Lynam, letter of 11 November 1949, IMC archives.
20 Phil Gribbon, email 2011.
21 *IMCJ* 1958–59; Bill Hannon in *IMCJ* 1986–87.
22 An Óige *Review*, August 1956; personal recollection.

23 *The Irish Times*, letter, 8 November 1962.

24 *IMCJ*, 1953–54.

25 Paddy McAteer, *80 Years of Youth Hostelling & The Story of The Mourne Wall Walk* (undated, HINI, Belfast).

26 An Óige *Review*, June 1956, June 1957, August 1956, September 1958.

27 Shipside, 'Pioneers'.

28 Drasdo, *Ordinary Route*, p. 152.

29 *IMCJ*, 1958–59.

30 V. N. Stevenson, 'The Wearin' O' the Green' in *IMC50*.

31 *IMCJ* 1956–57.

32 *IMCJ* 1955–56.

33 Winder, *IMCJ* 1955–56.

34 *Ibid.*

35 Con Moriarty interview October 2013. Related to him by Sean Ryan.

36 Kenny, *IMCJ* 1957–58.

37 Roy Foster, *Modern Ireland, 1600–1972* (London, 1988), pp. 594–95; Lord Killanin, Michael Duignan, Peter Harbison, *The Shell Guide to Ireland* (Dublin, 1995), p. 144; *Trinity News*, 19 November 1964.

38 *IMCJ* 1960.

39 Rothery conversation August 2012.

40 *IMCJ* 1960, Gribbon, *IMC50*.

41 *IMCJ* 1960.

42 *IMCJ* 1955–56.

43 *IMCJ* 1956–57.

44 Morrison, *IMCJ*, 1958–59.

45 *IMCJ* 1961.

46 *Ibid.*

47 *IMCJ* 1956–57.

48 Brian Kennedy, email 13 July 2011.

49 Lynam, *IMCJ* 1960.

50 Drasdo, *Ordinary Route,* p. 148.

51 Gribbon, *IMCJ* 1960.

52 *IMCJ*, 1958–59.

53 Winder, Kenny obituary in *IML* 13, winter 1989.

54 *IMCJ* 1960.

Chapter 4: Wet Face of the Dru

1 George Band, *Summit*, pp. 105–6.

2 *IMCJ* 1962.

3 *IMCJ* 1960, 1961.

4 Tony Ingram, interview May 2012.

5 Winder, 'Introduction' in *Rock Climbing Guide to Wicklow*, 1993.

6 Gerry Cairns, interview 2011.

7 *IMCJ* 1962.

8 *IMCJ* 1963.

9 Eddie Gaffney, conversation at the time.

10 *IMCJ* 1963.

11 www.climbing.tcdlife.ie/ accessed 9 July 2012.

12 *IML* 22, spring 1992.

13 *Ibid.*
14 *Ibid.*
15 S. Moore, S. C. Hiller and R. Bell (eds.), *Rock Climbs in the Mourne Mountains*, 1988 and 2010, historical notes.
16 *IML* 9, winter 1988. Letters page.
17 Tony Ingram, interview May 2012; Gerry Cairns, conversations.
18 IMC50, Golden Jubilee journal, p. 10; Niall Rice, interview May 2012, and subsequent talks.
19 IMC minutes.
20 Letters from Rothery, Donnelly, Lynam, O'Flynn, etc., IMC archives; Lynam, 16 April 1973, National Archives of Ireland, BR/2002/77/2.
21 Calvin Torrans, 'A History of Irish Rock-climbing 1940s to 1980s' in *Journal of Irish Mountaineering and Exploration Society*, vol. 2, 2005.
22 *Spillikin Club newsletter,* spring 1968.
23 *IMCJ* 1965.
24 IMC address list; Shay Nolan conversation.
25 www.climbing.tcdlife.ie/ Accessed 9 July 2012.
26 Minute Book, DUCC; TCD MUN/club/climbing,1/1.
27 Seamus Ó Colmain in Declan O'Keeffe, ed., *UCD Mountaineering Club 1961–2011: an incomplete history*, p. 4. (Hereafter *UCDMC history.*)
28 Alice Leahy, *With Trust In Place: writing from the outside* (Michigan, 2003), p. 190.
29 *The Irish Times*, 12 September 1994.
30 Spillikin Club stencilled guide 1967. (Sean Rothery has written in *IMCJ* 1968 that these crags were first found by Winder and Maguire in 1949.)
31 *Fair Head Rock Climbing Guide, 2002.*
32 *Spillikin Club newsletter,* May 1967.
33 *Ibid.*
34 Conversations with Noel Kavanagh, early 1960s.
35 Author's personal encounter in darkness with unknown personnel officered by someone with a British accent, followed by a fake bomb planted by one side or the other under the pub's thatched roof.
36 J. J. Lee, *Ireland, 1912–1985: politics and society* (Cambridge University Press, 1989).
37 John Forsythe, *IMC newsletter* 4, 1989.
38 *IMCJ*, 1968.
39 Mike Shea, in *Outdoor Kerry* December 1988 – March 1989.
40 *UCDMC 1961–2011.*
41 *IMCJ* 1961; personal experience.
42 *IMC newsletter* no. 2, May 1969.
43 *IMC newsletter* October 1969; *IMCJ* 1971.
44 *IMCJ* 1968.
45 Gribbon, email 2011; *IMCJ* 1966.
46 Memorial bulletin, IMC Hut Glendasan.
47 Niall Rice, interview summer 2012.
48 *IMCJ* 1965, 1968, 1971.
49 Frank Nugent, letter on behalf of Spillikin Club to IMC, 27 November 1970.

Chapter 5: Distant Ranges and Domestic Strife

1 *IMCJ* 1961.
2 *Ibid.*

3   *IMCJ* 1962.
4   Minute book DUCC; *IMCJ* 1962.
5   George Band, *Summit*, p. 107.
6   *IMCJ* 1962.
7   *IMCJ* 1965.
8   Conversation with Ingram, May 2012.
9   *IMCJ* 1963.
10 Minute Book DUCC.
11 *IMCJ* 1964.
12 *IMCJ* 1965.
13 *Ibid.*
14 Minute Book DUCC.
15 *IMCJ* 1968.
16 Torrans, introductory remarks at Goulding lecture 1990s.
17 Jim Perrin, *The Climbing Essays*. (The In Pinn, Glasgow, 2006).
18 Conversations with Tony Ingram and Kevin Shelley, May 2012.
19 *IMCJ* 1968.
20 *Ibid.*
21 *IMCJ* 1971.
22 *IMC newsletter* 3, 1969.
23 *IMCJ* 1971.
24 *Ibid.*
25 *IMCJ* 1961.
26 *IMCJ* 1961.
27 *Himalayan Journal* XXIII, 1961.
28 *IMCJ* 1962.
29 *IMCJ* 1964.
30 *The Irish Times*, 1 April 1967.
31 *IMCJ* 1965.
32 *Himalayan Journal* XXXIX, 1981.
33 *IMCJ* 1965.
34 *Ibid.*
35 *IMCJ* 1966.
36 *American Alpine Journal* 1969.
37 *IMC newsletter*, December 1968.
38 *IMCJ* 1971.
39 *Ibid.*

Chapter 6: Fianna Warriors and Hillwalking Challenges

1   Joe Lyons, *Wicklow Climbing Guide* (Mountaineering Ireland, Dublin, 2009), p. 17.
2   J. J. Lee, *Ireland, 1912–1985: politics and society* (Cambridge, 1989), p. 360.
3   Maureen Delamere, 'Tourism and Transport' in Adrian Redmond, ed., *That Was Then, This Is Now* (Dublin, CSO, 2000), p. 165.
4   Tony White, *Investing In People; higher education in Ireland 1960–2000* (Dublin, IPA, 2001), p. 242.
5   Ken Higgs, telephone conversation, December 2012; Steve Young, email January 2013.
6   *IMC newsletter* 8, October 1972.
7   Moore *et al.*, *Rock Climbs in the Mourne Mountains*, Mountaineering Ireland, Dublin, 2010.

8   *IMC newsletter* 8, October 1972.

9   *IML* 16, 1990.

10 Young, in Peter Woods, *Climbs in the Burren and Aran Islands* (MCI, 2008), p. 51; Jim Leonard, conversations.

11 Howard Hebblethwaite, 'History' in *Climbs in the Burren and Aran Islands*.

12 Ken Higgs, 'The Burren Sea Cliff 1972–1979' in *The Irish Climber*, (FMCI Dublin, 1985); telephone interview Ken Higgs 2012.

13 Irish climbing route database, www.climbing.ie.

14 Ricky Cowan, email January 2013. Greene is credited with the route in the Mourne guidebook.

15 Steve Young, email January 2013.

16 *Ibid.*

17 Sean Windrim, email March 2013.

18 Sean Windrim, telephone conversation, September 2013.

19 Ken Higgs, *Wicklow* (FMCI, Dublin, 1982), p. 15.

20 Windrim, conversation.

21 Steve Young, original manuscript submitted for an article in *IMC Journal* 1998.

22 *Dalkey Quarry Guide*, 2005.

23 Windrim, conversation.

24 Ken Higgs, 'The Burren Sea Cliff 1972–1979' in *The Irish Climber* 1985.

25 Dermot Somers, *Rince ar na Ballaí*, (Dún Laoghaire, Cois Life Teo., 2002), p. 15.

26 Sean Windrim, telephone conversation summer 2013.

27 Conrad M. Arensberg & Kimball, Solon T., *Family and Community in Ireland* (County Clare, third ed., Clasp Press, 2001).

28 Windrim, email.

29 Clare Sheridan, Calvin Torrans, *Fair Head Rock Climbing Guide* (MI, Dublin, 2002,), p. 10.

30 Dave Walsh, *IMC50*, p. 12.

31 Historical notes. *Rock Climbs in Mourne Mountains* (Mountaineering Ireland, Dublin, 2010).

32 John Codling, *IML* 13, winter 1989.

33 Tom Hand, *Mountain Log* 8, spring 1980.

34 Torrans, *The Irish Climber* (FMCI, Dublin, 1985), p. 27.

35 Interviews with Leonard, Walsh, Irving, Niall and Christy Rice, 2012.

36 Torrans in *Rock Climber* 4, February 1994/5.

37 Alan Tees, *NWMC Journal*, 50th anniversary edition.

38 *IMCJ* 1978.

39 *IMCJ* 1976.

40 *IMCJ* 1978, obituary.

41 Dave Walsh, *IMC50*.

42 Young, 'Flashes from the past' in *IMC50*.

43 Christy Rice, conversation, 30 January 2013.

44 *IMCJ* 1978.

45 Lynam, *IML* 26, spring 1986.

46 Niall Rice, conversation, 2013.

47 Irving, interview.

48 *IMCJ* 1978.

49 Seán Ó Súilleabháin, *Irish Walk Guides/1: South West* (Dublin, Gill & Macmillan, 1978). Tony Whilde, *Irish Walk Guides/2: West* (Dublin, Gill & Macmillan, 1978).

50 *IMCJ* 1971.

51 *IMCJ* 1973.

52 Uinseann Mac Eoin, 'Tom Quinn, intrepid mountaineer' in *IMCJ* 1978.

53 *North-West MC 50th anniversary journal; IMCJ* 1978, obituary.

Chapter 7: The Walker Spur and Freney Pillar

1 *IMCJ* 1971.

2 *Spillikin Club newsletter*, 1972.

3 Calvin Torrans, letter 2013.

4 Shay Nolan, interview 17 April 2013.

5 *IMCJ*, Silver Jubilee edition, 1973.

6 *Ibid.*

7 W. Cunningham, email May 2014.

8 *Alpine Journal* 1975.

9 Lindsay Griffin, email summer 2013.

10 Torrans, interview and letter, 2013.

11 *IMCJ* 1976.

12 Gerry Moss, email, 18 December 2012.

13 *IMCJ* 1976.

14 Torrans, interview and letter summer 2013.

15 *IMCJ* 1976.

16 *IMCJ*, 1978.

17 Harry O'Brien, email, 28 June 2013.

18 *IMCJ*, 1978.

19 O'Brien, 28 June 2013.

20 Tommy Irving, interview summer 2012.

21 *Mountain Log* 3, autumn 1978.

22 Irving, interview: *Mountain Log* 6, autumn 1979.

23 O'Brien, 28 June 2013.

24 *Mountain Log* 6 and 7, autumn and winter 1979.

25 *Mountain Log* 6.

26 *Ibid.*

27 *IMCJ* 1971.

28 *IMCJ* 1973.

29 Lynam, *IMC newsletter* January 1972. *Alpine Journal* 1972.

30 Shay Billane, *Spillikin Club newsletter* 1972.

31 *Alpine Journal* 1972; *Spillikin Club newsletter* 1972; *American Alpine Journal* 1973; *IMCJ* 1973.

32 *IMC newsletter*, 3, 2003, autumn (obituary).

33 *IMCJ* 1976.

34 *Mountain Log* 1, January 1978.

35 'Beyond the end of the habitable world', report of Irish Himalayan Expedition 1977.

36 *IMCJ* 1978.

37 *Mountain Log* 1, January 1978.

38 *Ibid.*

39 *Mountain Log* , autumn 1978; spring 1979.

40 *Mountain Log*, May 1978.

41 *Mountain Log*, autumn and winter 1979.

Chapter 8: Coastal Tour
1 See chapter 1.
2 *IML*, winter 1980.
3 *IML* 9, winter 1988; *IML*, winter 1982; *IML* winter 1988.
4 *IML* 16, winter 1982.
5 *Mountain Log* 17, spring 1983.
6 Howard Hebblethwaite, interview October 2013.
7 Stelfox, interview 2013.
8 Torrans, interview *IML* 48, spring 1998.
9 *UCDMC history*, interview and emails May 2013.
10 Sheridan, interview in *IML* 25, winter 1992.
11 *IML* 13, winter 1989.
12 Al Millar, 'Climbing history' in *Rock Climbs in Donegal*.
13 C. Torrans, *Irish Climber*, 1985.
14 Peter Owens, *Climbs in the Burren and Aran Islands* (MCI, 2008).
15 *IMC newsletter* 4, winter 1986.
16 Con Moriarty, interview September 2013; email 8 October 2013.
17 Mike Barry, interview November 2013.
18 Irish Climbing Route Database (www.climbing.ie) and Con Moriarty, interviews and emails autumn 2013.
19 Aidan Forde, 'Kerry Ice' in *IML* 1, winter 1986.
20 Con Moriarty, conversation September 2013.
21 Moriarty emails October and November 2013.
22 *IML* 44, autumn 1997.
23 Brian Callan, *IML* 21, winter 1991–92.
24 Conversation with Peter Kenny in 1950s.
25 *Mountain Log* 17, spring 1983; *Mountain Log* 26, spring 1986; *IML* 1, winter 1986.
26 *Mountain Log* 17, spring 1983.
27 *Mountain Log* 26, spring 1986.
28 *IMCJ*, 1955–56.
29 *Mountain Log* 8, spring 1980.
30 *IML* 3, summer 1987, letters page.
31 Paddy McAteer, *80 Years of Youth Hostelling and the Story of the Mourne Wall Walk*, (Belfast, 2011).
32 *Mountain Log* 24, autumn 1985; *NWMC Journal*, 50th anniversary.
33 *Mountain Log* 23, spring 1985.
34 Denis Rankin, *IMC50*.
35 *UCDMC history*.
36 *Westmeath Independent*, 6 July 2011.

Chapter 9: On Five Continents
1 Robbie Fenlon, interview 2013.
2 Dermot Somers, email March 2014.
3 *Mountain Log* 9, autumn 1980.
4 *Mountain Log* 10, winter 1980.
5 *Ibid.*
6 *Alpine Journal*, 1981.
7 *American Alpine Journal*, 1981 and 1995.
8 *NWMC Journal*, 50th anniversary.

9   Jack Bergin, Sean Maguire and Choc Quinn, various emails from April to August 2014.

10 'MEF Notes' in *Alpine Journal*, 1982.

11 Stelfox, interview May 2013.

12 Somers, *Rince ar na Ballaí*, pp. 37–38.

13 *Mountain Log* 9, autumn 1980.

14 Somers, *Mountain Log* 13, winter 1981.

15 *Mountain Log* 12, autumn 1981.

16 Somers, *Rince ar na Ballaí*, p. 66.

17 Based mainly on Somers own accounts in the various *Mountain Logs* already referenced, in *Rince ar na Ballaí*, and in conversations; Lorna Siggins, *Everest Calling: ascent of the dark side* (Edinburgh, Mainstream Publishing, 1994).

18 O'Brien, personal communication, June 2013; *Mountain Log*, autumn 1982

19 *Mountain Log* 15, autumn 1982; interview with Torrans and Sheridan 2013.

20 *Himalayan Journal* 39, 1981–82.

21 *Mountain Log* 15, autumn 1982.

22 *Mountain Log* 17, spring 1983.

23 *Mountain Log* 18, autumn 1983.

24 *Ibid.*

25 Goulding, conversations 2011 and 18 July 2014.

26 *Mountain Log*, autumn 1984.

27 *Himalayan Journal* 41, 1983–84.

28 *IMCJ* 1984–85.

29 *The Irish Climber* 1985.

30 *Mountain Log* 9, autumn 1980.

31 *Ibid.*

32 *Mountain Log* 18, autumn 1983.

33 *Irish Climber* 1984.

34 *Mountain Log*, spring 1985; *Irish Climber* 1985.

35 *IMCJ*, 1986–87.

36 Moriarty, emails autumn 2013.

37 Walsh, interview 2013.

38 Gerry Moss, personal communication October 2013.

39 *Mountain Log* 27, autumn 1986.

40 *Irish Mountain Log* 1, winter 1986 (henceforth *IML*).

41 *IML* 2, spring 1987; Dave Coulter, email, December 2014

42 Lance S. Owens, *American Alpine Journal*, 1987.

43 S. Swenson, *American Alpine Journal*, 1991

44 *IML* 3, summer 1987.

45 *IML* 6, spring 1988; *IML* 8, autumn 1988.

46 *IML* 2.

47 Lynam, *Himalayan Journal* 44, 1986–87.

48 Lorna Siggins, *Everest Calling* (Edinburgh, 1994), p. 28.

49 *IML* 8, autumn 1988.

50 Moss, personal communication October 2013.

51 *IML* 8.

52 *UCDMC history*.

53 *IML* 9, winter 1988.

54 *IML* 12, autumn 1989.

55 Con Moriarty, email November 2013.

56 Moss, personal communication October 2013.

57 *Himalayan Journal* 46, 1988–89.

58 *IML* 14, winter 1989.

59 *IML* 15, spring 1990.

60 *Ibid.*

Chapter 10: A Shift Sideways

1 Paul Harrington, interview November 2013.

2 *IML* 22, spring 1992.

3 *IML* 24, autumn 1992

4 *IMC50.*

5 *IML* 24, autumn 1992; *IML* 53, spring 2000.

6 *IML* 35, summer 1995.

7 *IML* 26, spring 1993.

8 *IML* 22, spring 1992.

9 *IML* 20, autumn 1991.

10 *IML* 44, autumn 1997.

11 *IML* 23, summer 1992.

12 *IML* 27, summer 1993.

13 *IML* 26, spring 1993.

14 *IML* 35, summer 1994.

15 *IML* 49, winter 1998.

16 *IML* 44, autumn 1997.

17 Helen Lawless, *IML* 35, summer 1995; Liam Reinhardt, *IML* 49, winter 1998; Con
     Moriarty, *IML* 44, autumn 1997; Philip Gormley, *IML* 40, autumn 1996.

18 Gerry Moss, *IMC newsletter*, spring 1998.

19 *IML* 23, summer 1992.

20 *IML* 31, summer 1994.

21 Paul Cullen, *IMC newsletter* autumn 1999.

22 *IML* 44, autumn 1997.

23 *IML* 28, autumn 1993.

24 Hebblethwaite, interview October 2013.

25 Paul Harrington, interview October 2013.

26 Somers, email November 2013.

27 Hebblethwaite, interview; *IML* 28, winter 1993.

28 Notes of interviews, details of which will be made available to authorised researchers.

29 Torrans and Sheridan, *Fair Head Climbing Guide.*

30 *Ibid.*

31 Sheridan, email March 2014 and elsewhere.

32 'Historical notes' in *Rock Climbs in the Mourne Mountains.*

33 *Rock Climber* 4, February 1994–95.

34 Rea, 'Historical Notes'.

35 Gribbon, *Peak Viewing* 8, 1980.

36 Lewis Carroll, *Through the Looking Glass, and what Alice Found There* (London, 1871).

37 George Band, *Summit*, p. 29; Doug Scott, *Big Wall Climbing* (Oxford University Press,
     1974), p. 5; Nugent, *In Search of Peaks*, p. 1.

38 Rea, letter in *IML* 9, winter 1988.

39 Hebblethwaite, *IML* 48, autumn 1998.

40 British Mountaineering Council, 'Archive statistics in Participation in climbing and mountaineering, (2013). www.thebmc.co.uk. Accessed 8 January2014.

41 Torrans, *IML* 15, spring 1990; *Mountain Log* 26, spring 1986; *IML* 12, autumn 1989; *IML* 26, spring 1993; *IML* 18, spring 1991; *IML* 22, spring 1992; *IML* 20, autumn 1991; *IML* 26, spring 1993; *Rock Climber* 4, December/January/February 1994–95; *Rock Climber* 5, April 1995; *Rock Climber* 1, January 1994.

42 *Rock Climber* 1.

43 *IML* 25, winter 1992.

44 www.ibisworld.com/industry/indoorclimbingwall.html accessed 8 January 2014.

45 British Mountaineering Council, 'Participation in climbing and mountaineering'; archive statistics. www.thebmc.co.uk Accessed 8 January2014.

46 Hebblethwaite, interview 1993.

47 *IML* 30, spring 1994.

48 *IML* 32, autumn 1994.

49 *IML* 46, spring 1998, obituary.

50 Moriarty, email November 2013.

51 *Ibid.*

52 *IML* 45, winter 1997.

53 *IML* 31, summer 1994, obituary.

Chapter 11: FMCI/MI, Rescue Training

1 Observed by author.

2 Brendan Walsh, typescript report, 9 February 2009.

3 *IMCJ* 1962.

4 Author's personal involvement with Dan O'Shea in having stretcher made with IMC funds.

5 Author's observation on the day.

6 Phil Wood, 'Well. Where's the Body' in *IMCJ* 1964.

7 *The Irish Times*, 12 January 1966.

8 *Ibid.*

9 IMRA report 1965/66 in *IMCJ* 1968.

10 *Ibid.*

11 Walsh; IMRA reports in *IMCJ* 1966/67.

12 Walsh; the O'Sullivan brothers of Killorglin who, in their email of August 2014, were anxious to downplay their own well-known role.

13 Galway Mountain Rescue Team website, www.gmrt.ie/, accessed 20 February 2014.

14 Sligo MRT, www.sligoleitrimmrt.ie.

15 *The Nationalist*, 24 October 1976.

16 Tramore Cliff and Mountain Rescue Association. www.cliffrescue.ie

17 Dublin–Wicklow MRT website, www.dwmrt.ie/, accessed 20 February 2014.

18 Glen of Imaal MRT website, www.wmr.ie/, accessed 20 February 2014.

19 Mayo MRT website, www. mayomrt.com/, accessed 20 February 2014.

20 Galway MRT website.

21 Donegal MRT website, www.mountainrescue.ie/node/538, accessed 20 February 2014.

22 Kerry Mountain Rescue Team, KMRT scroll 1980–89, www.kerrymountainrescue.ie/scroll/scroll80s.html. Con Moriarty, interview.

23 Department of Transport website; John Manning, email 15 June 2014.

24 *Irish Independent*, 4 June 2000.

25 *Peak Viewing*, winter 1978.

26 'Tollymore the Northern Ireland Centre for Outdoor Activities; Legal History' (unpublished draft document, 16 March 1992, Tollymore archive); Dick Jones, letter of 12 April 1975 (National Archive, BR/2002/77/2).

27 *The Irish Times*, 14 October 1969; *IMC newsletter* no. 2, 1969.

28 *Ibid.*

29 *Peak Viewing*, winter 1978.

30 *IMC newsletter* 4, 1970; *The Irish Times*, 10 March 1971.

31 Charles Haughey, budget speech, May 1969.

32 *IMCJ*, 1976.

33 Hansard, House of Lords debate 10 April 1973.

34 *IMC newsletter* no. 4, 1970.

35 IMC Belfast Section, minutes of section 19 August 1964, 30 October 1964, 8 June 1965.

36 *Ibid.*, 9 January 1969.

37 *Ibid.*, 5 December 1966; *IMCJ* 1963.

38 *IML* 40, autumn 1996.

39 IMC Dublin Section, minutes of 4 June 1969, 2 July 1969, 3 September 1969; Northern Section minutes 21 January 1971; letter from F. Nugent of Spillikin to IMC, 27 November 1970.

40 *Ibid.*

41 Seán Ó Súilleabháin, *IML* 40, autumn 1996.

42 National Archives, Mountain Heritage Trust, Doc. BR/2002/77/1.

43 *IML* 24, autumn 1992.

44 IMC minutes, 2 July 1969; Spillikin letter to IMC, 27 November 1970.

45 National Archives, Mountain Heritage Trust, Doc. BR/2002/77/2.

46 *IMCJ* 1976.

47 *IML* 53, spring 2000.

48 *IML* 3, summer 1987, letters; *IML* 42, spring 1997, letters.

49 *IML* 43, summer 1997.

50 K. A. Lowther, 'The Environmental Impact of Recreational Pressure on the Mourne Mountains' (unpublished MSc Thesis, QUB, 1987).

51 P. D. O'Leary, 'A comparative study of recreational capacity in the Mourne and Wicklow uplands' (unpublished MA thesis, NUI Maynooth, 1991).

52 *Ibid.*

53 *IML* 49, winter 1998, Simon Stewart, interview; 'How many in a group?' in *IML* 52, winter 1999.

54 W. and U. Breckle, *Abstracts of Conference of International Orienteering Federation.* University of Bielefeld 1988; K. A. Lowther, 'The Environmental Impact of Recreational pressure on the Mourne Mountains', unpublished MSc thesis, Belfast, QUB, 1987; T. Huxley, *Footpaths in the Countryside. Countryside Commission for Scotland,* Battleby, 1970; M. Drommy, 'Footpath trampling in the Wicklow Mountains. A study of its impacts on the soil and vegetation with guidelines for management', unpublished MSc thesis, University of Dublin, 1987.

55 Stewart, *IML* 49; McAteer, *80 Years of Youth Hostelling.*

56 *Mountain Log* 23, spring 1985.

57 *Mountain Log* 12, autumn 1981.

58 *IMC newsletter*, March 1977.

59 Saive Coffey, at symposium 'Recreation in the Irish Uplands', October 1989.

60 *IML* 54, summer 2000.

61 *IML* 49, winter 1998.

62 www.mournelive.com, accessed 1 June 2014.

Chapter 12: Winter on the Eiger Nordward

1 *IML* 16, autumn 1990.
2 Dermot Somers, 'South Pillar' in *IML* 80, winter 2006.
3 Somers, email November 2013.
4 *IML* 16.
5 Lindsay Griffin, *Mont Blanc Massif*, vol. II, (London 1991).
6 *IML* 16; letters/emails from Harry O'Brien, Calvin Torrans and Clare Sheridan.
7 *IML* 16.
8 *Ibid.*; Gerry Moss, email.
9 John Breen, email January 2014.
10 *UCDMC history.*
11 *IML* 22, spring 1992
12 *IML* 23, summer 1992.
13 *IML* 21, winter 1991–92.
14 *IML* 23.
15 Moss, email.
16 *IML* 25, winter 1992.
17 Orla Prendergast, email November 2013.
18 Sheridan, *IML* 28, autumn 1993.
19 *Rock Climber* 1, January 1994
20 *IML* 29, winter 1993.
21 *Ibid.*
22 Moss, email.
23 *IML* 33, winter 1994.
24 *Ibid.*
25 *Rock Climber* 4, December–February 1994–95.
26 Moss, email and interview November 2012.
27 *IML* 38, spring 1996.
28 O'Brien, emails, May and June 2013.
29 *IML* 38.
30 Stelfox, interview March 2013.
31 *Ibid.*
32 *IML* 42, spring 1997.
33 O'Brien, email.
34 Moss, email.
35 Prendergast, email December 2013.
36 *IML* 40, autumn 1996, obituary.
37 Paul Harrington, 'Eigerwand in winter' in *IML* 43, summer 1997.
38 *Ibid.*
39 *Ibid.*
40 *IML* 45, winter 1997.
41 *IML* 44, autumn 1997.
42 Ivan Counihan, emails September and October 2014.
43 Paul Harrington, 'Irish Mountain Info', in *IML* 50, spring 1999.
44 *IML* 48, autumn 1998.
45 *IML* 47, summer 1998.
46 Harrington, *IML* 50; obituary, *IML* 49, winter 1998; Hawkins, 'A weekend in the Alps' in *IML* 49.
47 Somers, 'South Pillar'.
48 *IMC newsletter* 4, winter 1999.

Chapter 13: Ama Dablam, Manaslu, Everest

1   *IML* 17, winter 1990; Kevin Higgins and John McEvoy, *Tyndall Mountain Club: a history,* (Kilkenny, 1991).

2   *IML* 18, spring 1991.

3   *IML* 16, autumn 1990.

4   *IML* 18.

5   *IMCJ* 1989–93.

6   *IML* 22, spring 1992; *The Telegraph* 11 February 2013, obituary.

7   Brendan Murphy, 'Ama Dablam 1990' in *Alpine Journal* 1991–92.

8   Pat Falvey, *Reach for the Sky,* (Cork, The Collins Press, 1997), p. 81.

9   *IML* 19, summer 1991: Falvey, *Reach for the Sky,* Con Moriarty, email and interview October 1993.

10 *IML* 19, summer 1991.

11 Siggins, *Everest Calling,* pp. 28–38.

12 *IML* 19; *IML* 20, autumn 1991; Siggins, *Everest Calling,* p. 38; *Sunday Tribune* 19 May 1991.

13 *Sunday Tribune,* 12 May 1991, 19 May 1991; comments of team members in 2013.

14 *IML* 23, summer 1992.

15 *IML* 24, autumn 1992.

16 *UCDMC history.*

17 *IML* 25, winter 1992.

18 *IML* 27, summer 1993.

19 *Ibid.*

20 Orla Prendergast, email December 2013.

21 *IML* 28, autumn 1993.

22 Dawson Stelfox, 'Everest Calling', in *Alpine Journal* 1995, pp. 15–24.

23 Robbie Fenlon, *AFAS News* no. 10, autumn–winter 1992.

24 Lorna Siggins, *Everest Calling: the Irish Journey* (Cork, The Collins Press, 2013), pp. 130–31.

25 Stelfox, *Alpine Journal* 1995, paraphrasing Hugh Ruttledge, *Everest 1933,* (London 1934), p. 161.

26 Siggins, *Everest Calling,* 2013, pp. 146–8.

27 *AFAS News,* no. 10, autumn/winter 1993.

28 Lorna Siggins, *Everest Calling: Ascent of the Dark Side* (Edinburgh, 1994); Siggins, *Everest Calling: the Irish Journey* (Cork, 2013).

29 'Expeditions and notes' in *Himalayan Journal* no. 51, 1994.

30 *Ibid.*

31 Falvey, *Reach for the Sky.*

32 *IML* 32, autumn 1994.

33 *IML* 34, spring 1995.

34 *Ibid.*

35 *Alpine Journal* 1996; *Saga Magazine,* November/December 1995, February 1996.

36 *IML* 39, summer 1996.

37 *American Alpine Journal,* vol 43, issue 75, 2001, p. 349; Jack Bergin conversation March 2014.

38 Pat Falvey, *Reach for the Sky.*

39 *IML* 38, spring 1996.

40 Rea, *Rock Climber* 7, July 1996.

41 Harrington, interview September 2013.

42 Falvey, *Reach for the Sky*, pp. 181–93.

43 *IML* 44, autumn 1997.

44 Falvey, *Reach for the Sky*, pp. 194–218.

45 *IML* 45, winter 1997.

46 *IML* 47, summer 1998.

47 Torrans, interview in *IML* 46, spring 1998.

48 Torrans, *IML* 49, winter 1998.

49 Gavin Bates, *IML* 49; Con Collins, conversation, February 2014.

50 Kieran O'Hara, *IML* 49.

51 *IML* 49.

52 Harrington, *IML* 50, spring 1999.

53 Prendergast, email December 2013.

54 Vera Quinlan, *IML* 50.

55 Moss, email November 2012; Moss, *IMC newsletter* winter 1999; Terry O'Neill, email January 2014.

56 Falvey, *IML* 54, summer 2000.

57 *Journal of the Irish Mountaineering and Exploration Society*, vol. 3, 2012.

58 Harrington, *IML* 53, spring 2000; Conor Reynolds, *IML* 53.

59 Harrington, *IML* 53.

Epilogue

1 Damien O'Brien, *The Time Has Come: Ger McDonnell, his life & death on K2*. (Cork, The Collins Press, 2012).

2 *IML* 76, winter 2005; *IML* 78, summer 2006.

Select Bibliography

Journals and Magazines
American Alpine Journal
An Óige Review
Cambridge Mountaineering, 1934
Climbers Club Journal
Irish Mountaineering Club Journal
Irish Mountaineering Club Newsletter
Irish Mountain Log
Journal of the Irish Mountaineering and Exploration and Historical Society
Mountain Log
North West Mountaineering Club, 25th Anniversary Edition
Outdoor Kerry
Rock Climber
The Alpine Club Journal
The Himalayan Journal
The Irish Climber
Saga Magazine
Walking World Ireland

Memoirs
Claude Wall Diaries, National Library of Ireland
Uinseann Ó Rathaille Mac Eoin, *Peaks and Summits* (1998), a monograph

Newspapers
Belfast News Letter
Connacht Tribune
The Irish Independent
The Irish Times
The Nationalist
Westmeath Independent

Irish Rock Climbing Guide Books (selected from over 100 versions and editions)
FMCI/MCI/MI
Bergin, J. and S. Gallwey (eds.), *Interim Guide to Rock Climbs in the Comeragh Mountains,* 1995, with Comeragh MC.
Browner, R. and H. Hebblethwaite (eds.), *Dalkey Quarry,* 2005.
Curran, M. (ed.), *Antrim Coast,* 1975.
Fogg, G. (ed.), *Ballykeefe Rock Climbing Guide,* 2002.
Gribbon, P. (ed.), *Mourne Rock Climbs,* 1957.
Lynam, J. (ed.), *Twelve Bens, Hill Walkers and Rock Climbers Guide,* 1985.
Lynam, J. and L. Convery (eds.), *Bray Head,* 1978.
Lyons, J. (ed.), *Wicklow Rock Climbing Guide,* 2009.
Moore, S., C. Hiller, and R. Bell (eds.) *Rock Climbs in the Mourne Mountains,* 2010.
Owens, P. (ed.), *Climbs in the Burren and Aran Islands,* 2008.
Tees, A. (ed.), *Rock Climbs in Donegal,* 2002.
Torrans, C. and C. Sheridan (eds.), *Fair Head Rock Climbing Guide,* 2002.

IMC
Gribbon, P. (ed.), *Mourne Rock Climbs,* 1957, with NITB.
Healy, E., B. McCall, M. Butler, B. O'Flynn (eds.), *Climbers Guide to Donegal,* 1962.
Kenny, P. (ed.), *A Guide to the Rock Climbs of Dalkey Quarry,* 1959.

Spillikin Club
O'Brien, H. (ed.), *Interim Guide to Fair Head,* 1971.
O'Leary. P. (ed.), *Interim Guide to Playground, Co. Cavan,* 1967.

Privately published
Johnson, H. C. (ed.), *Some Climbs in the Scalp,* 1958.
Stack, R. (ed.), *Gap of Dunloe,* 1995.

ALPINE GUIDES

The Alpine Climbing Group
Francis, G. H. (general ed.), loose-leaf, *Selected Climbs in the Mont Blanc Range,* 1954.

Alpine Club
Collomb, R. G. and P. Crew (eds.), 2 vols., *Selected Climbs in the Mont Blanc Range,* 1967.
Griffin, L. (ed.), 2 vols., *Selected Climbs in the Mont Blanc Range,* 2002.

Books and Articles
Allberry, E. C., 'Lugnaquilla' in *Cambridge Mountaineering* 1934.
Arensberg, Conrad M. & Solon T. Kimball, *Family and Community in Ireland* (Co. Clare, third ed., Clasp Press, 2001).
Band, George, *Summit: 150 years of the Alpine Club* (Collins, London, 2006).
Bardon, Jonathon, *A history of Ulster* (Belfast, Blackstaff Press, 2005).
Barrington, Richard, 'Henry Chichester Hart' in *The Irish Naturalist,* vol xvii, no.12, (December 1908).
Boylan, Patricia, *All Cultivated People: A history of the United Arts Club* (Gerrards Cross, Colin Smythe, 1988).

Brown, Terence, *Ireland: A Social and Cultural history 1922–2002* (Harper Perennial, London and New York, 2004).

Carroll, Lewis, *Through the Looking Glass, and what Alice Found There* (London, Macmillan, 1871).

Coleman, J. C. *The Mountains of Killarney*, (Dundalk, Dundalgan Press, 1948).

Crofton, J. W., 'Connemara' in *Cambridge Mountaineering* 1934.

Cullen, L. M., 'Politics and rebellion: Wicklow in the 1790s' *in Wicklow: history and society*, eds., Hannigan, K. & W. Nolan, (Dublin, Geography Publications, 1994).

Delamere, Maureen, 'Tourism and Transport' in Adrian Redmond, ed., *That was then, this is now* (Dublin, CSO, 2000).

Dickinson, P. L., 'A Rock Climb in Wicklow' in *Climbers Club Journal*, vol. xi, old series (1908).

Drasdo, Harold, *The Ordinary Route* (Glasgow, Ernest Press, 1997).

Falvey, Pat, *Reach for the Sky* (Cork, The Collins Press, 1998).

Foster, Roy, *Modern Ireland 1600–1972* (Harmondsworth, Allen Lane, 1988).

Gribbon, Phil, 'Our Golden Years of Irish climbing' in *Peak Viewing* no. 8 (Belfast, 1980).

Hankinson, Alan, *Geoffrey Winthrop Young; poet, mountaineer, educator* (London, Hodder & Stoughton, 1995).

Harrington, Paul, 'Eigerwand in winter' in *Irish Mountain Log* 43, summer 1997.

Haskett-Smith, W. P., *Climbing in the British Isles* (First ed. 1895, reprinted Dublin 1974).

Herman, David, M. Geraty, V. O'Hagan, S. Peel, B. White, *A Plan for Our Hills: A National Park for the Dublin & Wicklow mountains* (Irish Ramblers Club, 1986),

Higgins, Kevin, 'The first Celtic Tiger' in *Journal of the Irish Mountaineering and Exploration Society*, vol. 3 (2012).

Hill, Judith, *In Search of Islands: a life of Conor O'Brien* (Cork, The Collins Press, 2009).

Kiberd, Declan, *Inventing Ireland: the literature of the modern nation* (London, Jonathan Cape, 1996).

Kirkpatrick, W. T., *Alpine Days and Nights* (London, George Allen and Unwin, 1932).

Leahy, Alice, *With trust in place: writing from the outside* (Dublin, Trust, 2010).

Lee, J. J., *Ireland, 1912–1985: Politics and Society* (Cambridge University Press, 1989).

Lynam, Joss, 'A history of Irish Mountaineering', in *Peak Viewing* (Belfast, 1979, 1981 and 1982).

McAteer, P., *80 years of Youth Hostelling & the story of the Mourne Wall Walk* (Belfast, Hostelling International Northern Ireland, 2011).

Malone, J. B. *Walking in Wicklow* (Dublin, Helican, 1964).

Murphy, Brendan, 'Ama Dablam' in *The Alpine Journal*, no. 96 (London, 1991).

Nugent, Frank, *In Search of Peaks, Passes & Glaciers* (Cork, The Collins Press, 2013).

O'Brien, C. and P. L. Dickinson, 'Irish Mountaineering' in *Climbers Club Journal*, new series vol. 1, no. 1 (February 1912).

O'Brien, Damien, *The Time Has Come: Ger McDonnell, his life & death on K2* (Cork, The Collins Press, 2012).

O Colmain, Seamus, 'The underground years' in Declan O'Keeffe, ed., *UCD Mountaineering Club 1961–2011: an incomplete history.*

Ó Cuinn, Tomas, 'Glenreemore or Glenmalure. Where does the Fugitive Prince lie' in *Irish Mountaineering Club Journal*, 1964.

O'Keeffe, Declan, *UCD Mountaineering Club 1961–2011: an incomplete history.*

O'Leary, P., 'The Irish in Himachal Pradesh' in D. O'Keeffe (ed.), *Journal of the Irish Mountaineering and Exploration Historical Society*, vol. 3 (Dublin, Mountaineering Ireland, 2012).

– 'Bogda Ola' in, *Irish Mountain Log* 37, winter 1995–96.

Ó Suilleabhain, Sean, *Irish Walk Guides/1: South West* (Dublin, Gill & Macmillan, 1978).

Perrin, Jim, *The climbing essays* (Glasgow, The In Pinn, 2006).

Praeger, R. L., *Some Irish Naturalists* (Dundalk, Dundalgan Press, 1949).

– *The Way That I Went* (Dublin, Allen Figgis, 1980).

Quinn, P. Q., *Wigs and Guns* (Dublin, Four Courts Press, 2006).

Robinson, Tim, *Connemara: A Little Gaelic Kingdom* (Dublin, Penguin, 2011).

Rothery, Brian, *The Crossing* (London, Constable, 1970).

Rothery, Sean, *A Long Walk South* (Cork, The Collins Press, 2001).

Scott, Doug, *Big Wall Climbing* (Oxford University Press, 1974).

Siggins, Lorna, *Everest Calling: Ascent of the Dark Side* (Edinburgh, Mainstream Publishing Company, 1994).

– *Everest Calling: The Irish Journey* (Cork, The Collins Press, 2013).

Somers, Dermot, *Rince ar na Ballaí*, (Dun Laoghaire, Cois Life Teo, 2002).

– 'The Central Pillar of Freney' in *Mountain Log* 13, winter 1981.

Stelfox, Dawson, 'Everest Calling' in *The Alpine Journal*, no. 100 (The Alpine Club, 1995).

Torrans, Calvin, 'A History of Irish Rock-climbing 1940s to 1980s' in *Journal of Irish Mountaineering and Exploration Society*, vol. 2, 2005.

Trench, Terry, *Fifty years young: the history of An Óige*, (Dublin, An Óige, 1981).

Tyndall, John, *Hours of exercise in the Alps* (London, Longmans Green, 1871).

Webb, D. A., 'The hey-day of Irish Botany' in *The Scottish Naturalist*, December 1986.

Wells, Colin, *A brief history of British Mountaineering* (Mountain Heritage Trust, 2001).

Whilde, Tony, *Irish Walk Guides/2:West* (Dublin, Gill & Macmillan, 1978).

White, Tony, *Investing in people: higher education in Ireland 1960–2000* (Dublin, IPA, 2001).

Young, G. W., *On High Hills* (London, Methuen, 1944).

– *Mountains with a difference* (London, Eyre and Spotiswoode, 1951).

– 'From Genesis to Numbers' in G. Sutton, G. W. Young, W. Noyce, *Snowdon Biography* (London, Dent, 1957).

Index